Understanding Political and Public Identity

Understanding Political and Public Identity

Hercule Davidson

STATES
ACADEMIC PRESS
www.statesacademicpress.com

Published by States Academic Press,
109 South 5th Street,
Brooklyn, NY 11249, USA

ISBN: 978-1-63989-542-7

Cataloging-in-Publication Data

Understanding political and public identity / Hercule Davidson.
p. cm.
Includes bibliographical references and index.
ISBN 978-1-63989-542-7
1. Political psychology. 2. Identity (Psychology). 3. Identity politics.
4. Group identity. 5. Political participation. I. Davidson, Hercule.
JA74.5 .U53 2021
320.019--dc23

For information on all States Academic Press publications visit our website at www.statesacademicpress.com

STATES
ACADEMIC PRESS

Contents

Preface

The qualities, beliefs, personality, looks and expressions that make a person or group is called their identity. It shapes many aspects of human life, such as perspective and behavior. In the social sciences, the term identity is often used to describe the social identity, or the collection of group memberships that define an individual. The notion of political identity can be understood as an account of one's political self. It frequently refers to a specific political party affiliation. Public identity refers to the identity of an individual inside a group of people. The topics covered in this extensive book deal with the various forms of identity. While understanding the long-term perspectives of the topics, the book makes an effort in highlighting their impact in the society. Constant effort has been made to make the understanding of the difficult concepts of identity as easy and informative as possible for the readers.

All of the data presented henceforth, was collaborated in the wake of recent advancements in the field. The aim of this book is to present the diversified developments from across the globe in a comprehensible manner. The opinions expressed in each chapter belong solely to the contributing authors. Their interpretations of the topics are the integral part of this book, which I have carefully compiled for a better understanding of the readers.

At the end, I would like to thank all those who dedicated their time and efforts for the successful completion of this book. I also wish to convey my gratitude towards my friends and family who supported me at every step.

Hercule Davidson

Introduction

A detective story works when the conclusion is a surprise. If the butler (or frequently, these days, the home secretary or MI5) did it, that has to be hidden until the end, however many clues were scattered on the way. Non-fiction is under the opposite obligation. Readers want to know where the narrative is going. If capitalism is to blame, or is the solution to everything, that must be announced from the start. In practice the genres can be muddled. Accounts of human life can be presented as if they were a surprise which the evidence has revealed only as the story advances. But any account has to begin with some understanding about what is going on. So I will describe the assumptions that are illustrated, rather than proved or discovered, in the following chapters.

I have followed writers as varied as Pierre Bourdieu, who has argued for the importance of every aspect of human identity, and Gilles Kepel, who has pointed to the importance of religious belief, to present a picture of human life as more than a collection of material interests, and have assumed that identity might not precede or determine a conception of someone's self-interest, but will accompany it.[1] Identity cultivation, composed of both choice and circumstance, has been discussed in many ways, from theology's balancing of free will and predestination, through Marx's creativity within circumstance, to discussions such as Bourdieu's taxonomy of taste. The following chapters are not a presentation of a theory of social life, but an examination of what kinds of things can be said by starting with identity.

The chapters that follow are not of equal character, and readers who prefer the story to the justification of the plot may want to leave chapter 2 until the end, or skip it entirely. The book has five principle themes, which are no more than abbreviations of well-established ideas not only in the social sciences and humanities, but in theology and political theory and, quite possibly, art and artistic theory.

First, the identity paradox – the continual tension between identity as association with some broader group, ideology, or vision, and identity as distinctiveness by contrast within such groups, ideologies, and visions – is a continual tangle between the aspiration towards equality and the assertion of inequality.

Second, everything counts, no human activity is trivial or meaningless, and the visible and audible actions that constitute identity both individually and collectively – clothing and eating, speaking and moving, architecture and public spaces – are not best seen as expressions of some deeper, internal, or foundational essence. Any summary of identity is a summary of these components, not a description of a first principle, foundation, or source. When Pope satirised the social butterfly who might 'stain her honour, or her new brocade', he was mocking the value placed on clothing and bodily adornment, not disputing its importance, and was conveying in a few satirical words an understanding of the role of clothing which might have taken an academic commentator rather longer.[2] A commentator or describer of identities is therefore obliged to be a democratic empiricist, to begin by taking account of all aspects of behaviour, and may not dismiss anything as of no significance. Parsimonious accounts are parsimonious, and have the same disadvantage as parsimonious meals, plays, music, or literature. The metaphor of a mask is misleading too – it separates the person from the public, evident identity in a way which suggests that one is in some sense more real than the other, and that what is seen and heard is artificial, a pretence by a real person.

Third, the cultivation of identity in public and political life is conducted by people within contexts which provide them with both opportunities and constraints, and which, prior to their making choices, cultivate in them preferences, conceptions, and perceptions. The cultivation of identity is therefore a continual negotiation, and neither simply determined nor simply free. The constraints and the opportunities which form the context of choice are themselves the product of earlier actions. In the cultivation of identity as an interplay between choice and circumstance, circumstance may be the result of the actions or intentions of other people, and choice may be a choice to influence or control not only one's own identity but that of others.

Fourth, identity and interests are not alternative ways of describing individuals or groups, but are concepts describing different aspects of social life, so that the phenomena to which they refer stand in a symbiotic rather than a causal relation to one another, each presupposes the other, and an account in terms of one is not a denial of the reality of the other.

Fifth, general theories of causality can be monochrome or one-dimensional, and can never fully account for actual events and circumstances. By their very universality they exclude much that a fuller but more bifurcated account could give, but are nonetheless necessary components of accounts and explanations in conjunction with other descriptions of human social behaviour. Social life is composed of many purposes, contexts, constraints, and opportunities so that causes, effects, patterns, and relationships attributed to humanity as a whole will always refer to ideal and imagined events and circumstance, never to actual ones. General theories or narratives provide the necessary ingredients for complex or qualified accounts of real circumstances, not a sufficient or full account of what is going on. It follows that the apparently general accounts I give can themselves only ever serve as ingredients for narratives of geographically or temporally specific events, conditions, or patterns.

Each of these issues has been dealt with great skill and subtlety and at higher and higher levels of abstraction and universality by writers across the social sciences and humanities; an enterprise which I have not attempted to join. I have not tried to operate on a philosophical high wire whilst juggling a handful of conceptual plates. If this makes my working assumptions more arbitrary it will nonetheless, I hope, make them simpler and more immediately accessible.

These working assumptions mean that the following chapters are syntheses of several disciplines, not meticulous operations within any single one. Whilst they glean from history, political science, anthropology, law, and sociology, they do not make or attempt to make specific contributions to any one of them. To use a distinction made by Bourdieu in his discussion of art, they deal with the subject rather than with the study or depiction of the subject.[3] They draw on, and I hope engage with, accounts, explanations, and theories of several kinds, but as a scavenger rather than as a member of any particular academic community.

There is a footnote to this introduction. Pierre Bourdieu has argued that the most apparently trivial aspects of behaviour and taste and the most apparently grand, or sophisticated, are all parts of a coherent whole. Something similar might be said of accounts of identity, and of the range of accounts, descriptions, and histories in the humanities and social sciences. The theories of academics and the comments and recommendations of reformers, politicians, and ordinary citizens often seem surprisingly similar in substance while not in style, in dealing with such issues as the relation between the built environment and the character and quality of life, or the role of clothing in stating and constituting the status, or skill, or valued qualities of the wearer. Just as in music and architecture there is an unbroken though not even scale from the vernacular to the professionalised and back again, so can there too be in accounts of human identity. The academic work of seeing architecture and the arrangement and creation of public space as both aspects of the identity of regimes, communities, or classes, and means of cultivating those identities, can draw on and be sustained by the stated intentions of those who created these built environments, but whose concern was the expected impact, not the view of human identity which informed it. The institutional boundaries which seem to separate novelists from social scientists, dramatists from demographers, or poets from political scientists, are less easily insisted on in the productions of these different communities. Academic accounts raise the stated aspirations, expectations, and descriptions from particular locations and transmute them into broader, general accounts, which in their turn can inform the more particular. This book is no exception to that wide community of argument, explanation, and action which provides an unbroken though sometimes bumpy continuity from the vernacular to the academic. Plays, poetry, cinema, novels, cartoons, or theatre are not auxiliary illustrations for scientific work, but contributions in their own right to description and explanation. What follows cannot claim to be any more than a swift synthesis of some of this work, and its own contribution is by way of co-ordination and presentation, not discovery.

Since I have stated what I shall do, I should state also what I shall not. This limitation is a judgment not on the importance of matters and questions with which I do not deal, but on their volume and complexity, and on the possibility always of being able to speak and write only by setting boundaries to what is described. A major concern of those who have written about identity has been its ethical dimension. What are the implications for the conduct of public life of an understanding of the nature of human identity and human agency? I have not dealt with these questions not because they are not important, but because I have attempted something different and more limited, though some ethical preferences will unavoidably, and not necessarily damagingly, be associated with explanatory or descriptive assumptions or arguments. Nor have I set out to identify, or create, laws of human behaviour, but only to indicate some of the possible components of behaviour in particular times, places, and societies. This is in part because that would be a separate and substantial enterprise, but also because of a suspicion that too often apparent explanations of something are simply redescriptions of it as instances of a broader category. Alternatively, the explanation of one thing is simply the unexplained presence of another thing.

There are two further questions that I have not addressed, which is the downside of my attempt to treat everything that is evident as evidence. First, I have not considered the extent to which the actions, statements, and evident identities of people, and in particular of powerful people, leaders and rulers, are an aspect of simple greed, obsession, or megalomania. A modest reply to this criticism is that even if its grounds are accepted, the coinage of identity appears to be of very great value if it is thus used, and even if the purposes to which it is put are unacceptable, its role in public life has to be recognised and studied. Second, identification by association always requires that other members of the association, however distinguished from them a leader or an elite is, are friends or allies. The identity of the association will frequently be contrasted, with varying degrees of hostility, with that of other associations who, in the most extreme version of the narrative, will be presented as enemies. I have not discussed this element of identity cultivation between associations, though I have done so elsewhere.[4] Absence of consideration here does not imply lack of importance, simply distribution of attention.

Notes

1 Pierre Bourdieu, *Distinction: A Social Critique of the Judgment of Taste* (London: Routledge, 1986); Gilles Kepel, *The Revenge of God: The Resurgence of Islam, Christianity and Judaism in the Modern World* (Cambridge: Polity, 1994).
2 Alexander Pope, *The Rape of the Lock* (Oxford: Oxford University Press, 2007), p. 15.
3 Bourdieu, *Distinction*, p. xxvi.
4 Rodney Barker, *Making Enemies* (Basingstoke: Palgrave Macmillan, 2007).

1

A Study of Plumage

A strange creature in bright feathers; what you get is what you see

Replying to Burke's denunciation of the revolutionary regime in France, and his apologia for monarchy and aristocracy, Tom Paine famously complained that Burke pitied the plumage, but forgot the dying bird.[1] To which a reply – though not one made by Burke or other defenders of tradition, hierarchy, or the wisdom of elites – is that without the plumage, the bird is not a bird at all, and that observing plumage is one of the first ways in which we try to see what sort of a bird we are looking at, or even if it is a bird at all rather than some other creature entirely. Nor is the nature and function of plumage limited to making recognition possible. Plumage is just as necessary to the bird as it is to those who want to identify it. Without its feathers, the bird can neither fly nor swim, attract mates nor hide from predators. The feathers are neither additions to the bird nor expressions of the bird, they are part of what the bird is, as any bird spotter would have told Paine. But Paine was drawing on an ancient view of core versus superficialities, essence versus accidents, internal substance versus external display, which has served to set aside inconvenient evidence or dismiss some of what is seen as superficial or without significance, 'mere rhetoric' or epiphenomenal froth, while at the same time assuming an underlying but not immediately evident truth, nature, essence, or purpose. The disadvantage of such a view has always been that it provides an excuse for ignoring evidence, or explaining evidence which is acknowledged as the effect of some foundational feature or principle which is no more than a summary of what it seeks to explain.

What applies to birds applies with even greater force to humans, animals who wear not only their own skin and hair, but that of other creatures as well, adding to and extending their own plumage by creating for themselves second and third skins of clothing which are as much a part of who they are as are the feathers of the sparrow or the plumes of the peacock, and no more artificial than a sparrow's nest. Human plumage, as a tangible component of human identity, is not limited to clothing, however widely interpreted, but consists of the whole complex cultivation of both conduct and environment, from all the visible and audible elements of individual identity to the created physical environment which its members inhabit. Clothing and diet, language and architecture, all are part of the plumage of humans, which, being chosen and cultivated as well as given and received, can say even more than the plumage of the ostrich or the coot, since it is part of the cultivation of an identity which differentiates one society from another, one household from another, and one person from another. The plumage of a bird will show to which species it belongs; human plumage will show important elements not just of acquired or imposed but also of created and cultivated identities. If an initial impression is sought of what kind of society, government, polity, group, or individual is being looked at, then the visible, tangible, and audible expressions they give of themselves, and the ways in which they give them, are at the very least an essential first piece of evidence, the social anatomy of human identity. This elaborate human plumage is as much a part of who people are as the feathers of the crow are part of what makes it a crow.

The first answer to the enquiry, 'Why does taking account of human plumage matter?' is therefore informed by the distinction between free-range and battery data, and by democratic empiricism, the working assumption that whilst what can be observed does not provide explanations, it demands acknowledgment, and cannot be set aside as peripheral or epiphenomenal to some deeper or more parsimonious reality.[2] The second answer is that if there are consistent relationships between the cultivation of identity and other dimensions of public life, then plumage is one powerful indicator of other aspects of any society. The third answer is that it is important to understand identity as the ideological or cultural dimension of social life, a dimension which has always been there, but which was unduly neglected for much of the short twentieth century, particularly in accounts of political life. How people give meaning and justification for themselves, how they cultivate and present their identities, is a prominent element in the human history which both arts and sciences seek to describe, interpret, or explain. And the central paradox in that cultivation, between identity as association and identity as distinctiveness, is found in every component of identity.

This wider human plumage matters because it tells much about the character of the person, institution, regime, polity, or society which is being observed. In this view of things, expressed identity is not an instrument or shadow of some inner reality, but the thing itself; its powers and limitations are real, and are not under the control of some deeper self or purpose, but are the self and purpose, with its strengths and weaknesses. Acted out and observable identities, the 'habitus' of Bourdieu, have all the importance of the cloak which Clytemnestra threw over Agamemnon, in its constricting as well as its enabling possibilities. And like the one which enabled Agamemnon to be murdered, while it can be changed, precisely because it is a human creation it cannot be cast on and off instantly and at will. This lack of unfettered freedom in all the cultivations of identity is an important qualification to the view that since artefacts, whilst assigned meaning, are external objects they can be discarded and changed arbitrarily and at will. Cavallaro and Warwick have argued that 'dress, by encouraging us to make and remake ourselves over and again, renders the very idea of essence quite absurd.'[3] But it is not any illusory instant replacement of identity which calls into question the idea of essence, but rather the observation that when all the evident elements of identity have been considered, there is little if anything left to constitute any further reality.

Clothes construct the social person

It was in the tradition of Burke rather than Paine, though with rather different political intent, that Virginia Woolf included in her essay on gendered politics, *Three Guineas,* photographs of men in the elaborate regalia of their public roles – judges, generals, university vice chancellors, and bishops. Clothing, although it is only the most immediate aspect of cultivated identity, nonetheless is evidence and a component not just of personal adornment but of gender, status, and power. Each of the four roles is illustrated by Woolf with photographs of its full formal extravagance, with the judicial splendour of curls and scarlet unchanged in style since the eighteenth century; movement-constricting military uniforms weighted down with medals, braid, and ribbons; hats and cloaks and hoods in academic procession; and episcopal pomp laden with mineral embossment, the servants of God sparkling with the properties of Caesar.

The clothes people wore were for Woolf much more than superficial or insignificant display; they were significant social actions which anyone seeking to reform society needed to take seriously. The ceremonial dress of males:

> serves to advertise the social, professional, or intellectual standing of the wearer. If you will excuse the humble illustration, your dress fulfils the same functions as the tickets in a grocer's shop. But, here, instead of saying 'This is margarine; this pure butter; this is the finest butter in the market,' it says, 'This man is a clever man – he is Master of Arts; this man is a very clever man – he is Doctor of Letters; this man is a most clever man – he is a Member of the Order of Merit.'[4]

The clothing both claimed and constituted a status and transmitted a message. And whatever the practicality of the clothing that might be worn when a particular job was being done, the clothing which was worn when the status of the person doing the job was being proclaimed was of a very different character – flamboyant, dramatic, and ceremonial, wholly impractical but no less functional: 'Military uniforms, the non-functional kind which are not worn for fighting, glorify war and make a military career appear attractive.' For women who identified themselves as opponents of war, therefore, refusing distinctions, honours, and uniforms would both present a public identity which corresponded to the rest of their beliefs and actions and would 'do something, indirectly, to discourage the feelings that lead to war'.[5]

Woolf's account illustrates graphically that far from humans being, as Desmond Morris described them, naked apes,[6] they are clothed apes, and often very elaborately clothed ones. Their clothing is one of the things that distinguishes humans from other animals, and the clothes and all the other manufactured, constructed, and cultivated things with which people surround themselves, which they inhabit and in and through which they live, are essential components and constituents of identity, of status, function, and authority. The remarkable thing about the naked human ape is that there are possibly only two examples of the species, Adam and Eve, and even they did not remain without clothing for long. The transition from the Garden of Eden to the post-paradisiacal world was marked by the putting on of clothes. Even before their expulsion, Adam and Eve were provided with garments made of skins, thus marking them off from all the rest of creation: other animals wore their own skins, humans decked themselves in those of other animals. And not just skins, but buttons and bows, cloaks and hats, and all the artefacts which are part of human life. Woolf's advice to women on political tactics suggests an even more important role for clothing than that of label or price tag. Clothing is not simply an announcement of identity; it is part of identity, not an external addition, but an organic component. The clothing does not simply adorn or express the human identity, it contributes to constituting and creating it.

The importance of clothing as one of the first and most evident components of cultivated identity has long been recognised, and it is pleasantly appropriate that it was Woolf's nephew Quentin Bell who in 1947 drew on the arguments of Thorstein Veblen from the end of the nineteenth century to give an account of the central role of dress far beyond the simple functions of keeping humans warm and dry, and of the inadequacy of an unimaginatively narrow utilitarianism to grasp the fecundity of human actions and ambitions.[7] Veblen's description of bodily adornment and clothing as a means both of 'emulation' and of 'invidious distinction' was in terms of a single scale of ambition, greater and greater wealth, and to that extent assumes a single scale of valued appearance across an entire society.[8] But his account nonetheless presaged a broader notion of an identity paradox, where association might be sought for many reasons, and distinction equally grounded in many allegedly unique characteristics. Bell developed Veblen's argument to take in both a social and a totally private dimension of identity. Such was the dependence of people on their elaborately and minutely cultivated identities that even when no other humans could observe or hear them, the smallest detail of their constructed person was important to them. Commenting on this 'Robinson Crusoe syndrome', though not on Robinson Crusoe, for whom a hat on a deserted island constituted the difference between civilization and savagery, Bell observed that:

> it may frequently happen here, as in other moral situations, that the offender may be not simply the worst but in fact the only sufferer. A rebellious collar stud, a minute hole in a stocking may ruin an evening without ever being observed by the company at large. Our clothes are too much a part of us for most of us ever to be entirely indifferent to their condition: it is as though the fabric were indeed a natural extension of the body, or even of the soul.[9]

And once a person is away from the solitude of a desert island or a dressing-table mirror, it is the fabric, rather than the body beneath, which constitutes for everyone else the visible and tangible social identity.

Dress carries immediate social meaning, it is part of a person's identity, and it is both defended and sometimes threateningly asserted in its most minute detail. Recalling new shoes imposed in childhood, Jenny Diski described how 'it wasn't just the social disaster of such unfashionability that froze my heart: it was the fear that appearing to be the kind of person who wore such shoes might mean that that was the person I actually was. It wasn't just that my peers would despise me: I would despise myself.'[10] In Woolf's *Orlando*, a housekeeper's wedding ring was something from which she could not be parted for even a moment, since it defined her, and without it her very social existence seemed in peril. With it she was a respectable married woman. Without it her existence fell into confusion and disrepute. And not only her existence on earth: 'it was by the gleam on her wedding ring that she would be assigned her station among the angels and its lustre would be tarnished for ever if she let it out of her keeping for a second.'[11] In a similar way for a Protestant Orangeman in twentieth-century Northern Ireland, 'the sash my father wore' was both an expression of identity and a constituent part of the identity which it expressed. Clothes and scenery make the person, both for themselves and for others. There may or may not be an inner self so that we can say of someone that deep down they are superficial. But it is the outward construction with which we deal, and which constitutes, for social life, who we are.

The rituals and behaviour of public life are a visible and audible display which, in addition to being evidence of what they immediately express, communicate important messages about the meaning to be attributed to other ways in which people give an account and a justification of themselves and the roles they perform. In Woolf's case, clothing drew attention to the otherwise unacknowledged importance of gender distinctions. Men in Western society, who normally distinguished themselves from women by the unimaginativeness of their dress, their dark and uniform suits and subdued colours of shirts and ties, were quite different in their roles as the arbiters of state and society – as judges, university vice chancellors, bishops and generals – and were decked out with more feathers and frills and buttons and bows than could be found in the most extravagant display of women's ball gowns.

In public life, whether economic, religious, or political, dress is a constituent part and construction of how people see themselves, and how they see the other members of their society – a vision of a world which that dress at the same time constitutes. It is not only the prominent and the dominant who come in bright, or not so bright, feathers. The construction, cultivation, and display of external form is a part of all social life, and is an inherent dimension of the cultivation of social identity and social rank. Citizens and rebels, petitioners and demonstrators, exist through their attire just as much as do presidents and kings. Public identity is formed of all the visible, audible, and communicable aspects of a person and their actions and accoutrements. This identity explains and justifies who people are and what they do. And yet to put it in that way may suggest that a person, an action, and a meaning or justification are in some way distinct, so that one can chronologically precede and cause or influence the other. But each of these analytically distinct features is an integral part of an organic whole, each is a dimension or aspect of public identity, and each can influence and be influenced by the others, and has a character which, were it isolated and distinct (which it could not be), would be different. There is a necessarily integrated character to identification, that whilst it may be analytically distinct, concretely and historically it is not, and must be seen as an aspect of action, not as a precursor to it. Popular language has always recognised this, and when people talk of blue-stockings, Black Shirts, suits, anoraks, or hoodies, they are talking about the whole person, of whom the clothing is both an indicative and a constituent part. A fashion statement is not a superficial addition, it is part of who, socially and humanly, people are. 'Don't step on my blue suede shoes' is not an admonition to preserve the shape or cleanliness of footwear. Nor is the identity-forming role of clothing limited to the functional items which keep out cold and wet. Jewellery is not simply decoration, it is declaration. And the functions of jewellery wash over into ostensibly purely utilitarian items such as watches and mobile phones. The more expensive such small items are, the greater the proportion of their function is dedicated not to marking the time or enabling communication, but to constructing the wealthy identity of their possessor. When late twentieth-century social scientists looked at clothing and all the other elements of taste, they did so in a way which treated all aspects of cultivated identity as relevant and important; Bourdieu's 'habitus' was a the portfolio of taste which constituted social location, 'schemes of the habitus ... embed what some would mistakenly call *values* in the most automatic gestures or the apparently most insignificant techniques of the body – ways of walking or blowing one's nose, ways of eating or talking'.[12]

Yet whilst clothing is part of identity, it is not a physically inseparable part. It can be changed, and in changing, changes the identity of which it is a constituent component. Clothing is more easily changed than any other part of who a person is, and so a change of clothing can be used to create a change of identity, if not in the eye of the wearer, then certainly in the eyes of others. The audacious deception carried out by the man who became famous as the Captain of Köpenik depended on a uniform and a great deal of bravado, but by dressing as a Prussian officer Wilhelm Voigt became a Prussian officer in the eyes of those around him, commandeered a posse of soldiers, and confiscated 4000 marks from the city treasurer. It is a delicate philosophical point whether the posse of soldiers and the city treasurer saw a Prussian officer or someone posing as a Prussian officer, but the events up until the point of revelation would have been the same in either case; publicly, a Prussian officer was precisely what Wilhelm Voigt was. This instance casts light on the limitations of the theatrical or mask metaphor of identity. What happened was no different from what would have happened had Voigt been a genuine officer, because as part of a series of public events, that is what he was. Knowing in retrospect that someone was deceiving the world with his or her performance would alter the way events were explained, but not the way in which they were described. Just so did Mozart's Don Giovanni and Leporello by exchanging clothes enable Giovanni to evade his pursuers. But dressing as someone else has its perils. In Eisenstein's *Ivan the Terrible* it was by flattering the conspirators' candidate for the throne into wearing the royal robes that the tzar diverted the assassin's knife to the usurper whose cause it was meant to advance.[13] In an age without photography, film, television, or the Internet, faces were unknown beyond an immediate circle, while clothes proclaimed a king.

Renaissance theatre is full of identities mimicked or pretended by clothing or even by no more than a handkerchief. Nor is the age of visual familiarity immune to identity through dress, so long as it is collective rather than individual. At the beginning of Charles Gormley's film *Heavenly Pursuits*, the young priest from Glasgow, arriving at the Vatican, is asked if he can identify himself and, slightly puzzled, he points to his dog collar. It is sufficient.[14]

In politics, the colour of clothing is an immediate and simple way of signalling allegiance to a party, country, faith, or family. A Conservative might wear red braces, but would be unlikely to wear a red shirt. And yet it is on the face of it astonishing that so much significance should attach to the colour of items of clothing. But it has always and everywhere been so. One of the first things that the states of Europe did when they began putting their ordinary soldiers into uniform from the seventeenth century onwards, was to select distinguishing national colours: blue and yellow in Sweden, white in France, Red in Britain. When it came to revolutionary change, the identity constructed by clothing mattered even more. Lynn Hunt has described the importance of costume in revolutionary France:

> Different costumes indicated different politics, and a color, the wearing of a certain length of trousers, certain shoe styles, or the wrong hat might touch off a quarrel, a fistfight, or a general street brawl. During the Revolution, even the most ordinary objects and customs became political emblems and potential sources of political and social conflict. Colors, adornments, clothing, plateware, money, calendars, and playing cards became 'signs of rallying' to one side or another.[15]

The inclusions and exclusions of politics are paralleled by those of social life. The cartoons of H. M. Bateman made the point by parodying both exclusiveness and the naivety of those who are unaware of convention, but are part of a class or caste society where clothes mark distinction, exclusion, and superior knowledge. 'The man who ...' is a recurring figure who causes consternation by wearing the wrong clothes for a particular occasion or place, thereby not only announcing that he is an outsider, but offending insiders by not even being aware of their defining normalities.

When Kemal Atatürk wished to cast a new and distinctive identity for the Turkish state and its members, how Turks looked was treated as an important part of who Turks were, and the banning of the fez was not a sartorial whim, but a strand in the weaving of national identity[16] A little later, but with equally appropriate national and cultural location, Harold Nicolson, asked to suggest a uniform for Oswald Moseley's British fascist organisation, proposed the restrained English attire of grey flannel trousers and shirts.[17] Perhaps 'flannels' would have been the term used in Britain, instead of 'Black Shirts', had his advice been taken, although 'the wearing of the flannels' could never have had the same resonance as possessed in Ireland by 'the wearing of the green'.

Walking the walk

In their clothing, and in their language, their gestures, and the expressive environments of art, architecture, music, and decoration which they cultivate for themselves, humans are a species that exists and is created and cultivated through the whole complexity of social display, its manners and masques, scenery and costume, music and movement. How people move within public space is part of their cultural and political identity. It was entirely in keeping with the contribution that means of transport make to identity that Eliza Doolittle in Shaw's *Pygmalion*, once raised to the upper classes, should respond to the offer of a stroll across the park with 'Walk! Not bloody likely. I am going in a taxi.'[18] How you travel is who you are. The twentieth-century American poet Wallace Stevens made much the same point succinctly:

> I am what is around me ...
> One is not a duchess
> A hundred yards from a carriage.[19]

It was this dependence on a visibly expensive means of transport to create social status that so concerned Jane Austen's Emma Woodhouse, for whom the appropriateness of a possible marriage depended upon a tenuous indirect connection of an 'elder sister, who was very well married, to a gentleman in a great way, near Bristol, who kept two carriages'. When others did not travel in a style appropriate to their status there was great concern, and the novel's protagonist was much relieved when someone whom she otherwise admired, behaved with appropriate display after falling short by not using his carriage 'so often as became the owner of Donwell Abbey.'[20]

When pollsters ask respondents to compare politicians to cars, they are employing an important insight.[21] John Prescott *is* someone who has two Jags. This is, after all, a point that advertisers take for granted and which, if it were not so, would condemn most advertisements for cars as a waste of money. You are not just someone who happens to own a Hispano-Suiza; you are a Hispano-Suiza owner, a Hispano-Suiza kind of person. Sean O'Connell has pointed to the identity-expressing and identity-cultivating function of visible car ownership in the early days of the automobile: 'The car offered owners the chance to express their status and their distinction from less wealthy groups in society. It provided this not only in terms of its own existence as a sought-after consumer product, but also in the opportunity it gave to owners to translate the social space between them and "social inferiors" into geographical space.'[22] Conspicuous ownership made a very public statement about wealth and status. In Mel Brooke's film *The Producers*, spying a chauffeur sprinting out of a large and expensive car to open doors for his passenger across the street from his own shabby office, the theatrical impresario Max Bialystock calls out 'That's it, baby, when you've got it, flaunt it, flaunt it!'[23] The line is presaged many years earlier in Stanley Houghton's 1912 play *Hindle Wakes*, when the mill owner Natt Jeffcote asks rhetorically: 'Why did I buy a motor-car? Not because I want to go motoring. I hate it. I bought it so that people could see Alan driving about in it, and say, "There's Jeffcote's lad in his new car. It cost five hundred quid."'[24] It was an explanation which Veblen would instantly have recognised as an instance of both emulation and distinction. By the 1920s car ownership had spread across a wide enough social spectrum for manufacturers to tailor their models to contribute to the graded identities of their customers. A statement from Vauxhall observed that 'There is a class-consciousness in horsepowers, and the manufacturer has to build a model for every class.'[25] Boundaries which were in this way cultivated could be vigorously defended against those considered as interlopers. O'Connell comments of the Swallow Coachbuilding Company's SS1 sports car that:

> its comparatively low cost allowed new social groups to enter the sports-car niche. Hence its buyers came to be viewed as intruders in a sphere of motoring they had previously been unable to join, with the result that they were classified – by the 'Bentley Boys' and others amongst motoring's cognoscenti – as a motoring *nouveau riche* whose sense of good taste had not caught up with their purchasing power.[26]

More than 100 years after the motor car's arrival, it continued to play a role in group identity. The most extreme form of this was the exclusion of whole sections of the population – women – from driving cars at all, in nations such as Saudi Arabia.[27] Nor was the social role of the car a novelty in the identity-cultivating role of transport. In China, well into the early years of the twentieth century, wealth could be publicly asserted whilst the physical person could be concealed from the view of the masses in curtained sedan chairs, an older tradition serving the same function as clouded glass windows in large limousines.[28] Identification is cultivated by association of the individual with the group. But it is cultivated also by distinction between one group and another, and between one person and another within the group. Exclusion is the other face of solidarity, and the other component of identity.

Democratisation of societies and states has continued to be characterised by changes in the way that different groups travel. In the most steeply hierarchical societies, the upper levels of society and polity travel at such a remove from the mass of the population that they might not be viewed at all. Visibility to and recognition by the masses were irrelevant to the cultivation and confirmation of identity. When visibility could not be avoided, travel was arranged in a way which raised the elite above the mass of the people. A chevalier was raised above the crowd by his horse, and Yeats employed the 'high horse riderless' as his metaphor for an aristocracy vanished from the stage of public life.[29] But as the masses are mobilised, and even more as they are given some role in public life, seclusion is replaced by limited visibility. In Japan, the wedding of the then Crown Prince Akihito in 1959 was followed by an open horse-drawn carriage drive through Tokyo, another break with a tradition which until then had conveyed members of the imperial family in closed palanquins.[30] The presentation was of a royal family who were not only visible to the public, but receiving the approval, support, and acclamation of the public. That is something an absolute ruler, and even more so a semi-divine one, not only would not need, but would be compromised by seeking or receiving. The royal rulers of Japan had, like the monarchs of early modern Europe, been performers in a ritual without any popular legitimising audience. And as with monarchies elsewhere, the Japanese royal family moved from weddings out of the public gaze to a degree of public display at the time when the monarchy was moving towards a purely formal and symbolic role, but a role which, without the legitimation of privately celebrated power, drew legitimation instead from, however restrained, public presence and display.

The ways in which the identity of monarchy can be crafted can vary greatly. A royal yacht in late twentieth-century Spain will be a small sailing boat; at the same time in Britain, it was a floating hotel. In late twentieth-century Britain the remaining Edwardian grandeur of the monarchy was compared unfavourably with the more mundane style of the royal families of Scandinavian Europe. Earlier in the century such comparisons could be presented as merely comic. A Cummings cartoon in the *Daily Express* of 1953 shows the coronation as the cartoonist imagined it might have been arranged by Nye Bevan, with the horse guards on bicycles, the royal coach a shooting brake, and the peers in a double-decker bus.[31] But custom and practice can change, and assembled royal dignitaries may now find themselves at international weddings transported all together, as they were at the marriage of Prince Charles and Camilla Parker Bowles, in a Windsorian motor coach.[32] As with much visible identity, custom is easier to defend than innovation. When Tony Blair was reported to be considering the allocation of a special plane for prime ministerial use, it was mocked as '*Blairforce One*', an instance of presumption, whereas the United States President's *Airforce One* was regarded as a normal attribute of presidential presence.[33]

A society which mobilises more and more of the inhabitants of its territory faces a problem over the cultivation of hierarchy and exclusion. There may be a desire to maintain the distinctive identity of elites whilst at the same time not wishing to draw attention to the subordinate identities of the majority. It is in such circumstances that railway operators will retain the designation 'first class' whilst replacing 'second class' with 'standard class'. Airlines, similarly, use labels such as 'tourist' and 'economy', fine-tuning the distance between these and a retained 'first class' with the utilitarian meritocracy of 'business class'.

Politicians who wish to state their popular and populist credentials may sidestep even these euphemistic renamings. Whilst dictators and despots ride in state, elected, or hoping to be elected, leaders may walk or cycle. If they wish to cultivate not only their common touch but also their youth and vigour, they may even jog or run. However a person travels, identity is being cultivated and expressed. Not to travel is itself an aspect of identity. Simply to stand or sit in a public space can be part of homelessness, or political protests, or waiting for an acquaintance. It cannot be devoid of meaning. Moving or not moving, riding or walking, identities are being unavoidably displayed to the world. Social identity is constructed both by the use of one means of movement rather than another, and within each way of getting about. The range from steerage to the captain's table, or from one class of plane or train to another, can be paralleled even within simple walking. Romans characterised each other by their gait, and even their names reflected this. Gait was taken to be characteristic of social position, slaves hurrying and nobler Romans proceeding in a leisurely and dignified manner. Even families could be identified by how they moved, and Cleopatra's son Caesarion was deemed a genuine offspring of Julius Caesar by the way he walked.[34] Whether people move or are moved and carried, identity, and its tensions of solidarity and exclusivity are being constantly cultivated.

Talking the talk: how we speak

As for walking, so too for talking, as Eliza Doolittle demonstrated. To change the way you speak is to change who you are. Of all the components of identity, language is one of the most immediately evident, but even more than clothing marks humans off from other animals. Humans are, even more crucially than clothed apes, speaking apes. John Searle has placed language as the constituting phenomenon of human life, on which everything else depends, and at an only slightly less generalised level of argument, language can be presented as the fundamental constituting activity for human identity.[35] Its role is dramatically illustrated when collective identities are being challenged or asserted. The assertion of the role of Latin in the Catholic liturgy by the Council of Trent in the sixteenth century was as defining for the church's identity as was the shift to the vernacular by the Second Vatican Council in the twentieth.[36] Secular identity as much as religious identity is constructed, cultivated, and sustained by language. Language creates both common identities and separation and exclusion. Since the rise of modern nationalism, speaking and writing in the vernacular have been a part of the collective identity of a people or a nation, just as previously a more universal or less geographically rooted and restricted language had been part of the identity of elites: Latin for scholars and clergy throughout European Christendom; French for aristocrats and intellectuals in northern and eastern Europe, where the language at the court of Catherine the Great in Russia could be French, whilst in Prussia Frederick the Great could name his summer palace 'Sanssouci.' The widening of the community with which people identified beyond those who might, at least in principle, be immediately known and communicated with, by the accessibility of vernacular writings disseminated by what Anderson has called 'print capitalism,' placed language at the heart of the imagined communities of the modern mobilised nation.[37]

The language used, the prosaic substance of what is said, and the manner or accent in which it is said are all heavy with significance, but they do not exist independently of one another. Language, substance, and manner engage with each other, and in any one place and time there are conventional expectations of the character of that relationship. In Eliza Doolittle's case, the comedy arises from words associated with one way of speaking being presented in the accent of another way: 'It's my belief they done the old woman in,' pronounced in a cut-glass upper-class accent.[38] The comedians Alexander Armstrong and Ben Miller used a similar device in the twenty-first century with a sketch of Second World War Royal Air Force fighter pilots using the vocabulary of twenty-first century youth in the professional accents of the 1940s.[39] It is a dimension of identity recognised by writers across the generations. Changing the way you speak changes who you are, or who you are publicly. When Edgar in Shakespeare's *King Lear* wishes to conceal his identity from his blind father, he adopts a rustic accent and becomes a peasant and a stranger.[40] Fathers were not always so easily fooled, and Isaac almost sees through the deception of his son Jacob, who cheats his brother Esau of his inheritance by impersonating him before his blind parent, covering his arms with goat skin to imitate his brother hirsute limbs. Though Isaac is eventually convinced by his son's deception, when 'the hands are the hands of Esau,' he nonetheless thought that 'the voice is Jacob's voice.'[41]

Language is important, from the existence of separate languages for the ruling class or caste – Mandarin, Norman French – through the dialects of class to multicultural equality in countries such as the late twentieth-century United Kingdom. Writing in the early years of the eighteenth century, Maria Edgeworth could report that in Liverpool a wife with the wrong accent could cause embarrassment and impediment to the social aspirations of a newly wealthy husband.[42] There is no accurate means of recovering either the speech of the wife or that to which her husband aspired, but it is unlikely to have been an equally valued accent of identification in the same city, Scouse, which appears not to have developed until the end of the nineteenth century.[43] In 1928 the BBC's *Recommendations to Announcers* informed its readers that 'A man's social class will be more evident from the fashion of his speech than from any other fashion he adopts.'[44] Whatever the socially levelling consequences of the Second World War, language survived as a component of social hierarchy. Nancy Mitford's presentation of 'U' and 'non-U' drew only half-sceptical attention to the survival of linguistic class in the second half of the twentieth century.[45] The way in which we speak sends important signals of friends and enemies, people like us, and people who are regarded at best as different and at worst as hostile.

Just as distinctions of speech are part of a segmented society, the movement of language towards a median is part of a move towards greater equality, or at least less inequality. In England in the twentieth century, part of a wider democratisation was an erosion of distinctive upper-class ways of speaking. The change from 'huntin' to 'hunting' was not just the acquisition of a consonant.[46] But a greater democracy of language does not necessarily involve homogenisation. Whilst 'standard English', 'received pronunciation', or 'the Queen's English' may have become more familiar in the mouths of comedians and satirists than in the boundary beatings of class, regional dialects have flourished as a component of identity in public life.

Language, dialect, and accent can be learned, acquired, or cast off, and it is not only children who are skilled at fitting the voice to the occasion. The miners' leader Arthur Scargill could use the 'received pronunciation' 'U' for television interviews, but the northern 'U' for miners' galas, an ability which, far from marking him off from other political actors, provided only one more striking example of a widespread facility to match the voice to the political occasion.[47] Language may shape what can be said and how it can be said, but it can be put on and put off like a set of clothes. It does not either express some other aspect of identity, or determine it. But nor is that its significance. If a person has several languages for different settings, each contributes a part to an overall identity. Each is a public, social performance, not a 'real', hidden, secret inner identity. Identities do not need either to be always the same or to be coherent, in order to be real and substantial.

Even if language related in no way whatsoever to other aspects or dimensions of identity, it would nonetheless be part of the overall character of a person or collection of people. As a mark of identity, therefore, it can be as significant, or as insignificant, in expressing the boundaries and territories of identity, as religion, political allegiance, dress, or diet. Significant components of identity draw their significance not from any inherent character, nor from their being an expression of some underlying single principle of identity, but by being accorded significance by the possessor of those components, or by others. The languages which form part of an identity can be as varied as the clothing, and wearing overalls to work and morning dress to the horse racing at Ascot does not denote uncertain identity or a division between 'superficial' and 'real'. Language forms institutions and identities, and like all other dimensions of identity, is characterised by both association and distinction. Languages which distinguish one human community from another will themselves then be segmented in searches for individual distinction, and linguistic solidarity constantly fine-tuned to promote individual distinction.

What you eat (and how you eat) is what you are

Just as humans are clothed apes whose identity is significantly constructed and cultivated by their actions and by what and how they produce, so are they apes who eat and drink with a degree of sociability which both marks them off from all other animals and is part of the cultivation of their public identity. How food is prepared, how it is served, and how it is consumed can all form part of the consumer's identity. It is not only in tea ceremonies that identities are generated. Even when tea is more mundanely drunk, the way in which a cup is held is capable of making social statements. For one person to eat with another can be amongst the strongest forms of solidarity, or of the expression and cultivation of common identity. What people eat, which people eat what, how they eat, where they eat, with whom they eat, and in what relation to fellow eaters they consume – all and each constitute different cultures, different societies, different individual and collective identities. For the Oglala Sioux, the distinction between Indian and non-Indian foods was an important way not just of distinguishing themselves from Europeans, but of distinguishing between Indian tribes, and even between 'mixed bloods' and 'full bloods'.[48] For each of the three largest monotheistic religions, food and its common management has a major identity-sustaining role. The central ceremony of the Christian religion is a common and communal partaking of food and drink. The most familiar illustration of the discipleship of the original twelve Apostles is a depiction of the Last Supper, the community of the faithful sharing a common meal. For Christians, both in worship and in art, the Last Supper of Jesus and his disciples is the most powerful statement of the bond between them. The Christian Eucharist is in turn a celebration of a meal taken within Judaism, where Passover plays a major role of communal and religious solidarity, while the alternation of fasting and nourishment during the festival of Ramadan is one of the Five Pillars of Islam. Those who abstain from food by fasting are cultivating an identity as surely as those who by partaking in the Eucharist mark their membership of the company of the saved or the faithful. For each faith the common conduct of eating provides an identity-cultivation ritual.

It is because communal eating is such a powerful and ceremonial expression and cultivation of social solidarity that harm inflicted during eating is considered the worst form of treachery. To poison one's guests is to reveal the depths of one's own moral descent and one's departure from the society of civilised or socialised humanity. Conversely, the common table is the stage at which the solidarity of the family is cultivated, as is the solidarity of both secular and religious collegial bodies, clubs, corporations, and professional associations. Eating together expresses and cultivates a shared identity, and a sharing of the material resources which surround and extend that identity. It is for this reason that ostentatious failure to share food when seated with others causes deep offence. When Evelyn Waugh, at a time of great food shortage, sat at table with his family and consumed all the rare and hitherto unseen bananas which had been made available for his children, it was breach not only of courtesy but of solidarity and common identity.[49] Conversely, when the common identity is maintained, meals can be occasions not only for solidarity but for the celebration of that solidarity. In eighteenth- and nineteenth-century Britain, radical dining provided occasions for celebratory songs, toasts, and speeches, and a cultivation and consolidation of collective political identity in the face of a hostile dominant social and political culture.[50] When feasts become drunken excess they may be a custom more honoured in the breach than in the observance but, even then, they can celebrate and proclaim the character of their participants. As Martin Jones has put it, 'the sharing of food simultaneously builds an "in-group" and excludes an "out-group"'.[51]

Whilst eating around a common table is the most powerful indication of solidarity, membership of a distinct class of people can be exhibited publicly by individuals as an indication that they are not solitary or isolated, but part of a community whose identity they share and exhibit. Advertisers are well aware of this function of food, and can declaim that

'We are the Ovaltineys,' or confide, 'I bet he drinks Carling Black Label.' To eat or drink in the street can be seen as just as much an expression of identity as to dine in evening wear. The refinement of Chaucer's prioress in the *Canterbury Tales* is marked by the fact that when she eats,

> She leet no morsel from hir lippes falle,
> Ne wette hir fyngres in hir sauce depe.
> Wel koude she carie a morsel and wel kepe
> That no drope ne fille upon hire brest.[52]

Nebuchadnezzar's departure from the community of normal humans, conversely, was marked by his eating grass: 'he was driven from men, and did eat grass as oxen.'[53]

Like all aspects of identity, food culture, though powerful and persistent, is not immutable, and both grows and changes slowly, and can, in times when identity is challenged, be altered or innovative to deal with threats to solidarity. Sidney Mintz has described this potent, and manipulable, function of food in the case of introduction of the relatively unfamiliar Coca Cola to United States servicemen who, during the Second World War, had been deprived of other familiar contextual components of solidarity. Troops overseas:

> have not only been stripped of almost all of marks of their individuality (clothings, jewelry, coiffure), but because they are in a remote land, they also feel bereft of those material representations of their culture that are embodied in architecture and in linguistic forms (familiar buildings, signs, advertising). Under such circumstances, which can be alienating, objects that can 'carry' a displaced sense of culture, such as foods and beverages, take on additional potential power. Coca Cola turned out to be a nearly perfect symbolic repository.[54]

Mintz's account of the planned promotion and provision of Coca Cola gives a further dimension to Marx's observation that people make their own history, but do so in circumstances not of their own choosing. The consuming troops may not have chosen Coca Cola, but the military authorities did, and the circumstances were thus very much chosen, though in this case chosen by one group to be the circumstances of another. Whilst circumstances will at any single moment be the environment within which new choices are made or old ones sustained, they have themselves resulted from, directly or indirectly, human choice.

Just as the communal consumption and management of food cultivates solidarity, it provides at the same time opportunities for distinction or exclusion. Solidarity depends for its force on a boundary which divides the community from those whose identity bars them. The apocryphal Edinburgh snub to unwanted visitors, 'You'll have had your tea,' was a public denial of membership of a table. In the 1948 film *The Guinea Pig*, the young man played by Richard Attenborough horrifies the upper-class pupils at his boarding-school table by sopping up the remains of his meal with a piece of bread. It is in the same vein of observation of the identity-signifying role of food that, half a century later, Maggie Smith in the film *Gosford Park* spies a vulgar intrusion at the breakfast table: 'Shop-bought marmalade; how quaint.'[55] For Disraeli writing of the condition of England in 1845, food was as clear a marker of social division as the manners or morals of 'two nations; between whom there is no intercourse and no sympathy; who are as ignorant of each other's habits, thoughts, and feelings, as if they were dwellers in different zones, or inhabitants of different planets; who are formed by different breeding, are fed by a different food, are ordered by different manners, and are not governed by the same laws.'[56]

Whilst solidarity is cultivated by the culture of food, so also are distinctions within the group. Where one sits, whether one sits or serves, all construct identities and distinctions of superiority or inferiority. The hall of a college or a City of London livery company sets its members off from the world outside. But, at the same time, 'high table' is more distinguished than the commoners' table, and wily humility can conspire to achieve the former whilst appearing to choose the latter: 'When thou art bidden, go and sit down in the lowest room; that when he that bade thee cometh, he may say unto thee, Friend, go up higher: then shalt thou have worship in the presence of them that sit at meat with thee.'[57] Social status has been described with metaphors derived from placing at communal, but not common, tables: the lower orders are 'below the salt.'

Just as there are prohibitions on what a group, or sect, or faith, or nation, may eat in order to mark its character as at least equal to that of its rivals, so there are prohibitions which, by restricting access to particular foods to an elite, mark off that elite's superiority to and distance from the mass within the larger group, whether it is a college, a guild, a society, an organisation, or an entire nation. Swans in Britain are reserved for the royal table, whilst truffles and caviar, by their rarity and expense, can mark off those who consume them from the mass of their fellows. The gods have ambrosia, a food which is not so much barred to ordinary mortals as simply not available to them. If they transgress that barrier, as Adam and Eve did in eating a fruit that, whether or not it was reserved for God, was denied to them, then the defensive sanction of the deity is instant and absolute.

Whilst the privileged may cultivate their status by monopolising food, they can also cultivate it by sharing food, doing so on a scale sufficiently generous and extravagant as to mark off their own distinctiveness by their ability to provide for others what those others could not provide for themselves. When the prodigal son was welcomed with feasting on the fatted calf, his father was at one and the same time forgiving, and expressing his power to forgive and to nurture. To generously provide for others is to illustrate one's superior capacity, and to confer on them a benediction which they are thereby deemed to be unable to provide for themselves. Alternatively, the fortunate may use the generosity of their provision to impress those who would otherwise be considered their peers. The provision of food can, too, be a means of expressing gratitude for solidarity received from the guests. *Babette's Feast* is a culinary return of communal favours made even more luxuriant and elaborate when translated from text to film.[58]

Identities are both related to and independent of the universal necessity to feed. If all that were involved in eating was simple and straightforward nutrition, then the only differences of any significance between one group of humans and another would be the result of the availability of food, of climate and material habitat. But even when human society could be seen as closer to the natural life of foraging or hunting animals than is now the case, differences can be seen which cannot be explained by the presence or absence of food, or by the ease or difficulty of its consumption. Closely located communities in the Neolithic Middle East had widely different diets, one consuming available fish, another not consuming fish though it was available.[59] The rituals and practices whereby social eating is carried out are as much a part of the identifying function of eating as the food itself, and are not a simple reflex of the available raw materials. The history of oysters suggests a similar social construction, and flexibility, of diet, with the mollusc's progress from the seventeenth and eighteenth centuries' equivalent of fish and chips to the twentieth century's equivalent of caviar. The character of food culture is not determined by the material character of the food, and the same raw materials can, at different times and in different places, contribute to quite different identities. What is evident here is cultural distinction, not an uncultivated response to a universal, determining, physical human need.

The cultural basis of diet is part of the cultivation of identity, and of an identity which, in order to give meaning to itself, gives meaning to the surrounding world. Mary Douglas's account of the food regulations of Leviticus is of a taxonomy of the natural world which enables individuals and communities to identify their environment, but in so doing cultivate human wholeness and holiness.[60] Such individual and collective identity is composed of every kind of human action, construction, and cultivation. An individual, 'adjusting sights all the time, can see himself as a particular kind of person who would always do this sort of thing and never do that. "Moral style" is set collectively. At any given time the pervading cultural environment provides moral standards affecting every kind of resource. Food is inevitably brought within the moral perspective.'[61]

It is because the culture of food is part of the culture of identity that apparent slights to it can be so powerful. As Douglas puts it, 'Whenever a people are aware of encroachment and danger, dietary rules controlling what goes into the body would serve as a vivid analogy of the corpus of their cultural categories at risk.'[62] So cuisine is more than a symbol of other identifications, it becomes a parallel or supporting cultivation of distinctive identity, coherent with, rather than symbolic or expressive of, some other identity. To threaten a person's diet can be a major threat to his or her identity. In Vichy France, alienation from the Pétain regime and support for armed opposition greatly increased when the regime contaminated wine in June 1943 as part of their policy of requisitioning wine for fuel alcohol. Lucie Aubrac's description of vintage in defence of national identity adds one more dimension to the understanding of the Maquis: 'More than any rational arguments, more than any patriotic explanation, these glasses of heating oil adulterating a fine Pouilly-fuissé swung the winegrowers of the Mâcon hills to the Resistance.'[63]

Whilst food culture contributes to identity and solidarity, it contributes also to the exclusions which bolster identity by contrasting it with that of others who do not share one's common character. For George Orwell, food was an instant identifier of identity. 'Vegetarians' and 'fruit-juice drinkers' were badges of an alien or unorthodox identity in the same way as were 'pacifist' and 'feminist', and people who got their cookery from Paris were likely also to get their opinions from Moscow. The indigenous patriotism of the upper classes could be called into question by the restaurants they ate in, whilst the solid virtues of ordinary people were indicated by the fact that it was in their homes that a 'good slice of honest Yorkshire pudding' was most likely to be found.[64] For critics of Jesus, it was a mark of his departure from the society of the devout and the respectable that he ate 'with publicans and sinners.'[65]

Just as denial is simpler than assertion, in locating others expressions of distaste or disgust are easier than recipes and menus. The insults between Indians and Pakistanis in Salman Rushdie's *Shame* are couched in terms of their respective diets.[66] When the supporters of the American invasion of Iraq in 2003 wanted to stigmatise the weak or absent European, and particularly French, support for their enterprise, they ridiculed 'cheese-eating surrender monkeys.'[67] A old insult to the English was to call them 'les rosbifs', just as for Hogarth it was precisely the roast beef of old England that expressed so much about national character, and the hearty good health with which beef was popularly associated could be contrasted with the starved and pinched person of the French enemy.[68]

There is only one way in which one cannot eat pork, or shellfish, or black bread. There are, by contrast, an infinity of ways in which one can do so. The simplicity of taboo makes it an accessible and unambiguous way of cultivating identity. Not eating something is far more readily both employed and recognised than a particular way of eating something. Martin Jones comments that 'Our refusal to eat certain categories of perfectly edible food marks us out as belonging to one particular community, and definitely not belonging to another, foreign community, which in turn is characterized by the despicable practice of consuming that same foul foodstuff with relish.'[69] So with food as with all the other aspects of human identity, the least difference has significance for identity, and can sustain solidarity or difference with a force which owes little or nothing to the material reality of food, but to its powerful but also humanly cultivated character and significance. The college or city guild dining hall provides a microcosm of the paradox of identity – members in association apart from the world outside, and distinguished amongst themselves between high or head table and mere members.

Feathering the nest

The creation and nurturing of identity does not stop with the clothing and the accoutrements which attach directly to the person, or with language, movement, or food. Whilst birds build no more than nests, humans construct an architecture both grand and public, and quotidian and domestic – cities and cottages; patios, parks, and plazas; allotments and amphitheatres – which add a further dimension to identity. Humans construct not only their own nests but their own trees in which the nests rest – complex physical environments which, whilst they cater for material needs, also provide the setting for the cultivation of social identity. Identity is cultivated, and that cultivation involves and requires more than the character of the material person; the constructed environment is a part of the person's extended identity. Humans do not limit the creation and cultivation of their identity to the artefacts immediately next to their bodies; more than any other species they construct the material world in which they live and in so doing construct yet further their public identities. People are clothed by their architecture just as much as by their coats and hats. Plazas and palaces and houses and gardens contribute public and private space and scenery to the formation of identity. And just as there is an immediate and visible difference between a swan's nest and a weaver bird's nest, so the settings humans construct can be an immediate and visible dimension of their created and cultivated identity. From the suburban villa which both proclaims its villadom and replaces its number with a name lest it be thought to be just one more villa like all the others, to the presidential palace which proclaims both the grandeur of its occupant as the epitome of his or her people and the exclusion from that grandeur of ordinary subjects because of the uniqueness of that epitomisation, association and distinction are sought simultaneously and the inherent tension of identity cultivation is at work.

The built environment provides the clue to the dimension which is missing from accounts which present people as predominantly or solely the recipients of identity or the products of circumstance, training, education, or socialisation. However distant the connection, some person or people created, or contributed to the creation, of built environments, and whether it is the direct user of or visitor to that environment seeking an appropriate setting for and contribution to their own identity, or a planner, architect, politician, or client seeking a setting to influence others, people are making their own history in circumstances which are partly of their own choosing.

The complexity of dimensions which the built and cultivated environment introduces to an understanding of identity has led to both discussion and disagreement amongst commentators. Three broad viewpoints have emerged: an account of architecture as an instance of power exercised by elites; a denial of any simple connection between architecture and other aspects of identity; and an account of the built environment as a place of continual negotiation and change, where the physical world has no intrinsic meaning or function, and where both powerful and ordinary subjects and citizens mould, alter, ignore, or cultivate significance. This third view, although or because it is the most flexible and unpredictable, can be the most productive in apprehending the contribution to identity of the built and cultivated environment.

The first view nonetheless has great currency, if only because politicians, architects, planners, and reformers have frequently and eloquently espoused it, and there is a dimension of the history of the built environment which sustains it. Even when those who have sought to use architecture and the built environment as a means of maintaining or changing society have been frustrated or diverted from the start, their very difficulties have confirmed the optimism of the belief in the social and political effects of pavements, columns, and porticos. The account given by Carl Schoske of the development of the Ringstrasse in Vienna in the nineteenth century is of an extended and shifting contest between the defenders of military tradition, imperial conservatives, and reforming liberals to use the choice and location of government buildings, museums, and churches as part of a social and political programme of change, maintenance, or enhancement. When liberals succeeded in claiming former parade-ground space in 1870 and replacing it with a parliament building, this could be seen as 'a triumph of historical eclecticism and the most eloquent spatial expression of bourgeois power in the new capital.'[70]

The relationship between architecture and the character of society is taken for granted in archaeology: the building is taken to be the expression but also the context of the civilisation, when even the merest outlines of a house or village can provide evidence of social hierarchy, religious practice, and household culture. From the dusty remains of foundations, a whole settlement and its character can be rebuilt in the narrative of the excavating investigator. A worn paving stone or the outline of a courtyard or corridor can constitute the skeletal remains of an entire social order.

In everyday life the assumptions if not the methods of the archaeologist are applied to discern the identity which people are cultivating. The smallest artefact can constitute part of an expressed identity. A door knocker, a carriage lamp, or the pattern of a curtain serves as a shorthand summary for a lifestyle and a life; the curve of a drive or the shape of a flower bed sets down a conception of order and elegance and the discernment of the persons who enjoy them. When the 'women of the quality, the gentry and the middling sort' described by Amanda Vickery were contemplating the qualities of potential husbands, a prominent part of the possible groom's marriageable identity consisted of his house and its furnishings.[71] This was not merely a matter of assessing wealth but, equally importantly, of ascertaining character and culture. The hostesses of an emerging salon culture were well aware of the role and importance of domestic interiors in publishing their inhabitants' identity, and the expansion of visiting, and hence of parlours, in the eighteenth century was part of the theatre of social life where what mattered was 'the prestige of the stage, the props and the hostess that could stand up to the scrutiny of guests.'[72] Furniture and furnishings can shape an identity as substantially as can the turn of a staircase or an order of rooms. This was well recognised by the Scottish minister Andrew Boyd, who wrote in 1861 that 'the scenery amid which a man lives, and the house in which he lives, have a vast deal to do with making him what he is,' and 'We are all moral chameleons; and we take the colour of the objects among which we are placed.'[73] Robert Crawford's poem 'Us' records just such an identity at the point of its destruction:

> Now someone will bid for, then clear these rooms,
> Stripping them of us. We were that floral wallpaper,
> That stuck serving-hatch, radiograms polished and broken,
> Dogeared carpet-tiles that understood us,
> Our locked bureau, crammed with ourselves.[74]

Crawford is drawing attention to the way in which houses become homes, part of and confirming the identity of those who live in them. Alain de Botton makes a similar point when he speaks of an imaginary house whose 'owners have returned from periods away and, on looking around them, remembered who they were.'[75] This portrayal of a decorated and furnished house might seem to be countered by more austere versions of domesticity, the idea that a house is a machine for living in. But the modernist, rationalist conception of the built environment and Corbusier's conception of building, identify only a part of what is going on. Even people who choose to live in what they consider to be no more than a machine are cultivating a distinct identity for themselves – modern, utilitarian, and functional – and by choosing a rational and materially functional identity for their domestic environment, are cultivating an identity, initially private but potentially public, of themselves as modern, post-Romantic, and realistically ascetic. And these material settings for lives are permanent, solid, and unavoidably present, however flexible may be the human interpretation of them.

The theatrical metaphor used by Vickery for material settings has often seemed neatly appropriate for talking about the role of the constructed material environment in cultivating identity. Buildings and the disposition of public space can readily be compared to scenery, a stage of public life, and there is an immediate illumination in describing them as a setting for the generation of particular public identities of citizenship, empowerment, or subordination, as the theatres where the public drama is acted out. So Richard Beacham, in a study of imperial Rome, can write that the emperor Augustus's 'reconceptualization of the city went far beyond mere beautification or monumentalization: it became an essential and highly theatrical expression of the ideology of the principate.'[76] But the theatrical metaphor, having initially illuminated, can then dazzle and confuse. The cultivation of identity is not a matter of social costume and greasepaint; the roles which are performed on the public stage are not hung up like an actor's costume at the end of the day, but are dimensions of a sustained public persona. Bricks and mortar, stone and marble, are not like paper and cardboard, to be packed up at the fall of a curtain and replaced in the morning with different landscapes and cityscapes. Both publicly and domestically, buildings are there all the time, either as dwellings or as places of public work or assembly. In this role, they are a permanent context for the cultivation of identity. As a context, they are permanently present at both the public and the domestic level, and however weak or strong their influence on identity, it is not switched on and off with a cultural spotlight. Buildings have a solidity and permanence which gives them an advantage in longevity over clothing. The grander and more public they are, the greater the number of people for whom they form a context. Garments, however much they express common identity, are a part of single identities and attach to single persons and are individually employed, which gives architecture a potential to shape identity as well as to constitute it that is both thinner as an expression but potentially more powerful and longer lasting as an influence. There is a further difference between the built environment and other elements in the cultivating context of identity. Whatever the degree of spontaneity in the generation and influence of cultural contexts, a building is the result of a deliberate set of decisions and expectations. This is a feature of the built environment to which the theatrical metaphor, despite its limitation, draws attention: a play requires an author, a director, and a cast of performers – it does not simply happen. Architecture thus provides a pointer to the gap in any account which sees the person as the recipient but never the provider or creator of identity and its ingredients. Architecture both composes human character and is deliberately produced by it.

The assumption that social order and architectural order can sustain one another has been held by builders, designers, and planners in advance of any academic account, and later academic observation follows on from the working assumptions of earlier architects, planners, politicians, and reformers. In Augustus's Rome, the pageantry of the living and of the dead was both an expression of the grandeur of the patron or protagonist and a communication of that grandeur to the city and its populace. In this way it expressed both aristocracy and the authority of the populace. This was neither accidental nor unconscious, and Vitruvius was able at the time to observe that 'The majesty of the Empire has ... been expressed through the eminent dignity of its public buildings.'[77] The intentions and assumptions of the architects of Augustan Rome were not concealed, and the presentation of them to later audiences does not reveal hidden or accidental purposes, but a portrayal of vernacular ones. Murray Edelman's claim that the built public environment can be a response to 'the need to establish or reinforce a particular definition of the self in a public official'[78] was something that earlier politicians and improving elites would have applauded, and in describing how 'The theatre of Marcellus and its seating arrangements were fashioned to resemble a microcosm of society and to convey this hierarchy in visual terms,'[79] Richard Beacham was theorising from the intentional identity cultivation of Augustan Rome. The grids of well-drilled streets set out in decorous and spacious order in New York, Philadelphia, or Edinburgh's New Town proclaimed and encouraged a particular vision of social order.[80] And in describing this vision, academic commentators already have to hand the accounts of less theoretically ambitious contributors which can be expressed at a more general and abstracted level, and then fed back into the practice and cultivation of the architectural settings of identity. The debate over the city in Britain in the nineteenth century took for granted that the arrangement of streets, buildings, and public spaces not only expressed but shaped and cultivated identity. Churches were crafted with the expectation and hope that their character would contribute to an organic and sanctified society, just as art galleries and assembly rooms were advanced as part of a campaign of rational improvement of education, culture, and public life.[81] As Alexander 'Greek' Thomson, who made a distinguished contribution to the architecture of nineteenth-century Glasgow, put it, art had the responsibility for the 'furnishing of our minds with correct images.'[82] Building a city was much more than providing shelter from the weather and facilities for work, it was nurturing a garden in which the plants of wholesome humanity would flourish. When the leading citizens of nineteenth-century Manchester were discussing a museum, a library, or a college, the design and shape of the building was as important a part of the character of the envisaged human institution as the contents were of the services it would provide.[83] Bentham's widely used panopticon prison design sought to maintain order both by the central human supervision which the arrangement of space would make possible, and by the ordering of space itself, which placed people in neat hierarchies. Educational reformers in eighteenth- and early nineteenth-century Scotland frequently used a Benthamite panopticon arrangement of space in a desire to promote social order; the function of created space being no less powerful in civil society than in prisons.[84] In all of this, the creators of a material world were articulately conscious of what they intended and hoped for, and their testimony provides material for any account of the active human role in creating the circumstances within which identity is cultivated. The explanation of these intentions and these actions continues to inform both practice and explanation, and the social consequences of material environments are a commonplace of public discussion. What applies to the insides of buildings has been applied equally to their shaping of urban space, and the character and arrangement of streets, pavements, and open spaces. Three centuries after the municipal visionaries of Edinburgh and Manchester, the Conservative politician David Davis was able to speculate on ways of 'designing out crime.'[85]

Buildings, and the spaces which they contain and create. both state a social identity and shape and encourage one. They are training grounds where people learn and practise their roles and, as Murray Edelman put it, 'become the executives, the authorities, the psychotics, or the unreliable employees their settings tell them they are.'[86] The identity may be one of solidarity or of hierarchy and exclusion. Shops may, with their warm blast of air at the front door, say 'Come in,' but government buildings more frequently say 'Keep out' or 'You don't belong here,' or tell those who are allowed in that, compared with the possessors of the space to which they are given brief access, they are socially, as they are architecturally, diminished. Murray Edelman commented on such intimidatory architecture that it 'reminds the mass of political spectators that they enter the precincts of power as clients or as supplicants, susceptible to arbitrary rebuffs and favors, and that they are subject to remote authorities they only dimly know or understand.'[87] Even when the public are admitted to public buildings, they may be admitted only up to a certain point and no further than a clear boundary, and in ways which cultivate their status as permitted outsiders, not as rightful occupiers. Thomas Markus makes the point neatly: 'In public buildings there is a shallow visitor zone. Visitors interface with the inhabitants at some spatial barrier which prevents deeper penetration: the counter in shops and banks, the bar in pubs, the proscenium arch in theatres, the gallery space of museums. ... The person with the greatest power is at the tip of a tree, reached through corridors, stairs, outer and inner offices and waiting lobbies.'[88] The more elevated the sought-after identity, the grander and more extensive the stage. Just such a distancing of the apex from the periphery was constructed in the Reich Chancellery which Albert Speer designed for Adolf Hitler. The Chancellery required vast spaces to be traversed before reaching the Führer's office, though office was a very inadequate term for the grand hall at which the suppliant eventually arrived.[89] The distance the visitor had to travel, and the removal of the remotest areas from ordinary public access, was a human hierarchy as well as an architectural progression, an instance of what Markus has described when he commented that 'the number of layers of space one passes through from the outside of a building to reach an internal location ... map society.'[90] A similar use of intimidatory distance was used in the grandiloquently choreographed spaces of the Nuremburg rallies (figure 1).

There was nothing new in the political theatre of the Chancellery. The progression of visitors to the royal presence at Louis XIV's Palace of Versailles was through a series of courts, vestibules, and courtyards of increasing grandeur and remoteness. To enter the Hall of Mirrors was to be overwhelmed by the distances and soaring heights of the royal architectural presence, with vision vanishing in every direction in an ever repeated succession of gilt and reflected image (figure 2). When the king himself processed through the hall to his chapel, he occupied and commanded its spaces, spaces in which courtiers were observers and permitted visitors, whilst the mirrored spaciousness of the hall served on this and other grand occasions to give visible form to the magnificence of the monarchy. Nor was Versailles anything but one instance of a long history of architectural cultivation of hierarchy and elevation. Charles Goodsell comments that

1 Intimidatory space, Nuremburg

2 Reflected glory, Hall of Mirrors, Versailles

the 'rites of governance, while usually less dramatic than religious or magical rites, nonetheless invoke their own sanctity. Their formalistic, solemn format reminds those who are present of the grand and even mysterious compulsion of state authority.'[91] In the Mycenaean palace at Pylos, a 'truly elaborate series of routes separates the inside from the outside, constraining access through courtyards, vestibules, pantries, storerooms, lobbies, and entranceways. To move from the throne room to the exterior, a minimum of five spaces must be traversed.'[92]

The architectural presence of rule and government might have its grandest expressions in regimes with steep political hierarchies, but is evident in all political systems. The theatre of British constitutional monarchic democracy's rule in India was more restrained than totalitarian- or ancient-regime high opera, but Lutyens's New Delhi, completed in the second and third decades of the twentieth century, both proclaimed imperial grandeur and, by its insulating spaces, made clear the relations between rulers and ruled, the boundaries between the palace of government and the streets of mere subjects. The spaces between buildings were as important as the spaces within them in setting out inclusion and exclusion, the identities of

3 Imperial vistas, New Delhi

rulers and ruled (figure 3). When, after the end of British rule, Le Corbusier and Jane Drew planned the government buildings for an independent and democratic India in Chandigarh, the state capital of the Indian Punjab, a quarter of a century after Lutyens, what they produced, despite being part of a formal democracy, said more with its 'pedestrian-resistant' expanses of plaza about the independent authority of rulers than about the rights or participation of citizens.[93] Just as in New Delhi under imperial rule, public spaces defined the public, and defined them as subjects rather than as citizens. The grander the identity which buildings create for rulers, the smaller and lowlier by simple contrast is the identity of the ruled.

The new Brazilian capital Brasilia, designed by the architect Oscar Niemeyer and the town planner Lúcio Costa and completed in 1960 in a revived democracy, was similarly constructed in a way which functions in 'distancing the masses from the seat of courtly power' by the vast and intimidating spaces which surrounded its governing buildings.[94] The offices of government and legislation were viewed across acres of emptiness, constructing separation and distinction at the same time as they proclaimed superior presence. The very spaciousness which elevated the identity of ruling groups diminished the identity of excluded and ordinary subjects.

This importance of built space in cultivating identity was graphically and fictionally acknowledged in Richard Loncraine's 1995 film of Shakespeare's

Richard III, where the buildings of contemporary London were used as the context for an imaginative construction of a mid-twentieth-century dictatorship. High columns and grand staircases elevated the regal actors who possessed them, and raised them above the crowd. Those who had always felt that the University of London's Senate House had something of a fascist crematorium about it had their suspicions confirmed as Ian McKellen's Richard the Third strode in jackboots down its marble stairs.[95] It is not only political grandeur which can be cultivated in architecture.

All kinds of pre-eminence can be declared by built magnificence, and by elaborations of both structure and decoration such as those which led the Woolworth Building, opened in New York in 1913, to be described as 'the cathedral of commerce'.[96] The use of architecture and built space to cultivate social and political hierarchy is matched by their use to sustain it. John Nash, in planning the layout of Regent Street and its environs at the beginning of the nineteenth century, envisaged them providing 'a boundary and complete separation between the Streets and Squares occupied by the Nobility and Gentry' on the one hand and 'the narrow Streets and meaner houses occupied by mechanics and the trading parts of the community' on the other.[97]

Architecture is a built and chosen setting for human life, and can be designed for the whole range of social and political theatre. The democratic response to the architecture of distance and superiority is the architecture of transparency and access. Norman Foster's City Hall in London attempts a different statement from the architecture of dominance and exclusion, displaying the offices of bureaucrats and the deliberations of legislators to the public gaze even as they keep the public safely behind glass (figure 4). In the same way, citizens visiting Enric Miralles's Scottish Parliament building at Holyrood can rise above the spaces used by their elected representatives and peer down on them from above. The superiority of the citizen, whether or not achieved in practice, is nonetheless claimed, expressed, encouraged, cultivated, and enacted in architectural form.

The identity-cultivating and identity-confirming function of architecture is not limited to public buildings and public spaces. Within a domestic setting the construction and shaping of space can be part of the construction and shaping of the hierarchies, solidarities, and exclusions of the household. A round dwelling is more conducive to communal and egalitarian relations than a rectangular one, which can more readily be divided into zones of privilege or exclusion.[98] The principal was fictionally expressed in the equality within a knightly elite of King Arthur's round table. It is a function of space illustrated by the difference between theatrical and collegiate seating. A theatre audience, whilst observing, does not normally participate, and is ranked row on row apart from the performers. Rather

4 Open government

than being face to face, each row of observers sees only the backs of the row in front. Members of an ecclesiastical choir and directly participating clergy, by contrast, face each other on either side of a central aisle, as do legislators in the upper and lower houses of the British Parliament. Each side is then both observer and participant, actor and witness, with each, by observing, registering the active identity of the other.

But an account of architecture as simply an exercise of power in a single direction misses the feature of the very solidity of buildings and spaces which prevents them from possessing any inherent meaning. One response to this is a radical denial of any coherent relationship at all between the built environment and the rest of society and to insist, in the words of Eric Monkonnen, that 'It is all too easy to make what might be called the architectural fallacy: to read economics, politics, and society through buildings.'[99] Architecture and the construction of space are distinguished from other elements of identity in that they are not part of the immediate physical identity of any individual, but provide identity-shaping contexts, nests rather than plumage. They are, too, both slower and more permanent ways than other means of cultivating, constituting, and expressing identity. They cannot change or mutate with the speed of clothing or language, but once there, they are more solidly permanent, or semi-permanent. For this reason, paradoxically, their social meaning can change at least as radically as can that of other forms of constructed identity. The physical presence, being far more resistant to alteration than clothes or conduct, must, if there is to be change, be either effectively modified, or reassessed and re-presented – or demolished. In all of this, the built environment displays that general feature of identity cultivation which is embodied in all its instances. Making one's own identity in the face of a triumphal avenue or an intimidating palace or a cramping house may require different strategies from changing the way you dress, or speak, or move, but it is an instance of the same broad category, of the person as actor as well as recipient, agent as well as patient.

Architects and builders may have made decisions before the inhabitants arrive and without consulting them. They may, too, have had expectations about the consequences of their plans which were never fulfilled. The extreme version of this hope is the attempt to recreate old societies in new lands when, in Chris Abel's optimistic phrasing, 'people quite literally recreate familiar environments in alien locations, thus retaining that part of their identity which is their architecture.'[100] But New York is not York, nor New Hampshire Hampshire, and optimism cannot clone worlds. Dell Upton's account of the development of nineteenth-century cities in the United States is of a process whereby 'through everyday experience in and of the material world of buildings, spaces, and people – American urbanites developed active sense of themselves as individuals and as members of a new republican society', whilst at the same time the expectations of planners and reformers for the creation of calm and civilised order were frequently frustrated.[101] But the failure of plans is not the only way in which power is modified or diverted. In altering the social presence of architecture there are layers or levels of choice, cultivation, and creation, particularly in domestic settings. There are many things that can be done within a living space which develop its character without altering its structure. There is nothing inherent in the concept of power which restricts its location to the actions of an elite, and the advocacy of architecture as a means for more decentralised cultivation of the built environment can, in the support of such schemes as self-build, take and redirect an apparently extreme claim such as Abel's that people 'do not *have* architecture, therefore, but rather, a part of us *is* architecture. Architecture is a way of being.' Once the assumption of monopoly of agency is set aside, architecture can provide 'opportunities for those expressions of personal and social identity which come from having control over one's own home and neighbourhood.'[102] Sometimes, more substantial amendment than the choice of furniture or interior decoration is feasible. The stark minimalism of the workers' houses designed in 1923 by Le Corbusier for the Frugès factories in Lège and Pessac was fairly speedily transformed by their inhabitants with the addition of pitched roofs, shutters, and picket fencing.[103] Functional sparseness was attractive to architects and clients, but jarred with the actual inhabitants' idea of what a home should look like. The 1960s Bijlmermeer estate in Amsterdam was planned for an idealised average Dutch family, but incomers from Surinam with different family sizes and structures adapted the accommodation by knocking through both walls and floors.[104] The negotiation, conflict, or failure of communication between planners and users can be more comprehensive. Margaret Cameron in her account of American company towns, having dismissed architectural accounts which take the physical built environment as both simple and given, and as evidence of social, political, and industrial patterns and arrangements, reports results which were never the consequence of the ambitions of any one party, but where workers 'actively participated in the struggles to define their living and working conditions.'[105] The plans of builders and architects are never immune to the desires of users, and every skip in a city street signals further adaptation.

Where buildings are more substantial than individual homes, such reclothing is less easy, and reinterpretation is the more likely outcome. Classical buildings, as Markus comments, 'are as likely to be associated with 1930s European Fascism as with republicanism or humanism; the Modern Movement with democratic freedom as with doctrinaire bureaucracy.'[106] The meaning of stone and space may be at one time and one place intended and clear, but meaning is a human construct, and can evolve, erode, or be transformed. Anthony Alofsin comments on the Vienna Rathaus that 'At the end of the nineteenth century, people of the empire and Viennese citizens could read it as a combinatory sign of new civic power, imperial fortitude, urban revitalization, and sacred grandiosity. Today, while it houses many functions of city government, it reads as the locus of bureaucracy.'[107] The Parliament Building in Budapest was seen by its critics as Gothic and Germanic, but by opponents of Austrian power as British, democratic, and an expression of autonomy.[108] The flat roofs and simple lines of modernist design could be attacked by right-wing anti-Semites as marks of alien culture when employed by Mies van der Rohe at the Weissenhofsiedlung in Stuttgart, or used by Mussolini as an expression of the virtues of fascism.[109] This mutation of meaning places the severest strains on the interpretative skills of the archaeologist. It is an illustration, too, of the paradoxical limits by which grand buildings, or their architects and commissioners, are constrained in their ability to shape the social identities of individual citizens. The more removed from the daily, the immediate, and the domestic a building or an urban setting is, the greater the possibility that it can be dismissed, even by those who have to pass through it, as a distant display or backdrop, irrelevant to the business of normal life.

The immediate setting of space and structure is for the living. But the more grand and public and the less domestic a structure, the more it may express identities which outlive individuals. Some human constructions have no other function. Even in death, identities are cultivated, created, and demarcated. The dead can be given unique identity in the plumage with which they are interred. Discussing the traces of the life of early *Homo sapiens*, Martin Jones has observed that 'Pierced skeletal fragments, bones, shells, teeth, and ivory ... will be strung together in necklaces and headgear of buried bodies, emphasizing the face and head, and sometimes arms, in other words, the body as communicator, as social person.'[110] The collective solidarity of members of the armed forces is expressed in the ordered ranks of uniform stones in a military cemetery, just as the hierarchies of civil society and public life are marked out by the range of monuments, from elaborate miniature chapels to simple crosses, in civilian graveyards. The location and character of funerary monuments has proclaimed the virtue of teetotallers as readily as it has the indigent dependency of the poor.[111]

The dead can be part of the identity of the living as well as of their own. In eighteenth-century Britain, memorial sculptures and monuments to radical politicians could provide 'a rallying point for groups that stood outside and in opposition to constituted authority and established hierarchies.'[112] The living can recruit the dead in support of their assertion of identity and their challenge to identities which threaten or marginalise their own. In Edinburgh, the installation on Calton Hill of a memorial to Scots transported in 1793 and 1794 for sedition was an assertion of a contrary identity to that represented by statues of Pitt, Melville, and George IV in the streets below.[113] Whereas the dwellings of the living lost their function with the death of their inhabitants, the tombs and monuments of the departed, as the Viennese architect Adolf Loos observed, constituted an identity for as long as their fabric survived.[114] In republican Rome, the architectural theatre of the Forum provided an imposing setting for the funerals of prominent citizens which functioned 'both as homage to an individual and as powerful propaganda drawing the public's attention to the past accomplishments and future promise of the family staging the ceremony.'[115] In creating and honouring the habitations of the dead, the living embellish and sustain their own identities.

The dead link the living to the land in which they lie and on which their successors live. Movements of the populations on the Sino-Russian borders led to the Cossacks' reassertion of their own identity by the exhumation and reburial, with renewed Christian rites, of ancestors in land whose sacredness was proclaimed as a part of collective transcendental distinctiveness. The ancestors made the land sacred and distinct, and the land made its inhabitants sacred and distinct.[116] People are in part the places they inhabit, and if the place is grand enough, it is incorporated in a person's name: 'de,' 'von,' or an aristocratic title which dispenses altogether with the pronoun and substitutes the geographical for the familial whilst at the same time implying a familial claim to the named territory. The individual is greater than his or her mere body, and incorporates hills and fields, lakes and boulevards.

Those at first sight natural elements of human environment can, as the landed titles of aristocracy suggest, contribute one further dimension to human identity. The very seemingly prehuman source of the natural world makes it appropriate as a location and symbol of elements of human identity which lie beyond the immediately visible, tangible, or audible aspects of human bodies and human artefacts. Nature can be supernatural, but with a supernatural dimension that embellishes the identity of mortal humans.[117] Man may be made in the image of God, but the signs on earth of that divine casting and of other gateways to or manifestations of the supernatural are the result either of human cultivation, or of the attribution by humans of significance to aspects of the existing natural world. The sacred and magical places – trees, rivers, springs, and wells which were the outer boundaries of religious experience – provided both sources of continuing identity for those who felt the Protestant Reformation in the British Isles as a loss, and continuity for those who acquiesced in change but found sustenance in elements of continuity.[118] In cultivating sacred meanings in the natural world, men and women expand the dimensions in which their own religious identity is expressed and sustained. The cultivation of human identity in humanity's material environment does not stop with architecture, but grows outwards to shape an entire world.

Identity is everything we do

Woolf's call to political action illustrates the two poles of identity, whatever its form. At one extreme, cultivated identity is part of membership or association in a group, or class, or level of society. To that extent it is not chosen, but is the conventional appearance of who one is because of who one associates with; it is Bourdieu's habitus. But at the other extreme, it is possible to choose from existing possibilities and overcome existing restraints, refusing uniforms and honours. And it is the infinite number of possible points on that scale from the domination of circumstance to the maximum exercise of choice that characterises the variety of actual outcomes and the difficulty of ever predicting them all. Woolf's photographs also illustrate the paradox of identity, for however much the regalia of her elite males marks them off from the ordinary population, at the same time it allows them to set themselves apart from each other, and from those with whom they are in splendour associated – a vice chancellor not a mere dean, an archbishop not a suffragan bishop, a general with more medals than anyone else.

The paradox of identity is that this cultivated persona is pulled in two directions. On the one hand identity is cultivated by association, by membership of a group, or class, or religion, or profession. On the other hand identity is a step back from all those who might be considered similar. The first pole of identity is the whole complexity of conduct, appearance, and speech, which can be described as received rather than chosen by the members of a class, group, or caste, and which constitutes a part of their association with others – taste, as Bourdieu has labelled it.[119] The second pole is the cultivation of individuality, a refusal to be identified as merely an example of a general cultural species but as a special or exemplary instance of it.

Human plumage differs in one major quality from the plumage of birds: it can be put on and put off. But whilst this might suggest impermanence and unpredictability, plumage change is not usually carried out in a whimsical manner. Choices are made, but they are made in cultural contexts, and their non-trivial significance is often marked by rituals of transition. A change of plumage, whilst it is an opportunity which humans are markedly more privileged than other creatures in enjoying, is not necessarily made lightly, and will be marked by rubrics and rituals which declare to others the identity choices that are happening. Choices and changes and their accompanying rituals can be carried out in any mode of human action or production. Shifting identities can be cultivated by changing the ways and components of eating, just as existing identities can be consolidated by them. And eating as a mark of transition can be given its own rituals and rubric from wedding cakes to the feasts of Oxbridge colleges, the Inns of Court, or City of London livery companies. When George Orwell was welcomed into a hitherto seemingly menacing congregation of stevedores, navvies, and sailors in a rough lodging house with "Ave a cup of tea chum,' it was as much of a culinary ritual as the grandest state banquet, and as little to do with the mere sustenance of life.[120] Other rites of transition from one professional, religious, or other social status to another will be marked by formal ceremonies of passage, investitures, graduation ceremonies, ordinations, baptisms, weddings.[121]

One of many components of changes or embellishments of identity may be a change of name. 'Christian names' were at one time precisely that, and those entering monastic orders may still acquire a new name for their new identity. For the grandest and most publicly prominent changes of identity, from cardinal to pope, or heir to the throne to monarch, a change of name proclaims the new person. The Emperor of China left family and personal names behind, Albert Windsor becomes George the Sixth, Joseph Ratzinger becomes Benedict the Sixteenth, and Professor Hugh Trevor-Roper becomes Lord Dacre.

In all of this, identity is negotiated in the engagement of individual action with social contexts, and the restraints and opportunities which existing identities present to individuals. Choices are continually made, and in being made amend and cultivate the range of identity which provides the starting point and context for any further individual decision. And as with every concrete event or situation, the point on the scale from impossible unconstrained freedom to equally impossible wholly determined action will differ, and the degree of circumstantial or coercive and legal sanction in the cultivation of identity will be specific to time and place. In the United Kingdom it is convention alone which leads women on marriage to change their family name to that of their husband. In Japan, a law of 1896 requires married couples to have the same surname. Convention has favoured the male partner in retaining his existing family name rather than adopting his wife's, but has not required it. And in 2015 five Japanese women unsuccessfully sued their government over what they contested was an unconstitutional violation of their rights.[122]

Whilst identity is the fluid product of a negotiation between structure and agency, accounts and theories which aspire to universality tend to construct their argument around a single cause or function or source of identity, from a near determinism where culture is independent of any individual, who is left no effective freedom or choice, to an account of the constant presentation of self as a free agent. The most extreme point at the determinist end of the scale sees coercion by the state, or in societies with limited government by churches or other state-like institutions, as enforcers of conformity. Gary Watt has argued that clothing functions to 'instantiate the power and authority of the political State.'[123] A milder point on the scale concentrates on convention. But the force of convention and the application of law are only ever single factors in the cultivation of identity, and no temporally or geographically specific instance can be explained solely by their analytical deployment. A duffle coat or a pair of green wellington boots can be as much a part of identity as a party rosette, but the absence or presence of beards, which might be a fashion statement in contemporary Europe, can be coercively governed in Taleban-controlled areas of Afghanistan, while in revolutions outward appearance can be violently regulated and penalised. What might cause beams or bemusement in Kensington could evoke bludgeons in Kabul.

Conclusion: the tension between equality and inequality

The never-ending cultivation of human identity involves artefacts and ornamentation, culture and customs, in the creation of collective and individual distinction along the tense polarity between solidarity and individual distinction. Human societies are structured around these cultivated identities, not at either of its theoretically possible but practically implausible polls. And whilst when the search for identity through solidarity is focussed on a whole community or nation it becomes an aspiration towards equality, the politics of equality is played out along these lines of tension and opposition. The pull towards solidarity is constantly countered by the opposite pull towards group and individual distinctiveness and, frequently, group and individual superiority and inferiority. Whenever visible and audible character appears to express equality, there soon begins a recession towards rank, or hierarchy, or exclusion, or ascendancy. The dilemmas of an egalitarian society were soon apparent in revolutionary France. The passion for equality to accompany liberty and fraternity included a reaction against any appearances which under the old regime had marked superiority or privilege. But '"dressing for equality" foundered in practice, first on gender and then on politics ... Bodies without signs were unreadable and therefore suspect or dangerous.'[124] So the revolution substituted the distinctions of office for the distinctions of rank, marking its leaders and cadres with the very distinctions it denied to monarchy, aristocracy, and clergy.[125]

Whenever equality is established, there are immediate efforts to make distinctions within it. The very processes which make artefacts the insignia for wider and wider circles of a population are both reacted against and promoted by the aspiration to individual uniqueness. Advertising applauds how products sold in the thousands will make their possessor stand out from the crowd, whilst brand labels become the only distinction between one mass-produced car, or suit, or pair of jeans and another. Mass clothing feeds an aspiration towards distinctiveness just as every other form of equality or solidarity leads to aspirations towards singularity and exclusion. But it does not create it.

It is unwise ever to be dismissive about 'mere appearance'. If you know the house, and the office, and the wardrobe, and the breakfast, you are getting close to the whole public person. And since for most of the time, in order for orderly relations with the rest of humanity to occur, we need swift and unambiguous signals, we use them and read them. It is what makes us the clothed ape. The constructed person and the person's constructed setting are not a representation of or a clue to that person's identity; they are that person's identity, whatever secret and unexpressed reservations or alternatives the person may have.

One form of social life, politics, has frequently been compared to a theatre, and the performances of its participants as masks. Erving Goffman distinguishes between the performer and the performance, though once all the things which he describes as performance have been gathered together, there is nothing left to be attributed to any other identity or self. Either the self is the performance, which is cautiously suggested when Goffman writes that 'the very structure of the self can be seen in terms of how we arrange for such performances' and when he refers to 'producing and maintaining selves', or the self consists of awareness or self-consciousness, experiencing 'fantasies and dreams' but having no character. Whichever solution is employed, the identity of a person is a social and public thing, not some inner reality.[126] David Runciman has drawn attention to the complexity of the metaphor of mask and theatre in discussing political action and political association.[127] In his discussion of hypocrisy in public life, he speaks of 'the masks of politics and what lies behind those masks', and of masks as concealing 'whom one really is', though this distinction between a public front and a deeper reality is qualified when, referring to La Rochefoucauld's description of hypocrisy, he comments that 'the concealment turns out to be a form of amelioration ... Hypocrites who pretend to be better than they really are could also be said to be better than they might be, because they are at least pretending to be good'.[128] But both metaphors, of theatre and of masks, when filled out, can move the account towards according the dramatic presentation its own reality, rather than being a pretence for obscuring a deeper, more real, identity. Ferdinand Mount has argued that:

> the idea that there is a *real* (efficient, useful) politics which is masked by an *unreal* (superficial) sham show is one of the most potent delusions of our time ... The myths and rituals which a regime has allowed or, more usually, encouraged to grow up around itself often reveal something very significant about the real nature of that regime – the essentially populist, good-humoured, consensual nature of Macmillan's Toryism, the aristocratic, activist liberalism of the Kennedys, the autocracy of de Gaulle.[129]

It is possible to take the equal value of onstage and offstage underlying Mount's argument further, and to insist that the show is not even adequately seen as an indication of what lies beneath, but is a public reality in its own right. This is to move even further from a metaphor of masks which would assume or imply that in private, or in more secluded company, a real identity emerges and a false public identity is hung up like a selkie's skin on a coat hanger. But whatever the disjunctures between one dimension of identity and another, a public identity is a real feature of public life, whatever else may be said about it. And whilst there are people, such as spies, who lead two lives and are in that way two people, most identities survive the transition from the relatively public to the relatively private with little damage or moderating, and serve equally well in both. The problem about the inner man or the inner woman is that they are invisible. The outside is all we have to go on. Alternatively, if it is suggested that the mask is permanent, then the mask is the person and the metaphor collapses. And when one distinction goes, another arrives. Even when there is no one else about, the material construction and cultivation of identity goes on. Robinson Crusoe alone on his island showed himself civilised by means of a hat, and did so in the absence of anyone but himself to appreciate his wearing of it. For whilst the drama of identity is composed of public show, the most important member of the audience can be the actor himself or herself. And unlike the life of the theatre, the audience is ever-present, the costumes always there, and there is no dressing-room retreat or curtain close.

The mask metaphor may suggest the view that external actions may be either an expression of or a camouflage net for a secret or inner self. But even if the visible and audible presentation of self is paralleled by some private, lesser, or unexpressed self, as a person living in society and relating to other people it is the external and acted self which is real. The identities which people create are the only ones they have, and if there are secret dreams, unless they receive some expression, they remain secret, and dreams. Quentin Crisp made the point neatly when he said that if for forty years a pig farmer has been saying that really he was meant to be a ballet dancer, by that time pigs were his style.[130]

Whilst any identity may be composed of many layers and aspects, all the layers need not be of equal importance, and people do not defend all dimensions of identity with equal vigour. What is missed in a one-dimensional, plucked, account and in the search for the one true identity is the complexity and potential instability of the variegated whole. Identity and its cultivation provide the script and the scenery for the human drama, but it is not a drama with a universally coherent plot or a harmonious cast. People cultivate an identity not only for others, but for themselves, and the safest working supposition is that there is coherence, rather than incoherence, between what is done in the sight of the audience, front of house, and what is done backstage. Rulers, leaders, and everyone else, in other words, should be taken at face value unless there are good reasons to believe otherwise. The drama of identification is not conducted with reference to scenery, theatrical effects, and the construction of expressive contexts only in its more public aspects, but in its more secluded or private ones as well. The identity constructed or cultivated by the larger public stage set is normally consistent with, or seeking consistency with, that cultivated by the more immediately personal plumage and scenery.

Human life is endlessly diverse, and once the same understandings are used in giving an account of it as are used in giving accounts of the rest of existence, the only meaning the term 'human nature' can have is 'everything that humans do'. Eating, speaking, moving, dressing, singing, dancing – all go to make up the complexity that is human identity. Accounts in terms of essences or essentials will always be one-dimensional or monochrome, and without being untrue, will be of limited illumination. However comprehensive an account of the cultural setting within which, despite themselves, people operate, or which they may choose as a means of identity cultivation by association, the contrary pull of individual assertion and the possibilities of eccentric dissent and innovation create the permanent lurking promise of surprise, disruption, and unpredictability. That does not make the understanding of human life easy, but it prevents it from being uninteresting or predictable.

Notes

1 Thomas Paine, *Rights of Man: Being An Answer to Mr. Burke's Attack on the French Revolution* (London: Watts & Co., 1937), p. 15.

2 Rodney Barker, 'Hooks and Hands, Interests and Enemies: Political Thinking as Political Action', *Political Studies*, 48:2 (2000), 228.

3 Dani Cavallaro and Alexandra Warwick, *Fashioning the Frame: Boundaries, Dress and the Body* (Oxford and New York: Berg, 1998), p. 116.
4 Virginia Woolf, *Three Guineas* (London: Penguin, 1993), p. 137.
5 Woolf, *Three Guineas*, p. 138.
6 Desmond Morris, *The Naked Ape* (London: Jonathan Cape, 1967).
7 Quentin Bell, *On Human Finery* (London: Hogarth Press, 1976).
8 Thorstein Veblen, *The Theory of the Leisure Class: An Economic Study of Institutions* (London: Allen & Unwin,1924), pp. 40, 70.
9 Bell, *On Human Finery*, p. 19.
10 Jenny Diski, *A View from the Bed and Other Observations* (London: Virago, 2003), p. 33.
11 Virginia Woolf, *Orlando* (London: Penguin, 1974), p. 170.
12 Bourdieu, *Distinction*, p. 468.
13 Sergei Eisenstein, *Ivan the Terrible, Part 2* [film] (Moscow: Mosfilm, 1958).
14 Charles Gormley, *Heavenly Pursuits* [film] (London: Channel Four Films, 1985).
15 Lynn Hunt, *Politics, Culture and Class in the French Revolution* (Berkeley: University of California Press, 1984), p. 53.
16 Eric Hobsbawm, *Age of Extremes: The Short Twentieth Century 1914–1991* (London: Michael Joseph, 1994), p. 209.
17 Harold Nicolson, *Diaries and Letters 1930–39*, edited by Nigel Nicolson (London: William Collins, 1966), p. 89.
18 George Bernard Shaw, *Pygmalion* (London: Penguin, 1946), p. 80.
19 Wallace Stevens, 'Theory', in *Harmonium* (London: Faber, 2001), p. 108.
20 Jane Austen, *Emma* (London: J. M. Dent, 1922), pp. 146, 170.
21 Hilton Holloway, 'Volvo plays party politics', *Autocar*, 10 June 2011, www.autocar.co.uk/blogs/autocarconfidential/archive/2011/06/10/volvo-plays-party-politics.aspx (accessed 18 June 2011).
22 Sean O'Connell, *The Car and British Society: Class, Gender and Motoring 1896–1939* (Manchester: Manchester University Press, 1998), p. 79.
23 Mel Brooks, *The Producers* [film] (Beverly Hills: MGM), 1968.
24 Quoted in O'Connell, *The Car*, p. 188.
25 O'Connell, *The Car*, p. 23.
26 O'Connell, *The Car*, p. 24.
27 Jason Burke, 'Saudi women get behind wheel in protest against driving ban', *Guardian*, 18 June 2011, pp. 20–1.
28 Antonia Finnane, *Changing Clothes in China* (London: Hurst & Co, 2008), p. 1.
29 W. B. Yeats, 'Coole and Ballylee 1931', *The Collected Works of W. B. Yeats Volume I: The Poems*, revised 2nd ed. (New York: Simon & Schuster, 2010), p. 245.
30 Kenneth J. Ruoff, *The People's Emperor: Democracy and the Japanese Monarchy, 1945–1995* (Cambridge, MA: Harvard University Press, 2001), p. 222.
31 Frank Prochaska, *The Republic of Britain 1760–2000* (London: Penguin, 2001), illustration 17.

32 See www.info-britain.co.uk/prince.charles.camilla.wedding.photos/ (accessed 29 October 2009).
33 Philip Webster, '"Blair Force One" is on order, but it's for the Queen and Brown', *The Times*, 23 May 2007, www.timesonline.co.uk/tol/news/politics/article1826731.ece (accessed 30 November 2010).
34 Mary Beard, 'Highway Codes: What Romans Thought Walking Was For, and What They Might Have Talked About as They Walked', *The Times Literary Supplement*, 5693 (11 May 2012), p. 3.
35 John R. Searle, *The Construction of Social Reality* (London: Allen Lane, 1995); John R. Searle, *Making the Social World: The Structure of Human Civilization* (Oxford: Oxford University Press, 2010).
36 Françoise Waquet, *Latin: Or the Empire of a Sign*, translated by John Howe (London: Verso, 2001).
37 Benedict Anderson, *Imagined Communities: Reflections on the Origin and Spread of Nationalism* (London: Verso, 2006), pp. 45–7.
38 Shaw, *Pygmalion*, p. 78.
39 Alexander Armstrong and Ben Miller, *RAF fighter pilots sketch*, www.armstrongandmiller.co.uk/video_raf_pilots.html (accessed 22 June 2011). (The version the author consulted is no longer available, but this can now be viewed at www.youtube.com/watch?v=r_b1Y-Rl_Uo.)
40 William Shakespeare, *King Lear* (London: Methuen, 1957).
41 *The Bible, Authorized King James Version* (Oxford: Oxford University Press, 2008), Genesis 27:22.
42 From a quote in Marilyn Butler's *Maria Edgeworth: A Literary Biography*, quoted in Amanda Vickery, *Behind Closed Doors: At Home in Georgian England* (London: Yale University Press, 2009), p. 16.
43 John Belchem, '"An Accent Exceedingly Rare": Scouse and the Inflexion of Class', in John Belchem and Neville Kirk (eds), *Languages of Labour* (Aldershot, UK: Ashgate, 1997).
44 Quoted in Andrew Taylor, *A Plum in Your Mouth* (London: Harper Collins, 2006), p. 235.
45 Nancy Mitford (ed.), *Noblesse Oblige: An Enquiry into the Identifiable Characteristics of the English Aristocracy* (London: Hamish Hamilton, 1956).
46 Ross McKibbin, *Classes and Cultures: England 1918–1951* (Oxford: Oxford University Press, 1998), p. 27.
47 John Honey, *Does Accent Matter? The Pygmalion Factor* (London: Faber, 1989), p. 149.
48 William K. Powers and Marla M. N. Powers, 'Metaphysical Aspects of an Oglala Food System', in Mary Douglas (ed.), *Food in the Social Order: Studies of Food and Festivities in Three American Communities* (New York: Russell Sage Foundation, 1984), p. 47.
49 Auberon Waugh, *Will This Do?* (London: Carroll and Graf, 2003), p. 67.
50 James Epstein, *Radical Expression, Political Language, Ritual, and Symbol in England 1790–1850* (Oxford: Oxford University Press, 1994).
51 Martin Jones, *Feast: Why Humans Share Food* (Oxford: Oxford University Press, 2007), p. 163.

52 *The Works of Geoffrey Chaucer*, edited by Alfred W. Pollard, H. Frank Heath, Mark H. Liddell, and W. S. McCormick (London: Macmillan, 1925), p. 3.
53 *The Bible, Authorized King James Version* (Oxford: Oxford University Press, 2008), Daniel 4:33.
54 Sidney W. Mintz, *Tasting Food, Tasting Freedom: Excursions into Eating, Culture, and the Past* (Boston: Beacon Press, 1996), p. 27.
55 John Boulting and Roy Boulting, *The Guinea Pig* [film] (London: Pilgrim Pictures, 1948); Robert Altman, *Gosford Park* [film] (Sheperton, UK: Sheperton Studios, 2001).
56 Benjamin Disraeli, *Sybil, or The Two Nations* (Oxford: Oxford Paperbacks, 2008), pp. 65–6.
57 *The Bible, Authorized King James Version* (Oxford: Oxford University Press, 2008), Luke 14:10.
58 Gabriel Axel, *Babette's Feast* [film] (Copenhagen: Nordisk Film, 1987).
59 Jones, *Feast*, pp. 162–5.
60 Mary Douglas, *Purity and Danger* (New York: Russell Sage Foundation, 1984).
61 Mary Douglas, 'Standard Social Uses of Food: Introduction', in Douglas (ed.), *Food in the Social Order*, p. 11.
62 Mary Douglas, 'Deciphering a Meal', *Daedalus*, 101:1 (1972), 79.
63 Lucie Aubrac, *Outwitting the Gestapo*, translated by Konrad Bieber and Betsy Wing (Nebraska and London: University of Nebraska Press, 1993), p. 51.
64 George Orwell, *The Road to Wigan Pier* (London: Gollancz, 1937; Penguin ed. Harmondsworth, UK: Penguin, 1962), p. 152; George Orwell, 'The Lion and the Unicorn', *The Collected Essays, Journalism and Letters of George Orwell, Volume II: My Country Right or Left, 1940–1943*, edited by Sonia Orwell and Ian Angus (Harmondsworth, UK: Penguin, 1970 [1968]), p. 95; George Orwell, 'In Defence of English Cooking', *My Country Right or Left*, p. 58.
65 *The Bible, Authorized King James Version* (Oxford: Oxford University Press, 2008), Matthew 9:11; Mark 2:16.
66 Salman Rushdie, *Shame* (London: Picador, 1984).
67 Gary Younge and Jon Henley, 'Wimps, weasels and monkeys – the US media view of "perfidious France"', *Guardian*, 11 February 2003, www.theguardian.com/world/2003/feb/11/pressandpublishing.usa (accessed 7 February 2017).
68 Linda Colley, *Britons: Forging the Nation 1707–1837* (New Haven, CT: Yale University Press, 1992), pp. 33–4.
69 Jones, *Feast*, pp. 162–3.
70 Carl E. Schorske, *Thinking with History: Explorations in the Passage to Modernism* (Princeton, NJ: Princeton University Press, 1998), pp. 116, 157–71.
71 Vickery, *Behind Closed Doors*, pp. 100–1.
72 Vickery, *Behind Closed Doors*, p. 295.
73 Quoted in Deborah Cohen, *Household Gods: The British and Their Possessions* (New Haven, CT: Yale University Press, 2006), p. 26.
74 Robert Crawford, 'Us', in John Burnside, Robert Crawford, and Kathleen Jamie, *Penguin Modern Poets 9* (London: Penguin, 1996), p. 81.

75 Alain de Botton, *The Architecture of Happiness* (London: Pantheon, 2007), p. 11.
76 Richard C. Beacham, *Power into Pageantry: Spectacle Entertainments of Early Imperial Rome* (New Haven, CT: Yale University Press, 1999), p. 130.
77 Quoted in Beacham, *Power into Pageantry,* p. 130.
78 Murray Edelman, *The Symbolic Uses of Politics* (London: University of Illinois Press, 1964), p. 98.
79 Beacham, *Power into Pageantry,* p. 126.
80 Dell Upton, *Another City: Urban Life and Urban Spaces in the New American Republic* (New Haven, CT: Yale University Press, 2008); C. Philo, 'Edinburgh, Enlightenment and the Geographies of Unreason,' in D. N. Livingstone and C. W. J. Withers (eds), *Geography and Enlightenment* (Chicago: University of Chicago Press, 1999), pp. 372–98.
81 Tristram Hunt, *Building Jerusalem: The Rise and Fall of the Victorian City* (London: Weidenfeld and Nicolson, 2004), p. 87.
82 Quoted in Hunt, *Building Jerusalem,* p. 236.
83 Hunt, *Building Jerusalem,* pp. 239–47.
84 Thomas A. Markus, 'The School as Machine: Working Class Scottish Education and the Glasgow Normal Seminary,' in Thomas A. Markus (ed.), *Order in Space and Society: Architectural Form and its Context in the Scottish Enlightenment* (Edinburgh: Mainstream, 1982), pp. 201–61.
85 David Davis, 'Designing Out Crime ...' *BBC One, Politics Show,* 3 December 2006, http://news.bbc.co.uk/1/hi/programmes/politics_show/6193304.stm (accessed 1 February 2012).
86 Murray Edelman, 'Space and the Social Order,' *Journal of Architectural Education,* 32:3 (1978), 5.
87 Edelman, 'Space,' 3.
88 Thomas A. Markus, *Buildings and Power: Freedom and Control in the Origin of Modern Building Types* (London: Routledge, 1993), p. 14.
89 Charles Goodsell, *The Social Meaning of Civic Space: Studying Political Authority through Architecture* (Lawrence: University Press of Kansas, 1988), p. 4; Deyan Sudjic, *The Edifice Complex: How the Rich and Powerful Shape the World* (New York: Penguin Press, 2005), pp. 20–8.
90 Thomas A. Markus, 'Introduction,' in Markus, *Order in Space and Society,* p. 5.
91 Goodsell, *Social Meaning,* p. 12.
92 Jones, *Feast,* p. 190.
93 Lawrence J. Vale, *Architecture, Power and National Identity* (New Haven, CT: Yale University Press, 1992), p. 113.
94 Vale, *Architecture,* p. 127.
95 Richard Loncraine, *Richard III* [film] (Beverly Hills: United Artists, 1995).
96 Gail Fenske, *The Skyscraper and the City: The Woolworth Building and the Making of Modern New York* (Chicago: University of Chicago Press, 2008), p. 265.
97 Quoted in Rodney Mace, *Trafalgar Square, Emblem of Empire* (London: Lawrence & Wishart, 1976), p. 33.

98 Jones, *Feast*, p. 140.
99 Eric H. Monkonnen, *America Becomes Urban: The Development of U.S. Cities and Towns, 1780–1980* (Berkeley, CA; Los Angeles; and London: University of California Press, 1988), p. 14.
100 Chris Abel, *Architecture and Identity: Responses to Cultural and Technological Change*, 2nd ed. (London: Routledge, 2000), p. 149.
101 Upton, *Another City*, p. 1.
102 Abel, *Architecture and Identity*, pp. 150, 141.
103 De Botton, *Architecture of Happiness*, pp. 163–5.
104 Rowan Moore, 'We think we shape the homes we live in, but how much do they shape us?', *Observer, New Review*, 12 August 2012, p. 16.
105 Margaret Crawford, *Building the Workingman's Paradise: The Design of American Company Towns* (London: Verso, 1993), p. 7.
106 Markus, *Buildings and Power*, p. 4; Robert Bevan, *The Destruction of Memory: Architecture at War* (London: Reaktion, 2006), p. 12.
107 Anthony Alofsin, *When Buildings Speak: Architecture as Language in the Habsburg Empire and its Aftermath, 1867–1933* (Chicago: University of Chicago Press, 2006), p. 29.
108 Alofsin, *When Buildings Speak*, p. 128.
109 Sudjic, *The Edifice Complex*, p. 36.
110 Jones, *Feast*, p. 96.
111 Alex Tyrell, 'Preserving the Glory for Preston: The Campo Santo of the Preston Teetotalers', in Paul A. Pickering and Alex Tyrell (eds), *Contested Sites: Commemoration, Memorial and Popular Politics in Nineteenth-Century Britain* (Aldershot, UK: Ashgate, 2004), pp. 127–45.
112 Paul A. Pickering and Alex Tyrell, 'The Public Memorial of Reform', in Pickering and Tyrell, *Contested Sites*, p. 8.
113 Alex Tyrell and Michael T. David, 'Bearding the Tories: The Commemoration of the Scottish Political Martyrs of 1793–94', in Pickering and Tyrell, *Contested Sites*, p. 30.
114 Edward Hollis, 'Reality Checkpoint', *Cambridge Alumni Magazine*, 57 (Easter Term 2009), p. 25.
115 Beacham, *Power into Pageantry*, p. 38.
116 Leigh Brauman, 'Border Country', *Cambridge Alumni Magazine*, 62 (Lent 2011), p. 31.
117 Alexandra Walsham, *The Reformation of the Landscape: Religion, Identity and Memory in Early Modern Britain and Ireland* (Oxford: Oxford University Press, 2011).
118 Walsham, *Reformation of the Landscape*, pp. 233 ff.
119 Bourdieu, *Distinction*.
120 Orwell, *The Road to Wigan Pier*, p. 133.
121 Jones, *Feast*, p. 219; Pierre Bourdieu, *Language and Symbolic Power*, edited by John B. Thompson, translated by Gino Raymond and Matthew Adamson (Cambridge: Polity, 1991), pp. 119–21.
122 Reuters in Tokyo, 'Japanese women in court fight to keep their surnames after marriage', *Guardian*, 11 December 2015, www.theguardian.com/world/2015/

dec/11/japan-supreme-court-rule-one-surname-law-married-couples (accessed 14 January 2016); Justin McCurry, 'Japan upholds rule that married couples must have same surname', *Guardian*, 16 December 2015, www.theguardian.com/world/2015/dec/16/japanese-court-rules-married-women-cannot-keep-their-surnames (accessed 14 January 2016).

123 Gary Watt, *Dress, Law and Naked Truth: A Cultural Study of Fashion and Form*, Kindle ed. (London: Bloomsbury Publishing, 2013), Kindle location 148–50.

124 Sara E. Melzer and Kathryn Norberg, 'Introduction', in Sara E. Melzer and Kathryn Norberg (eds), *From the Royal to the Republican Body: Incorporating the Political in Seventeenth- and Eighteenth-Century France* (Berkeley: University of California Press, 1998), p. 9.

125 Richard Wrigley, *The Politics of Appearance: The Symbolism of Dress in Revolutionary France* (Oxford: Berg, 2002), pp. 59–86.

126 Erving Goffman, *The Presentation of Self in Everyday Life* (London: Penguin, 1971), pp. 244–6.

127 David Runciman, *Pluralism and the Personality of the State* (Cambridge: Cambridge University Press, 1997).

128 David Runciman, *Political Hypocrisy: The Mask of Power, from Hobbes to Orwell and Beyond* (Princeton: Princeton University Press, 2008), pp. 226, 10.

129 Ferdinand Mount, *The Theatre of Politics* (London: Weidenfeld & Nicolson, 1972), pp. 8–9.

130 Quentin Crisp, in performance at the Duke of York's Theatre, London, *An Evening With Quentin Crisp*, 1978.

2

Identity Cultivation

Taking people seriously; what you see is what you get

A can of paint can be sold with the slogan 'It does just what it says on the tin.' People are more than paint, but what can be seen and heard matters in social life. I have made the democratic empirical assumption that feathers and flags, clothes and gestures, voice and manners, and all the other expressions and features of identity, are not signs of who people are; they are what people, as social beings, are, and constitute their social identity. Whatever secret thoughts people may have which they communicate to no one, as social persons people exist in relation to other people, and what they do and what others see and hear is who they are. Identity is a visible, audible, and tangible social creation and cultivation, and is expressed in all the varied actions which people carry out and all the various contexts both which they create and cultivate for themselves and which they find created and cultivated already by others. Identity is a complex of circumstance and choice, of collectivity and individuality. This identity and its associated meaning and justification are cultivated and expressed as a dimension of public action: language, dress, the choreography of government and of politics, and the shapes and sounds of social and public life. The physical, created dimensions of identity, from clothes to architecture, are not only the constructed material setting for action, but are also themselves public actions which cultivate, generate, and constitute social persons.

To say that artefacts are part of identity is different from attributing purpose, character, or meaning to artefacts. Artefacts, using that term to refer to anything which is the creation of human labour, do not speak. It is the ways in which people inhabit, wear, or use them which give them their meaning. So although meanings are socially embedded in created objects and environments, it is not always easy or even possible to read that meaning once the original actors are departed. The physical presence of Stonehenge may be solid and tangible, but its social meaning is obscure and contested, and may always be impossible to discern with any certainty.

Because the significance of artefacts is socially cultivated, new and different significances can be generated around them. The swastika as an ancient Hindu symbol of well-being was reproduced in Europe on the book covers of Rudyard Kipling and, with quite different significance, in the regalia of the Nazi Party. It has no inherent meaning, but has possessed real and substantial social ones. The identities which were expressed and sustained by Stonehenge or by swastikas were not arbitrary or capricious. But they were identities created and cultivated by a particular people at a particular time, and for them, and for any one of them, constituted an external reality in relation to which their individual character and the character of the their collective life was formed.

The understanding that people are what they do is to be found in one form or another across a wide swathe of accounts of human social life. It is approached though not fully realised by the distinction made in survey studies of opinion and choice between stated preferences and revealed preferences, in which it is argued that people's 'real' preferences about, for instance, food, are indicated not by what they say about their tastes in answer to questionnaires or in conversation, but by what they actually eat. Stated wishes, in other words, are trumped by acted wishes, the actions of the outward, public person. A revealed preference in this sense is part of the real and public cultivation of identity, a stated preference is a mere aspiration. But the narrative of preferences can be taken further, since it is possible, having made the assumption about the reality of the public, expressed identity, to see even expressed preference as significant – a statement, not an intention to make a statement, revealing what it is that the speaker, actor, wants to be seen or heard and so creating a public dimension of that person's identity. Everything that is done, in other words, is to be treated neither as evidence of something else, an inner or core reality, nor as a deceit covering 'real' identity, but as a component part of the public reality of the person, group, or society. It is an extension to the whole gamut of action not so much of the aphorism, 'You are what you eat', as of the claim that 'What you eat is who you are.' But what you say you want to eat is also part of who you are. The 'realist' distinction between expressed and revealed preferences is not realist enough. Everything that is done is real, and contributes to identity. Just as human nature is everything that humans do, so human identity is composed of all the actions, cultivations, and creations which humans undertake.

The apparent contrast between what people say and what they do, between verbal action and all other kinds of action, can be replaced by a distinction between the various kinds of things that they do. The rejection of the view that if there is a contrast between statements and other actions then only the other actions are real has a long history. Hypocrisy is not just, as La Rochefoucauld put it, the compliment that vice pays to virtue. The aphorism is a recognition that even when you want to do the very opposite of what you promised, you have to frame your betrayal in the language and values to which publicly you are committed. This may not be an iron restraint, but it is a restraint nonetheless, and a restraint placed by one part of identity upon another. And while identity may always move towards coherence, it will never achieve a point where it can be expressed in a single statement, or deduced from a single principle or description. To that extent, duplicity and hypocrisy are features of the continuous pluralism of identity and the dynamic stress and collision between its different aspects.

This view, or something very much like it, informs the account of public life given by historians. Lynn Hunt in her work on eighteenth-century revolutionary France argues that dress and ritual do not express some other or distinct reality, but are themselves an important and distinct element of reality. 'Such symbols did not simply express political positions, they were the means by which people became aware of their positions. By making a political position manifest, they made adherence, opposition, and indifference possible. In this way they constituted a field of political struggle.'[1] This understanding of things adds a further dimension to Robert Browning's lament for the lost leader:

> Just for a handful of silver he left us,
> Just for a riband to stick in his coat[2]

A riband in your coat can be a prize as much sought after as a pig or a pension if it is part of a new, or enhanced, or modified identity. Browning's allusion is dismissive of buttons and bows, but they can be as much a component of the cultivation of identity as banners or creeds. In a violent football crowd, the colour of a sweatshirt can be all that is needed to brand a person as friend or foe. Bitter, violent, and deadly religious conflicts have been pursued over the extent of a monk's tonsure, the cut of a beard, or the tailoring of a woman's headscarf. One of the many roles assigned to God by his followers is as an autocratic editor of *Vogue*.

To accept everything people do as components of who they are is an application of a broad democratic empiricism: a recognition of the need to take people seriously and to give an account of what they actually do; the statements they make; the manner in which they present themselves; the identities, both public and private, which they construct and cultivate for themselves. People appear to care deeply about the plumage and the plazas, patios, and palaces which are part of their identity and the choreography and staging of their lives. But just as nothing that people do can be discounted as irrelevant to who they are, so statements which seem contradicted by other actions are nonetheless actions themselves, which have to be accounted for in the description and interpretation of what, and who, is happening. There is no such thing as 'mere' rhetoric.

The importance of paying attention to all the dimensions of identity when observing different people and different human actions arises not from any underlying or essential character of which the various aspects of identity are an expression, but because human social life is composed of all the aspects of its identity, each one of which contributes to the whole; take them all away, and nothing, no essence or founding principle, remains. That is why an identification of any single aspect or component of identity or character does not provide an adequate account, something which can be achieved only by observing the complex and particular whole.

Identity as a dimension of action; we cannot see into people's souls

While identity is visible and audible, not secret or internal, the audience for it is not only other individuals or groups, but the actor or actors themselves. Whatever conclusions may be drawn from that, it does not undermine the argument that social existence is external, and that whatever may lie within the impenetrable corridors of the soul, identity or character is in the first place public identity or character. The phrase 'external show' is one I will avoid, since the suggestion of an inner reality which is expressed by external action is not one I have found helpful. As the advertiser's slogan has it, 'What you see is what you get.' When Queen Elizabeth I declared that she did not wish to make windows into men's souls, a brave if politically unwise reply would have been that that was not possible anyway. All that could be known was what people say and do, and all of that is on the public side of any window.

There might seem to be in such an argument a dismissal of the subjective life, the thoughts and feelings of individuals. The reply to such a charge is partly in terms of evidence, that souls cannot be known, all that can be known are statements, in whatever form, about them. The important point about external action is that all external actions must be considered, and all the contexts of that action. If a voter is taken to the polls at gunpoint and coerced into voting for the government candidate, it would not so much be a denial of her expressed wishes to describe her as a supporter of the government, as a setting aside of the whole complexity of actions which constituted and set the context for the placing of her cross against the president's name. A full account of her actions would be quite different from a full account of the actions of someone who had voted freely.

The cultivation of identity is the expression or communication, either to oneself or to others, of a narrative or description of a person, or collectivity of persons. It might seem that the cultivation of an identity and its communication are two distinct activities, or at least two distinct stages of a single activity, that a narrative would be a statement about something beyond itself. But a narrative of identity *is* the identity, and it is difficult to imagine its cultivation unless it is being communicated either to the narrator as expressed self-consciousness or to others as action, or to imagine a communication of identity which was not at the same time its cultivation. There could not be a narration of which no one at all was aware, for in that case there would not even be a narrator. In telling a story – and the story can be told using all the modes of communication, of which language is one only – persons or collectivities cultivate meanings and justifications whereby what they are and what they do is both explained and given normative sanction. This tripartite activity of cultivating identity in a way which provides and nurtures meaning and justification is a dimension of all human action, and is what distinguishes action from mere reflex behaviour. The cultivation of identity in this manner, involving the creation or attribution of meaning and justification, is not prior to or subsequent to action, but is a component or aspect of it. Identity is created and cultivated in being expressed, and whatever its character was before such communication or expression is modified or enhanced. Statement and cultivation are simultaneous, and jointly aspects of a single action.

It will be evident that this is a view of things derived from Max Weber's definition of 'social action': 'We shall speak of "action" insofar as the acting individual attaches a subjective meaning to his behaviour – be it overt or covert, omission or acquiescence.'[3] But I have added to Weber's selection of meaning the cultivation of an identity which incorporates both meaning and justification. There is a qualification, too, or a redefinition, of Weber's 'subjective meaning'. Weber comments tantalisingly that his subjective meaning can be 'overt or covert'. But if it is covert it is not known, and if it is overt it is subjective in the sense of being expressed by a subject, but not in the sense of being internal as against external.

The use of the term 'cultivation' avoids the two poles of claiming an inherent identity on the one hand, or suggesting a whimsical or unlimited power to construct identities on the other. Identities are both generated and received, a perception which the term cultivation catches since cultivation is the care and direction, the nurturing and the shaping, of something which already exists, but is used to secure something other than its original form or character. Cultivation involves both nature and nurture, and in the cultivation of identity people both selectively work with and selectively appeal to the first, and cultivate through nurture, the second, identities which are influenced and affected, but not effected, by their own aspirations. The word cultivation is preferable to construction to describe this activity, since the elements of cultivation, unlike those of construction, are dynamic and flexible rather than inert, and continue to change in ways which may react to the intentions and actions of the cultivators and to context and contingency. The term cultivation catches, too, the elements of both conservation and growth and change. This human intent is most obvious (though not obviously strongest) at times of innovation and revolution. What frequently occurs at such times, as well as an attempt to dispense with old identities, is the rapidly perceived need to construct new ones whose function but not whose character is essentially the same as that of those they replace.

Cultivation catches not only both nature and nurture, but a range of related distinctions: between vertical and horizontal accounts, between action and structure, and between culture and the choices and conflict which inhabit all societies and prevent them from ossification. Not only is action best understood as a whole, which is not the same as homogeneous or undifferentiated, but the various activities which are associated with it – meaning, justification – are best understood as part of it. To describe myself as a Muslim or a Christian, a socialist or a conservative, is not simply to make a neutral taxonomic observation, but to assert my value and the value of the beliefs with which I construct and cultivate my identity. In speaking, I nurture my identity and enhance what, as I describe it, is already changed, by however so little, by my verbal or written action.

It is no accident that a similar perspective can be found being developed by political scientists studying issues such as legitimation, for when an identity is cultivated, so too at the same time is a justification or legitimation of that identity. To say who we are is to say, not subsequently or later as a defence, but simultaneously and as part of the same statement, what our authority is. The account which I have given of government in *Legitimating Identities*, and which Ian Clark has given in his discussion of legitimation in international society, is of external, visible, and audible practices, rather than of inner, inferred realities' justifications.[4] Government, as an activity, is not supported or enabled by legitimation or coercion but is composed of them. 'In the same way that erosion of legitimacy does not lead to crisis of government, so the bestowal of legitimacy does not cause international stability: it is but another way of describing such stability as already exists. In short, legitimacy and stability are not two separate, and causally related, conditions.'[5]

To speak in this way of action as meaningful and justified behaviour is to go beyond behaviourism or materialism in either its Marxist or utilitarian, liberal, rationalist forms. It provides a way of saying something intelligible about the ways in which people relate and combine for public action, public meaning, and public identification, whether as members of faiths, or as political actors, Hindus or Muslims, fascists or transformationalist socialists.[6] An account of what people do, of all the many kinds of action which they perform, is an account of who they are. Action, whether of speech, or comportment, or dressing, or dancing, is then not external or additional to the person, but part of what constitutes the person. Actions, and the motives and meanings which are part of them, are not then separable from identity, they are components of it. In a similar way, Patrick Gardiner has argued that 'to speak of a person having a motive, aim or plan is to make a shorthand, and often rather indefinite, statement about him.'[7]

'Mere rhetoric'

In talking in this way of an identity which is cultivated with external – in the sense of visible or audible – forms, a stand is being taken against both the view that there is an inner reality which the external forms express, and the view that such expression is secondary or instrumental to some other aspect of the person or collectivity, their interests or ambitions. R. H. Tawney once remarked caustically that in 1918 the Labour Party had declared itself a socialist party, and had believed that it thereby became one.[8] But this eloquent criticism could lead one to ignore the contrary, or at least complementary, fact that a great deal of what people and organisations are as social beings is precisely what they do and that what they say is part of that doing. The question is not, therefore, was the Labour Party 'really' a socialist party after 1918, but what did it mean when it declared itself one, what did it imagine describing itself as one involved, and how did this declaration relate to other actions of the party? None of this involves, or need involve, rejecting or bypassing the neat incisiveness of Tawney's remark. A formal statement does not determine all the other aspects of a party's character, and its meaning and function will not be best understood by relying entirely on the explanations given by the party itself. But claims and rhetoric will always have a significance, and the task is not to dismiss that significance, but to determine as exactly as possible what that significance is. Choosing to describe oneself as socialist is not insignificant, and is a claim to a character different from that of conservatives, or liberals, though even that broad suggestion will need specifying in relation to who is making such a claim, where, when, and to whom.

So I want to dismiss the account of human life as fractured between ideas and interests, or between rhetoric and action. Human identity is all of a piece, or, rather, all of a patchwork, and if words and the material cultivation of identity were of no significance, they would not be employed. This is the importance of Marx's distinction between a class in itself and a class for itself. If a group can be attributed with some common characteristic by an observer, but does not itself express a common identity, it cannot be accurately described as a class. There is a difference, in other words, between a taxonomic similarity and a social identity. For the true empiricist, everything that exists is significant. But 'significant' can be a misleading word, since it suggests that the importance of actions is as signs or signifiers of something else. But they are important also in themselves, not as clues, but as components.

Action is complemented by what it creates, and so modifies its own circumstances

Cultivation, as action with already existing resources, captures the double dimension of structure and act, context and innovation. 'Men make their own history, but they do not make it just as they please; they do not make it under circumstances chosen by themselves, but under circumstances directly encountered, given and transmitted from the past.'[9] This much-repeated sentence of Marx is true as far as it goes, but it does not follow to their conclusion the implications of its own insight. The past is not very distant, and is composed of all that has been done, so that any action is immediately a part of the past and hence of the context or circumstances in which further action is carried out. The history which men make is instantly a part of both their identity and the circumstances in which that identity is cultivated. Some, at least, of the circumstances in which men make their own history have been made by them and chosen by them, as well as by others. People who express themselves by particular actions – whether of dress, or speech, or the use or construction of objects or built environment – cultivate their identity as much as they express it and, in acting, produce something that was not there before, rather than communicating a previously unheard or unspoken character. So with a group or nation, an expression of collective identity is never adequately described as such, since what is expressed is modified in the act of expression.

Equilibrium and symbiosis, coherence and consistency

Whilst the continual search for coherence and the making of choices – actions at both an individual and a collective level which pursue that aim and at the same time alter the circumstances in which it will be pursued – are a central feature of human life; there can be a tension not just between various actions, but between 'actual' action and aspiration. On the other hand, aspiration can be divided between 'secret' aspirations which, by their very nature, will remain secret and unknown, and expressed aspiration, which is a form of action.

If the relation between the various aspects of human action is seen as symbiotic, then the ensuing account will be of a relationship which will seldom if ever be static, but will be characterised both by tensions, and by tendencies to equilibrium. There will be a continual but not in detail predictable search for coherence in reaction to cognitive dissonance. Something similar is described by Mary Douglas in her account of dietary rules as a construction of an ordered relationship to experience for the cultivation of holiness and completeness.[10] The search for coherence has affinities with rational, as contrasted with rationalistic, action as described rather differently by Michael Oakeshott: a cultivation of coherence on the basis of existing resources, habits, and traditions.[11] At the same time, this search will be a form of dynamism, in which each choice in pursuit of harmony necessitates further choices.

In such a process, there are three tendencies at work: towards equilibrium to avoid incoherence, towards control of the discordant, and towards stability or security so that identities and landscapes are predictable. All three of these could be subsumed under a single category, the tendency to harmony. Weber's punctual bureaucrat, who arrives at his office on time each morning because not to do so would conflict with his own sense of himself as a dedicated professional, provides an example of such coherence, or impetus towards coherence. Geoffrey Hawthorn employs a similar conception, borrowing the phrase 'necessary identity' from Bernard Williams and describing 'an identity such that someone who has it feels bound to act in ways that maintain their identity in the eyes of others'.[12] If the relationship between the dimensions of identity is symbiotic/organic rather than mechanical/mathematical, that does not change the expectation of possible coherence, but it does change the expectation of automatic coherence, and requires an expectation of the frequent possibility of non-correspondence between one aspect of identity and another. If we are not dealing with fixed components in a rigid mechanical structure, then all the various activities in which people engage, and all the various ways of perceiving and understanding those activities, may be relevant as part of the total phenomenon. Clothes, or plumage, can be as relevant as diet or dogma, and compliance or resistance as relevant as circumstance, tradition, or coercion.

The question then arises of what, if anything, can be predicted about the likely outcomes when there is incongruence within a population or territory. Is one factor in general more powerful than another? In states, does rulership normally have a built-in advantage, whatever its identification, whether religious, economic, ethnic, or cultural? One response to that question is that the answer is contained in the question, in that if such an advantage could not be identified, the person or persons enjoying it would not helpfully be described as rulers, and that for such a description to be appropriate, such an advantage must be discernible. In that case this fits, or at least is not inconsistent with, Patrick Dunleavy's criticism of rational-choice accounts of party competition: political leaders are Procrustean, and have both the capacity and the will, if not to replace reality, then at least to readjust it to their convenience or advantage.[13]

Should we expect differences in the ways in which different kinds of rulers react to incoherence? Do despots of various kinds pay less attention to telling stories to their subjects? Or does that depend on what they want from them? It is easier to tell an extravagant story about yourself if it is addressed to a limited audience. The greater the audience, the greater is the possibility of laughter. And to begin with, despots have less need to pay attention to large audiences. John Prescott's two Jags, for which he was pilloried in the United Kingdom, would not have been so widely and publicly derided in China, but in a democracy they were cause for merriment.

The recognition of the search for harmony or coherence raises the question of sincerity. A charge often made against those who are seen as greedy, unscrupulous, tyrannical, or devious, is that they must know the difference between right and wrong, must be aware of their own wickedness, and that therefore any account they give which reconciles their actions against their fellow humans with a pattern of meaning and justification must by hypocritical or deliberately intended to deceive others. But there is another account available, which by no means reduces the force of charges of oppression or greed, but does replace the charge of hypocrisy on the grounds that it oversimplifies to the point of distortion what is actually going on, and takes as the starting point the assumption that it is plausible or even likely that views which one person considers implausible are genuinely held by another person, and that incoherence is more common than conscious and deliberate deceit. Two illustrations from religious discourse may fill out this point. Evangelical Christians can sometimes be heard dismissively talking of the 'intellectual difficulties' of those who do not agree with their demands, the implication being that those who express such 'difficulties' recognise the force of the evangelical claim, and are constructing barriers against it. It does not require one to be sceptical about religion as such to see the inadequacy of such an account. Similarly, Islamists may attack what they describe as Western decadence for refusing to acknowledge the truth of Islam, again with the implication, or overt claim, that those in the West who are not Muslims are in some sense, as another discourse might put it, 'in denial'. Again, one does not have to be an opponent of Islam to see the inadequacy of such an account. There is a frequent tendency to assume or to argue that those whose conduct one regards as wrong, unacceptable, or abhorrent, cannot possibly believe that how they are acting is right, and must be insincere or hypocritical. It is both intellectually much more difficult and morally and ideological disconcerting to start from the premise that there is a real or potential harmony or at least modus vivendi between people's stated beliefs and the rest of their behaviour, and that even the most, to the observer, repellent conduct can be in harmony with the stated values and beliefs of the actor. This is one of the reasons why the debate amongst historians and social scientists over slavery in the United States has on occasion been so heated. To the opponent of slavery, it has frequently seemed difficult not to believe that there must have been at least an element of hypocrisy in the justifications which the beneficiaries of slavery gave for the society in which they lived. Such a view assumes that there must be standards of right and wrong which are both independent of human societies, and self-evident to all individual humans. One version of this view sees such intuitive or rational apprehension of moral criteria as following from the common rationality of a common humanity. The essential character of humanity transcends, or underlies, or is both historically and logically prior to, the values and practices of particular cultures or societies. The other version sees a universal apprehension of moral criteria as involving a metaphysical dimension which is revealed to or grasped by properly religious or spiritually attuned persons.

The first version can be queried by referring to the varieties of human morality, the second by the observation that whatever the alleged source of metaphysical criteria, they can only ever be heard, or read, in the actions of humans. This was the point satirically presented in Salman Rushdie's *The Satanic Verses* when, however hard the angel tried, he always found himself speaking not his own words but those of the prophet whom he was addressing.[14]

The search for coherence is best understood not as people trying to explain or justify what they know to be wrong, since there is no knowledge of right and wrong independent of our knowledge of what people do and believe. Conceptions of right and wrong can only be conceptions of human beliefs, and the search for coherence is then a response to the existence of difficult, contrary, or opposing views rather than of, necessarily, an attempt to square consciences which are either innate and independent of any other human action, or in direct contact with a moral realm distinct from and superior to the lives and actions of humans. This personification of morality is part of the search for a coherent or harmonious sense of self. For self-identity is told, unless the self is unrealistically solipsistic, in terms derived and developed from the narrated and acted-out identities of the range of knowable human actions. To act incoherently is to act in a way which disrupts this narrated self.

But the response to this apparent dilemma is that analysis and interpretation are distinct from moral evaluation, and that one is not compromised by the other. To explain how it was that people in the sixteenth and seventeenth centuries could believe in the existence of witches and in the need to torture and kill those whom they considered in league with the devil is in no way to make a moral judgment on their actions, nor does it prevent one subsequently from doing so.

The most sustained and substantial way in which coherence can be sought by cultivating identity is through association of the individual with a group, association, or collectivity of people – the observation of concrete identity made by Hegel using the example of war when he argued that physical survival was subordinated to an identity enhanced by association with the group or community.[15] There is, however, a paradox here. Identity is cultivated by identification with a group. But at the same time identity requires distinction, and the drawing of lines of demarcation and contrast both between the person and other persons, and between the collectivity which gives the person a more substantial identity and other collectivities. The first distinction is then between a person and his or her associates, a distinction among friends, the second a distinction between one's own association and competitors or even enemies. This is why Orwell's reassurance to the middle classes that they need not fear sinking down into the mass of the population, 'you have nothing to lose but your aitches,' was historically negligent.[16] The desire to sustain identity by association with others is most commonly complemented by the desire to underline identity by distinguishing the association from which one draws support from other, different, associations. The point was expressed fictionally by Philip Roth at the conclusion of *Portnoy's Complaint* where his protagonist visits Israel and finds his sense of identity, which in New York had been delineated by the presence of large numbers of people who were not Jews, shaken by a society in which even the muggers were Jews.[17]

Simple accounts are simple

Human action can be seen as one or a series of meaningful behaviours, in such a way that the material and the cultural or intellectual cannot be separated, however much they may be analytically distinguished. This view is inimical to the kind of construction of distinct and rigid categories of beliefs, desires, and behaviour which characterises some recent accounts of rational humanity, whilst recognising the usefulness of such distinctions at an analytical, but not at an interpretative, level.[18] It is similarly inimical to an insistence on 'parsimonious' or single-factor explanations. Such explanations frequently slide into saying either that all factors other than the one singled out and narrated are mere reflexes, or that they are unimportant, and that whether or not they change with the 'core' dimension is not of significance or importance either to the living or the understanding of human life. Either conclusion is unsatisfactory and arbitrary, since it is deductive rather than inductive, and dismisses as proper subject of enquiry precisely what, either empirically or historically, is actually going on.

To employ the view that I am supporting means giving up the chance of making confident predictions about the course of events. It is fairly straightforward to predict that changing one element in a historical situation will have consequences for other elements, and for the character of the whole. But the nature of those consequences will be formed out of the relations between the changed element and all the other elements, and on their mutual influence. No particular or specified character can be predicted as a result of such a change in one element. It may well not be possible, therefore, to make predictive or explanatory accounts, but only to chart change.[19] This limitation on what can be said is presented fictionally by Umberto Eco in his account of the great detective who, despite being surrounded by a sequence of criminal acts, never succeeds in predicting any of them, but only in retrospectively interpreting them.[20] Even this change can be difficult to fit into easy taxonomic boxes. The elements of identity may be generalisable, but the particular combinations are frequently unique in a way which makes broader generalisations difficult or inadequate, and parsimonious accounts unrealistic.

In very different ways, Trobriand cricket and the Constitution of the Soviet Union under Stalin each illustrate this point. Cricket was introduced to the Trobriand Islands off the north-east coast of New Guinea by Methodist missionaries, but the islanders, whilst still retaining the English game and its rules as a rough framework, built on this framework an exotic ritual of provocation and communal celebration, with dancing, ritual taunts and boasting, and teams of up to sixty a side – a formalised celebration of inter-village rivalry.[21] If all that was considered were the formal rules and the names given to elements in the game or ritual, then what was played on the Trobriand Islands was cricket. But if the narration was of everything that was going on, a very different and far more deeply textured account of a unique ritual would be given. If one had considered the Soviet Union in the 1930s in the light only of its published laws, then the account given would have been of a working liberal democracy, albeit with methods of representation based on class and occupational groups, rather than on geographical constituencies. This is more or less what Beatrice and Sidney Webb did in their much-derided *Soviet Communism: A New Civilisation?* Having described the administrative and constitutional complexity of the Soviet Union, the Webbs went on to say that 'in each department, structure and function are intertwined with each other and with a wealth of voluntary associations and spontaneous individual activities'.[22] Such a view would have been difficult to sustain for a moment had the authors gone beyond the official documents and the narratives of officials. As an account of those two sources, it had a degree of truth. As an account of the Soviet Union in the 1930s, it was largely worthless save as, and this was important, an unwitting account of one part of the way in which the regime chose to present itself to outsiders. In each case, a formal set of rules, to be recognised by all participants, was introduced, and in each case the result was, whilst an adaptation or employment of those rules, not one that could in any way have been predicted from looking at the rules in isolation and trying to read from them a resulting set or pattern of actions. One response to this account would be to say that had the rules been followed in the way that was intended by those who drew them up, then the result would have been predictable. But that is to say no more than that had things been different, they would have been different, and that had the rules been literally followed, they would have been literally followed. Even that apparent tautology can be questioned, since however precisely rules are drawn up, they are not like the bud which contains within itself all the features of the flower. And even that analogy has to be qualified: the precise shape and colour of the flower is conditioned by temperature, humidity, soil, and the actions of animals, birds, and insects. Actions will be composed of many other factors than the words of a legal or sporting document, and these factors will be necessary before those formal words can be interpreted, applied, or ignored.

Just as the Trobriand islanders created their own distinctive activity out of the imported game of cricket, practices and resources of all kinds, imported or imposed on existing societies or cultures, can be processed and employed to sustain traditional or existing ways of living. When the Oglala Sioux, following the Treaty of Fort Laramie in 1868, were cut off from their existing food source of buffalo and placed in dependence on government rations, they transformed these alien ingredients into versions of their own traditional cuisine. Cattle were not slaughtered in the manner of white people, but cut loose and then hunted with arrow or rifle, and renamed 'spotted buffalo'.[23]

What this means is not that history, or social science, is 'one damn thing after another', but that there is an intermeshed and interacting dynamic of many things all at the same time or, if there is a chronological sequence, a continual and continuous movement amongst changing elements so that there is no artificial stable or timeless point at which one can say that things now begin, and are caused by what follows rather than by what precedes that point. The constant proliferation of identities, the interplay between individual and collective choice and previously cultivated circumstance, together with the tension between identity as association and identity as uniqueness and exclusion, raises the question of the relationship between the many aspects of identity and the extent to which it is causal or symbiotic. If the components are both contingent on and particular to the phenomenon described, it makes no more sense to talk of changing one in order to change others than it does to inject warm blood into a lizard in order to turn it into a mammal. There is a need to be sensitive to the complexities of actual relationships. Certain kinds of positivist social science might be inclined to see a mathematical relation between one aspect of identity and another, of the kind that if you alter one term in an equation or formula, the others are necessarily adjusted: the world is like a spreadsheet. And although numbers can change, there is an immutability about the components so that they can change only within their quantity, not their quality. But the existence of a particular component of identity does not necessarily indicate the existence of other features of rule, in the way that the presence of '2' in the equation '2 + a = 5' necessarily indicates the presence of '3' in 'a'.

This does not mean that general analyses have no purpose. Their contribution is to refine the language which is then applied to specific phenomena. Human action is a comprehensive but never coherent whole. No one dimension is consistently a cause or treatable as an independent variable. All dimensions are variable, and any one of them is fully understood only in its relation to others, and never independently. Conversely, an understanding of the whole will always depend on an account of the contribution of the various aspects both to each other and to the overall character of the phenomenon or event. This makes abstraction and generalisation necessary at the level of the clarification of language (I prefer that way of putting it to talking of a clarification of concepts), and makes history and particularity, narrative and interpretation, necessary at the level of actual human action. So the two secondary themes or dimensions of this book are analysis and interpretation, the one general and about the clarification of language, the other specific and about the narrative or interpretation of human action. This creates difficulties in the way of a science of human action, or even of human behaviour. The fullest account will always be a particular one, having more of the character of history or a novel than of a scientific treatise. But any such account must be also about the manner and dynamics of change. The insistence on particularity and the non-privileging of any one factor entails the belief that what is separated at the level of general analysis must be organically integrated at the level of interpretation. But the biological symbiotic metaphor goes only so far, since human action and human choice alter the materials of identity in a way that a biological organism cannot alter its components. In that sense even a single human is more analogous to an entire non-human species over an extended period than to any single non-human animal.

Instances of front of house: wizards, spies, hypocrites, and politics

There is an account of action and identity which describes a very different reality from the one that I have depicted, which might be called the Wizard of Oz syndrome. In the film derived from Frank L. Baum's book, the wizard, when finally encountered, turns out to have a public identity utterly different from his private one. The public identity, maintained by tricks and gadgetry and reputation, is of a powerful and barely human magician. The reality, taking cover behind a screen and controlling the theatrical equipment, is a small and insignificant fairground entertainer from Kansas. In this account, public figures have a mask which is worn for effect, and which bears little if any relationship to their actual identity. The 'wizard' has an identity behind the theatrical pretences, but it is quite different from the one which is created for the world to see and hear. The Oz view differs from the theatrical metaphor in drawing attention to what the analogy of identity to drama ignores: the reality of the actor behind the role. But it moves in the opposite direction, and whilst the theatrical metaphor ignores the actor, the Oz metaphor ignores the role. To dismiss the wizard as unreal is to set on one side the clear effect on others that the created magical identity had. An account of the politics of Oz which ignored the wizard because he was a creation of artifice would truly be unrealistic. The wizard was a public presence, and events would make no sense without a presence which, whatever its relation to an actual person, was an effective participant in public events, and without which the four travellers would never have undertaken their journey along the yellow brick road.

A different instance of disjuncture between public and private realities is spies, who, whilst presenting themselves as sharing an identity with one group, nation, or community, present themselves in other, and concealed, circumstances, as sharing identity with a quite different party, state, society, or community. The Philby phenomenon is an instance of a particular kind of Wizard of Oz syndrome, save that, unlike the Wizard of Oz, spies have a real community to whom they do not necessarily dissemble. The ability to maintain two identities in this particular way can, however, be associated with a disposition to proliferate personas, so that no group to which the spy professes allegiance can be sure that there is not another, or are not others, to whom he or she is making equal, but more reliable, professions of loyalty.[24] But the spy is only the most extreme example of a feature of public life which Weber identified in his essay on politics as a vocation. The responsibilities which a politician takes on, argued Weber, are not compatible with a commitment to simple and absolute truthfulness, and mean that other methods are sometimes necessary to secure public well-being.[25] Runciman's discussion of hypocrisy stands in this Weberian tradition, while there are many and varied instances of differences between public and other identities, from the verbal constructions of democratic politics to the courts of both Peter the Great and Joseph Stalin, where the back of house was conducted with either an informality or a ribald boisterousness that was not echoed at all in the public performance.[26] Discord between front of house and back of house is not restricted to public and political affairs, though it will be on a grander scale there. It may be simple deception, of which Jacob's pretence that he was Esau in order to obtain his brother's inheritance is only one of the earliest described instances. But in each case, whatever the concealments and pretences involved, the public face is an effective reality; were it not so, the person who employs it would not bother to do so. The manipulation of identities involved in deception depends on the effective presence of both or all versions.

Interests versus identity

One reason why what Paine called plumage has been too readily dismissed, and not only by Paine, is the view that whatever importance is attached to it, it is not the whole bird. Identity, it can be argued, is better understood not as plumage or fur, which are an integral part of the beast, but as a coat which can be worn or discarded according to circumstance, and which is a means to achieving the goals and desires of the wearer, not part of the wearer's essential character. A person or a collectivity of persons, it can be argued, has interests in pursuit of which identity is an external show, and not even an external indicator of an internal reality, but like the resources of an actor in a theatre, the infinitely changeable materials for pursuing whatever it is that the essential or substantial interests of the person dictate.

In such a view, interests and identities are distinct phenomena, interests are objective and unavoidably demanding, whereas identities are not only cultivated but constructed, and not only constructed but sloughed off and replaced. The Vicar of Bray is the metaphor for this view of things: identities, in the sense of ways of life, religious practices, manners of living, are all in the last resort subordinate to objective interests, and will adapt to serve or defend them. The eponymous cleric of the song who declared that 'whatsoever King may reign, I'll be the Vicar of Bray, Sir,' fitted his theology and his liturgy to the ruling orthodoxy as determined by the monarch as lay governor of the Church of England. But another view is possible, that he was not a man without any identity, whose character at any one moment was a simple cover for or reflex of some objective material character. On the one hand, his principal identity was as the Vicar of Bray. On the other, the far from merely reflective or superficial or epiphenomenal significance of religious practice is confirmed, not shown to be of no significance, by the need for the imaginary cleric to have such scrupulous regard for it. Religious practice is entirely real. As Jack Goody has remarked, 'it is doubtful whether one can regard religion as an *expression* of identity ... Religion is not an expression or a handle so much as a major constituent of such identity.'[27]

A view of human life which distinguishes between interest and identity occurs in a variety of places and a variety of shapes and forms. For Marx the interests of the working class were objective facts, which might not be matched, depending on the level of correct consciousness, by a proletarian identity. In this view, interest comes first. But if interest is seen as material, economic, or a matter of physical survival and flourishing, a reversal of priorities occurs in the distinction which is made between economy and culture. Work is sometimes described as the characterising human activity. But when work is positively described, in the way that it is by William Morris in 'Useful Work Versus Useless Toil', the conventional equation of work with production is displaced by work as creation, and a creation which can be the creation of the person as readily as the creation of objects or commodities.[28] Once creation becomes the creation and cultivation of identity, a view of human life is possible as, potentially, a comprehensive rather than a fragmented activity. The candidates for essential, true, universal, or fundamental interests which will be set against the transient garb of identity are themselves flexible and varied, just as are identities.

The argument for prioritising those aspects of a person which are seen as interests rather than identity can fall back on the modified view that identity, fully comprehended, includes what are normally termed interests, and that this aspect of identity takes priority over others. If to be someone who likes warm dry weather, freedom from assault, meat and green vegetables, and a waterproof house is to have particular components of identity, it can be further argued that these components will be more solidly established, and defended, than others. If identity is described as everything that makes a person or a group what they are, then some aspects of that identity can nonetheless be given priority over others: survival, security, nutrition, shelter. But this argument would ignore the fact that these aspects are not necessarily given absolute and universal priority, otherwise people would never fight or go to war, a point which Hegel's parable of the slave and the master is intended to argue.

There are therefore two principal qualifications to this concept of the priority of basic needs. First, the placing of such requirements above other requirements of identity – whether religious faith; national military assertion; ascetic denial; loyal defence of friends, family, or household; or the acquisition of athletic or heroic prestige – cannot be predicted or assumed to be ubiquitous or universal. It will be contingent. Second, the manner of requiring even such seemingly basic goods is tailored, and confined, by personal or group identities which form the manner of eating or preparing food, of housing, or of clothing as a protection against wet or cold. Everyone, or at least most people, will eat, but not the same things, and what is a delicacy to one group or person will be repulsive and inedible to another. The work people do is part of who they are. It is frequently the first dimension of their identity that is expressed to or evident to other people. It is, like other dimensions of identity, both a matter of opportunity and a matter of constraint. One may not be compelled to be a nurse or an airline pilot, but nor, if that is what you are, can you immediately become an accountant or a dentist.

It will be clear from what I have said so far that I am not convinced by or sympathetic to the view that interests and identities can be seen as separate features of a person or group, whilst recognising both its force and its prevalence. In its various forms, from Marxism to rational choice, it rests on a conception of human life which is utilitarian, and narrowly so. It is important to put things in that way, since it is possible to conceive of a utilitarianism which was not so constructed, but which conceived utility in a way which provided a place for what I have described as identity, for altruism, and for self-denials and self-sacrifices which a conventional utilitarianism might have difficulty in accommodating. So Kristen Monroe is able to argue, in describing those who at great risk to themselves aided Jews in Europe under the Nazis, that:

> For the morally commendable, the ethical values of human well-being and the sanctity of life had become so intricately integrated into their basic sense of who they were that their commitment to these values shaped the central core of their identities. It thus became unthinkable for altruists intentionally to engage in behavior that would contradict the essence of their identity.[29]
>
> To have turned away from the Jews would have meant turning away from one's self. By showing us this, the rescuers remind us how important our ties with others are in preserving our own identities.[30]

This is similar to the argument of Erik Ringmar, that:

> people act not only in order to win things, but also in order to defend a certain conception of who they are. We act, that is, not only because there are things we want to have, but also because there are persons we want to

> BE. In fact, this latter kind of actions must be the more fundamental since it only is *as some-one* that we can have an interest *in some-thing*.[31]

Identity constrains: that was the point made in defence of the private detective Philip Marlowe, played by Humphrey Bogart in Howard Hawks's 1946 film of Raymond Chandler's *The Big Sleep*, who had been dismissed as amoral and opportunist. On the contrary, ran the counter-narrative, he was a white knight coming to the rescue of a lonely old man. Identities are far more than masks, and constrain those who wear them in ways which they would not necessarily anticipate, but would still consider appropriate for who they were and what they believed in. The rule of law might have operated in general in the eighteenth century in the interests of a dominant or ruling class, but, as E. P. Thompson has commented, 'the rulers were, in serious senses, whether willingly or unwillingly, the prisoners of their own rhetoric', and there will always be 'men who actively believe in their own procedures and in the logic of justice'.[32]

Some have argued, in a manner derived from a quote of Weber's, that ideas and, by extension, ideas about who one is and therefore identities, can be seen as 'switches' which direct the train of self-interest along one railway track or another.[33] This seems to me to artificially separate conceptions of identity from conceptions of need or interest, but also to apply the metaphor with insufficient imagination. If the role of ideas or, in the case of the account which I am presenting here, of identities, is to be acknowledged, it might be more illuminating to see them not as controlling the points on which the train runs, but as constructing the individual or group as a train rather than as a sailing dinghy or a pony and trap in the first place. Unless one perceives oneself as, for instance, a Scot, one cannot perceive an interest in defending Scottish interests against an English-dominated London parliament and government. Unless people first conceive of a class of cyclists, or motorists, and identify themselves with one or the other or both, they cannot have an interest in road use.

Because people are constituted by identification, it is not possible to say that interests cause identity, or ideas and values cause action, since all of these described features of human life are what compose the identity in the first place. The metaphor of identities as like clothes and therefore as secondary or superficial presents, in fact, not a clinching argument for those who want to assert the primacy of some utilitarian essence, but a trap into which their claims collapse. The trap was first set by Thorsten Veblen in *The Theory of the Leisure Class* when he argued that clothing, real clothing not metaphorical clothing, was used not only or even principally for warmth or protection: 'the greater part of the expenditure incurred by all classes for apparel is incurred for the sake of respectable appearance rather than for the protection of the person.'[34] And the appearance is the entire social presence, so that Jones and Stallybrass discussing Renaissance Europe can argue that to 'understand the significance of clothes in the Renaissance, we need to undo our own social categories, in which subjects are prior to objects, wearers to what is worn.'[35] The observation need not be limited to the Renaissance. Arthur Hocart complained of those for whom:

> only economic interests can create anything as solid as the state. Yet if they would only look about them they would everywhere see communities banded together by interest in a common ritual; they would even find that ritual enthusiasm builds more solidly than economic ambitions, because ritual involves a rule of life, whereas economics are a rule of gain, and so divide rather than unite.[36]

This is an insight which has been advanced against a narrowly material conception of interest in economic theory, and in economic theories of choice, to propose an economics of human life which is less universally homogeneous, and more aware of the particularities of identity.[37]

Private identity and public gaze

Robinson Crusoe cultivated an identity on an island before the arrival of any other humans. But once there was even one other person present, his social identity was engaged with that other person since a social reality depended on a society, however minimal. In Thornton Wilder's play *Our Town*, when a family member returns on her birthday, as a ghost, no one can see or hear her and in an important sense she does not, therefore, exist.[38] Pretence does not create something socially unreal, since even a deliberate attempt to present a new or 'deceitful' account of oneself creates a different self, which becomes at least part of who you are as a public reality and presence.

People create their own identities. But they do not do so with unrestricted freedom. They can work only with the materials to hand, but those materials are cultivated both by themselves and by others, and once an identity is created, and the external setting for it shaped, that setting and that identity become themselves factors both facilitating and constraining further identity cultivation. Brasilia, as a city for cars, makes walking difficult or impossible. That does not mean it cannot be modified but, unless it is, it constrains how its inhabitants can act. But the example of Brasilia draws attention to the pervasiveness of human agency in the creation of identity. Whilst people create their own identities, identities are created also by others.

This cultivation of the identity of others will in part be through the management, creation, or arrangement of material environments and resources. But it will also be carried on through descriptions of identity and the ways in which those with the power to do so define the character and the existence of groups and categories of people. Ian Hacking has referred to this understanding of things as 'dynamic nominalism', the view that a process is discernible whereby in describing a category of human action, one contributes to creating that category, alters the actions of those one describes, who are thus 'moving targets':

> We think of many kinds of people as objects of scientific inquiry ... They are moving targets because our investigations interact with them, and change them. And since they are changed, they are not quite the same kind of people as before. The target has moved. I call this the 'looping effect'. Sometimes, our sciences create kinds of people that in a certain sense did not exist before. I call this 'making up people.'[39]

Hacking's account denies static realism, but avoids saying that there is nothing real but only our narratives out there. Dynamic nominalism can be observed whenever an authoritative account develops or calls into existence a social category. Marc Raeff has described the ways in which modern states have contributed to the creation of social classes in order to make the general business of government, and the particular business of raising revenue, easier and more successful.[40] The Blair government in the United Kingdom, following the bombings of 7 July 2005, called a meeting of 'leaders and representatives of the Muslim community', and in so doing cultivated, even if they did not create, that community, and gave new or enhanced identity to a group of middle-aged men and their subsequent ability to make demands on those whom they could, with increased or new authority, describe as members of their community. Each of these cultivations is an instance of a wider process which occurs whenever accounts are given of others. Dynamic nominalism is not limited to language; artefacts of all kinds can perform in a similar way, creating new realities and new identities.

The generating of new identities, or the enhancement of existing ones, may involve a contrast between the defining group or association and others with whom they contrast themselves. Other groups or associations may then be at best inferior, and at worst hostile or threatening.[41] In this way identity can be not only a positive account of the defining group or association, but one which subordinates others as auxiliaries to that identity, or as possessed of an inferior status or quality which by its difference enhances that of the describing group. But it is not only at the level of groups and associations that the observer and describer can influence the identity of the observed. If people are categorised by others in terms of broad, general categories, their actual identity can be distorted and the ways in which others treat them be equally and deleteriously affected. A distinction can then be made, in the way in which both Charles Taylor and Axel Honneth have done, between recognition which sees someone in their own terms, and reification which attributes to them a simplified and distorted identity as one instance of an ostensible real and objective category.[42] The concept of understanding and failure to understand being used here follows from a distinction made by Collingwood between description, which freezes an account as a series of general categories, and expression, which responds to the particularity of individuals or events. Using a graphic metaphor, Anthony Appiah has talked of the Medusa syndrome, a gaze which turns living matter to stone and freezes the complexities of individual identity into narrow, stereotyped simplicities.[43] The direction of this way of talking about identity is to an insistence on individual uniqueness against an approach which continually subordinates the particular into rigid general categories. In the arguments of David Owen, this tradition has moved even more clearly towards and potentially beyond a pluralist conception not only of identity but of the means of recognising different identities.[44]

The composition of identity

The Burke and Paine exchange suggests a distinction between substantial identities and external and superficial ones, but if the metaphor is pursued even only a little way, it can be insisted that feathers do not cause birds, and birds do not cause feathers; rather, they are each part or aspects of a single, though complex, whole. Discussing changes in religious belief and perception, and the visual depiction of the crucifixion in medieval Europe, Jean Seaton asks 'whether the image of the dead Christ, the *imago pietus*, existed before the piety it served or whether the piety was the product of the pictures – or, finally, whether the pictures were a response to a new need.'[45] One further answer is that the piety was composed of such things as the images, and cannot be separated from them since it is a single word used to sum up a complex phenomenon or series of actions. In the study of identity it is not possible to take out one element to see what happens. There are few, if any, randomised controlled trials, and experiments with human identity in its social entirety would require both unbelievably large research grants and unimaginable powers of imperial or possibly divine intervention. The option sought in the film *Help!* by Professor Foot, who was 'out to rule the world ... if he can get a government grant', is not available.[46] And even if it were, it is impossible to step into the same revolution twice.

An explanation which dissects something out as a cause is never quite what it seems. It is not saying *post hoc ergo propter hoc*, but that this is an instance of a class of phenomena where *x* follows *y*, and that as a member of this class of phenomena, this is how it behaves. In one sense, that is a causal explanation, in another sense it is a tautologous redescription. Why does this creature have warm blood and suckle its young? Because it is a mammal. But it is just as accurate to say that it is a mammal because it has warm blood and suckles its young. So the explanation is saying no more than that this mammal is a mammal because it is a mammal.

The fuller the account of any set of events or circumstances, the more, and the less, is explained. For a full account, which is logically impossible and is only ever an aspiration, never an even remotely graspable achievement, would present all component elements as part of the phenomenon described, leaving nothing out as either cause or consequence. Paradoxically this does not mean that nothing can be explained. Each particular thing can be explained in terms of its immediate precedents, but things in general cannot be, for the reason illustrated by the chicken-and-egg paradox.

The fullest accounts will always be particular, even though the presuppositions and expectations, the words and stories, from which answers are constructed will be derived from and will return to generalised dialogues. The manner of understanding applies both the assumptions of democratic empiricism and a preference, in the many parallel juxtapositions of theoretical types, of recognition over reification, and a sensitivity towards individuality over the Medusa gaze. But in order to describe particular identities, it is necessary to use words which refer to general characteristics. A language which was entirely related to only one instance or identity would be incomprehensible to anyone else, even though in order to describe the particular it will be necessary to employ combinations of general terms. How else would speech be possible? The description of identity will draw on the general, though never ubiquitous, tension between association and distinction. Distinction will be in part composed of a cultivation of special or more developed characteristics within a group or association, whereas association will perhaps never be with one group or association alone, and in this overlapping of associations, further possibilities of distinction may be available.

Notes

1 Hunt, *Politics, Culture and Class*, p. 53.; Lynn Hunt, 'Freedom of Dress in Revolutionary France', in Melzer and Norberg (eds), *From the Royal to the Republican Body*, pp. 224–49.

2 Robert Browning, 'The Lost Leader,' in Tom Paulin (ed.), *The Faber Book of Political Verse* (London: Faber and Faber, 1986), p. 279.
3 Max Weber, *Economy and Society*, edited by Guenther Roth and Claus Wittich (London: University of California Press, 1978), p. 4.
4 Rodney Barker, *Legitimating Identities: The Self-Presentations of Rulers and Subjects* (Cambridge: Cambridge University Press, 2001), p. 24: 'Crises or erosions of legitimacy do not cause crises or erosions of government. They are a constituent part of what crises or erosions of government are.'; Ian Clark, *Legitimacy in International Society* (Oxford: Oxford University Press, 2005).
5 Clark, *Legitimacy in International Society*, p. 247.
6 Thomas Linehan, 'Communist Activism in Interwar Britain: Motivation, Belonging and Political Religion,' *Socialist History*, 32 (2008), 1–17; J. P. Nettl, 'The German Social Democratic Party 1890–1914 as a Political Model,' *Past and Present*, 30 (1965), 65–95.
7 Patrick Gardiner, *The Nature of Historical Explanation* (Oxford: Oxford University Press, 1952), p. 134.
8 R. H. Tawney, 'The Choice before the Labour Party,' in *The Attack and Other Papers* (London, George Allen & Unwin, 1953), p. 58.
9 Karl Marx, 'The Eighteenth Brumaire of Louis Bonaparte,' in Karl Marx and Frederick Engels, *Selected Works in Two Volumes*, Volume 1 (Moscow: Foreign Languages, 1962), p. 247.
10 Douglas, *Purity and Danger*, pp. 51–71.
11 Quoted in Efraim Podoksik, 'Overcoming the Conservative Disposition: Oakeshott vs. Tönnies,' *Political Studies*, 56:4 (2008), 857–80.
12 Geoffrey Hawthorn, *Thucydides on Politics: Back to the Present* (Cambridge: Cambridge University Press, 2014), p. 21.
13 Patrick Dunleavy, with Hugh Ward, 'Party Competition: The Preference-Shaping Model,' in Patrick Dunleavy, *Democracy, Bureaucracy and Public Choice: Economic Explanations in Political Science* (Hemel Hempstead, UK: Harvester Wheatsheaf, 1991), pp. 112–44.
14 Salman Rushdie, *The Satanic Verses* (London: Allen Lane, 1988).
15 Shlomo Avineri, *Hegel's Theory of the Modern State* (Cambridge: Cambridge University Press, 1972), pp. 196–7.
16 Orwell, *The Road to Wigan Pier*, p. 204.
17 Philip Roth, *Portnoy's Complaint* (London: Vintage, 2005), pp. 253–5.
18 Barker, *Legitimating Identities*, pp. 117–19.; Barker, 'Hooks and Hands.'
19 This is discussed with great clarity and insight in Geoffrey Hawthorn, *Plausible Worlds* (Cambridge: Cambridge University Press, 1991).
20 Umberto Eco, *The Name of the Rose* (London: Harcourt, 1983).
21 Gary Kildea and Jerry Leach, *Trobriand Cricket: An Ingenious Response to Colonialism* (London: Royal Anthropological Institute, 1974).
22 Sidney Webb and Beatrice Webb, *Soviet Communism: A New Civilisation?* (Liphook, UK: the authors, 1935), p. viii.
23 Powers and Powers, 'Metaphysical Aspects,' pp. 61–5.
24 Ben Macintyre, *Agent Zigzag* (London: Bloomsbury, 2007).

25 H. C. Gerth and C. W. Mills (eds), *From Max Weber: Essays in Sociology* (London: Routledge & Kegan Paul, 1948), pp. 120–1.
26 Runciman, *Political Hypocrisy*; Ernest A. Zitser, *The Transfigured Kingdom: Sacred Parody and Charismatic Authority at the Court of Peter the Great* (Ithaca and London: Cornell University Press, 2004); Simon Sebag Montefiore, *Stalin: The Court of the Red Tsar* (London, Weidenfeld & Nicolson, 2003).
27 Jack Goody, 'Bitter Icons', *New Left Review*, Second Series, 7 (January/February 2001), 19.
28 William Morris, 'Useful Work versus Useless Toil', in A. L. Morton (ed.), *The Political Writings of William Morris* (London: Lawrence and Wishart, 1973), pp. 86–108.
29 Kristen Renwick Monroe, 'Identity and Choice', in Kenneth R. Hoover (ed.), *The Future of Identity: Centennial Reflections on the Legacy of Erik Erikson* (Lanham, MD: Lexington Books, 2004), p. 80; Kristen Renwick Monroe, *The Heart of Altruism: Perceptions of a Common Humanity* (Princeton: Princeton University Press, 1996); Kristen Renwick Monroe, *The Hand of Compassion: Portraits of Moral Choice during the Holocaust* (Princeton: Princeton University Press, 2004).
30 Monroe, 'Identity and Choice', p. 86.
31 Erik Ringmar, *Identity, Interest and Action: A Cultural Explanation of Sweden's Intervention in the Thirty Years War* (Cambridge: Cambridge University Press, 1996), p. 3.
32 E. P. Thompson, *Whigs and Hunters* (London: Allen Lane, 1975), pp. 263–4.
33 Judith Goldstein and Robert O. Keohane (eds), *Ideas and Foreign Policy: Beliefs, Institutions, and Political Change* (Ithaca and London: Cornell University Press, 1993), pp. 11–12.
34 Veblen, *The Theory of the Leisure Class*, pp. 167–8.
35 Ann Rosalind Jones and Peter Stallybrass, *Renaissance Clothing and the Materials of Memory* (Cambridge: Cambridge University Press, 2000), p. 2.
36 Arthur Maurice Hocart, *Kings and Counsellors: An Essay in the Comparative Anatomy of Human Society*, edited by Rodney Needham (Chicago and London: University of Chicago Press, 1970), p. 35.
37 George A. Akerlof and Rachel E. Kranton, *Identity Economics: How Our Identities Shape Our Work, Wages, and Well-Being* (Princeton: Princeton University Press, 2010).
38 Thornton Wilder, *Our Town and Other Plays* (London: Penguin, 2000).
39 Ian Hacking, 'Making up People', *London Review of Books*, 28 (2006), 16, www.lrb.co.uk/v28/n16/hack01_.html (accessed 5 May 2007).
40 Marc Raeff, 'The Well-Ordered Police State and the Development of Modernity in Seventeenth- and Eighteenth-Century Europe: An Attempt at a Comparative Approach', *American Historical Review*, 80 (1975), 5; Marc Raeff, *The Well-Ordered Police State: Social and Institutional Change through Law in the Germanies and Russia, 1600–1800* (New Haven, CT: Yale University Press,1983).
41 I have said little or nothing about the role of enmity in this book, having discussed it at length elsewhere, in Barker, *Making Enemies*.

42 Jeffrey C. Alexander and Maria Pia Lara, 'Honneth's New Critical Theory of Recognition', *New Left Review*, 220 (November/December 1996), 126–36; Renante D. Pilapil, 'From Psychologism to Personhood: Honneth, Recognition, and the Making of Persons', *Res Publica*, 18:1 (2012), 39–51; David Owen, 'Reification, Ideology and Power: Expression and Agency in Honneth's Theory of Recognition', *Journal of Power*, 3:1 (2010), 97–109; Bert van den Brink and David Owen (eds), *Recognition and Power: Axel Honneth and the Tradition of Critical Social Theory* (Cambridge: Cambridge University Press, 2007).

43 Kwame Anthony Appiah, *The Ethics of Identity* (Princeton: Princeton University Press, 2005), pp. 105–10.

44 Owen, 'Reification, Ideology and Power'.

45 Jean Seaton, *Carnage and the Media: The Making and Breaking of News about Violence* (London: Allen Lane, 2005), p. 109.

46 Richard Lester, *Help!* [film] (Los Angeles: United Artists, 1965).

3

Leadership in Religion and Politics

Association and distinction in the leadership of religion and politics

In 1521 Martin Luther, appearing before the Diet of Worms, declared that he was bound 'by the Scriptures to which I have appealed, and my conscience is taken captive by God's word, I cannot and will not recant anything, for to act against our conscience is neither safe for us, nor open to us.'[1] It was a statement which illustrated the extreme contradictions involved in the cultivation of identity by both association and distinction. On the one hand, Luther expressed an identity which was as far as possible beyond and above his single person, 'captive by God's word.' Identity through association and solidarity could hardly go higher or further. But, on the other hand, he asserted his own conscience against the prevailing view of the church of which he was a member and by whose professed faith he also identified himself, claiming possession of a conscience which distinguished him from other members of the collective as a unique individual because of a particular understanding of the collective identity which all shared. While his identity was shaped around solidarity with the deity, Luther was claiming to be an authoritative source of knowledge of what that deity's purposes or identity was. So having established identity through association in two directions, to the Christian church and to God, Luther then established a unique and distinguished position in relation to each. Luther's claim to solidarity with the Word of God was an instance of a recurrent presentation of religious identity where solidarity is both necessarily engaged with and at the same time distinguished within a human community, and a transcendental, divine, or other worldly one. A Dalai Lama is infused with a spiritual personality which survives across generations; a priest in a church which asserts apostolic succession is in a direct line of spiritual descent through the laying on of hands; association and solidarity are asserted with both worldly and otherworldly identities. But since deities never speak save in private and in secret to religious leaders, those leaders will claim special insight into the mind or words of the deity – association coupled with distinction.

Secular identity lacks the ultimate solidarity and immunity from human reasoning of spirituality, but it can still claim a transcendent distinction, rising above but not beyond the egalitarian assertion of association with its subjects or followers. And the grander the practice or claim of leadership, the grander the expression of distinction. When Virginia Woolf chose illustrations of male flamboyance, her selections were from both the secular and the spiritual governing elites. Humanity as a whole might be distinguished by its plumage, but bishops, judges, generals, and monarchs appeared to engage with special intensity in the embellishment, in all possible ways, of the human person. An ordinary soldier might earn and wear a few medals, but a general will wear dozens, and a president scores. The political and social elevation of an elite is enmeshed with the elevated intensity with which its identity at the head of a hierarchy is cultivated. The general wears a uniform to show he is a soldier, but the grandeur of the uniform at the same time insists that he is not like other soldiers and is even more military than they. Clothes are one medium only; methods of transport, the way people speak, and the buildings within which and amongst which they move constantly tell stories about who people are. But whatever identity is cultivated and by whatever means, elites cultivate it publicly most and to the greatest number of observers. That is one of the things that characterises them as elites. They are not the only people who do so, nor do they necessarily do so more successfully or more imaginatively than others. But they will do so more intensively, and in doing so they tell stories about their magnificence, the nature of their authority, their difference from ordinary people, their knowledge and understanding, and their power. As religious leaders claim or assume privileged access to transcendent truths, political leaders will both appeal to and rise above those whom they lead by claiming knowledge of what the followers would themselves know or seek if they were fully informed or properly rational. All government and political leadership will to some degree rely on the arguments put forward in idealist political theory, that government has insights and understanding which will differ from the actual insights and understanding of the governed, but will be, as Bernard Bosanquet put it, 'the real Will, or the Will as logically implied in intelligences as such.'[2]

The very solidarity which nurtures identity is at the same time fine-tuned, qualified, or exaggerated in order to cultivate its uniqueness. This paradox is particularly evident in the identification which rulers, leaders, and elites of one kind and another cultivate for themselves, and their complex identification of both contrasts and affinities with the rest of a population. Whilst the cultivation of identity in at least two directions, association and distinction, is to be found in all kinds of circumstances, the leaders of government and religion display an exceptional distance between the two forms, and one which by the scale of the claim to distinction can put the claim to association under strain.

Religious leadership

Whilst identity is cultivated in part by association with all manner of groups and cultures beyond the individual person, religion is potentially the most powerful of these because the collective identification is not only with a group wider than the individual, but with a being, dimension, or level which transcends all humanity and is attributed with absolute authority. When identity is cultivated in terms of or in relation to religion, it makes the greatest possible claims of identity by association. The person or group is enmeshed with a metaphysical person or level, and thus claims an identity as a channel, representative, or agent of that person or level. Cultivation of the same kind takes place with reference to nations, castes, or ethnicities, but the metaphysical claim is the most absolute in what it claims, and as the most removed from human contingency, it is the ultimate pole in the tensions of identity.

Whilst the authority claimed is so great, the elements of identity which are thereby authorised can still seem minute, peripheral, or trivial. When the Celtic and Roman churches were manoeuvring for supremacy in the seventh-century British Isles, one of the contentious issues, attributed with such importance that it divided the two communities, was the manner in which monks tonsured their hair.[3] An issue between the old believers and the conventionally Orthodox in seventeenth-century Russia was whether one crossed oneself with two fingers or with three. But this seemingly scarcely visible difference bore the weight of major theological understandings about the Trinity and the nature of Christ.[4] In matters of religion, just as in seemingly more secular matters, a ribbon awry can be crucial. Since the authority claimed for such identity is transcendent, the most elaborate constructions and creations are employed to shape an identity as far removed as possible from the mundanely human. Woolf's illustrations of formal male finery included a bishop clothed from head to toe in gilt and embroidery, with so little mere bodily person evident that only the face and hands were unconcealed by stitched splendour. Religion has not been unique in its employment of clothes, rituals, and architecture in the creation and cultivation of identity, but it has been consistent in their use not only across time and place, but across faiths, and has done so in great style.

Whilst the character of religious identity will forever be referred to an external, metaphysical, or divine source, the phenomenon is essentially the same as with all other kinds of social character. Humans cultivate all manner of identities, religious and secular, which provide meaning and justification for their behaviour and are constituted by it. Even when those meanings and justifications appear to be external to the person, and to derive from some divine source, they exist only insofar as that person expresses them. For people to say that they are obliged to act in a certain way because the doctrine of their faith requires them to is another way of saying that they are members of that faith, and that that membership is a part of what constitutes their identity, and, further, that their understanding of what that membership entails, whilst specific to them, has at the same time the ultimate sanction of extra-human authority.

Whatever the nature or existence of divinity, all that can be known is what people do. That may be one way of interpreting the opening sentences of the Gospel According to St John: 'In the beginning was the Word, and the Word was with God, and the Word was God.'[5] All that can be known is what is said, and so 'the Word was God' could be inverted to claim that God was the word. The perception of icons in the Orthodox church is similar, where it is understood that there is no necessary connection between the divine and its human representation and where, as Rowan Williams puts it, there are 'no *natural* visible symbols of the divine, in political structure or in art.'[6] Yet, at the same time, it is the human creation, not the divine infinite, which is accessible to human cognition and perception. Religion may be the word of God, but all its evident or accessible components are the construction of humans – a point made, and causing great offence, in Salman Rushdie's *The Satanic Verses*. Since the divine can only express itself to humans in human form or to human perception, it can only ever be a human experience and communicated by human creation. The charge frequently made against Rushdie's novel was that it insulted the Prophet Mohammed. But there was an additional and perhaps as strong or even stronger reason why the book caused such distress and anger. The angel in the novel who tried to convey divine messages to human leaders found that he was always speaking their words, not his own. The divine was the creation of people, who then claimed unique authority over others on the basis of doctrine and invocation which was presented not as something they had themselves created, but as a set of higher truths of which they were no more than a channel. The authority invoked when it is said that a person is a channel for the divine is immense. But so is the challenge to a person whose identity is cultivated or constructed in this way when the divine authority is questioned. This can explain the fury with which some religious individuals and groups responded both to the publication of Rushdie's book in 1988 and to the award many years later in 2007 of a knighthood to the author in the Queen's birthday honours. If the transcendent or divine can never be directly known, then all statements about it are humanly created metaphors, shorthands, or symbols, and as such have no more, nor less, authority than any other human creation. For those whose identity depends on a different narrative, such a view is corrosive of their public existence.

The dependence of the divine upon the human was graphically instanced shortly after the expression of anger over the June 2007 knighthood. In the summer of the same year in Nepal, a young girl who had been identified as a 'living god' was disqualified by older male religious leaders for having visited the United States, and having done so without permission.[7] It is usually perceived as an attribute of divinity that it has an authority quite beyond human choice or reason. For divinity to be subject to human reconsideration and recall in this way suggests a different relationship between religious leadership and religious authority from that normally presented by those leaders.

This dependence of the invoked authority on the invoker, of the existence of superhuman beings on the acts of those who say they believe in them, is illustrated fictionally in J. M. Barrie's *Peter Pan*, where the dying fairy Tinker Bell is revived by the worldwide reiteration of children's belief in fairies.[8] A similar reduction to more mundane scale of an apparently grand claim is briefly observed in a very different work of fiction, Joyce's *Ulysses*. When Stephen Dedalus takes offence at a remark that he is someone 'whose mother is beastly dead', his companion apologises, 'I didn't mean to offend the memory of your mother,' to which Dedalus retorts that the offence is not to his mother, but to him.[9]

Religious reformers generation after generation demand a return to the inner spirit and a stepping back from the reliance on ritual and moral etiquette: rend your heart, not your garments. But the cultivation of religious identity reverts again and again from human spontaneity to human creation, and perhaps even in its most spontaneous forms, can never be anything else. The account of Christianity given by Hegel, of a steady movement from inner zeal to outer conformity, could be repeated for other religions, since inner zeal can only be evidenced by outward behaviour which, to be communicable, has to take a shared form and so is already on its way to being institutionalised and formalised.[10] Speaking in tongues is a self-defeating attempt to circumvent this process, but cannot avoid communicating religious style and religious identity. Religious truths are expressed through vestments, architecture, painting, music, sculpture, and all the creative actions of which humans are capable. The expression of divine truth and by association of the identity of the faithful will frequently be acknowledged to be beyond human cognition, so that human actions and human creations are needed as metaphors of an infinite and unknowable identity. So arises the seeming paradox of a truth and an identity which is further removed from human life than any other, but which is nonetheless approached by a fuller and more extravagant use of human creativity than any other more apparently mundane or material arena, both in the immediate garments, words, music, and movements of the faithful and in the artefacts which they produce. That is the logic of the icon lurking within the apparently merely strategic advice of Bishop Jewel in Reformation England, that singing by the laity in and around divine services 'sadly annoys the mass-priests and the devil. For they perceive that by these means the sacred discourses sink more deeply into the minds of men, and that their kingdom is weakened and shaken at almost every note.'[11] Religious dissension seldom remains for very long at the level of theological dispute. It involves rival human identities, which are expressed in human actions and human artefacts. The smallest aspect of dress or deportment, the shape or location of a symbol or token, can carry the weight of major communal antagonisms. In Poland in the autumn of 2010, following the death of the president and ninety-five others in an aeroplane disaster, the most immediate visual token of national mourning was the national flag with a black band across its surface. But the placing of an unassuming wooden cross in front of the presidential palace by a group of Scouts was followed by a prolonged dispute between conservatives and right-wingers, who surrounded it to prevent its removal, and secularists, who argued that religion and politics should be separate in a modern state.[12] A few pieces of wood carried the weight of major ideological and theological disputes.

The human expression of divine truths does not rest for long at simple symbols, while the greater the complexity and elaboration of the words, the images, the music, the architecture, the sculpture, the vestments, or the pictures, the more distinctive becomes the role of those who can understand, create, manage, or orchestrate the rich profusion of human creation. The progress from direct and spontaneous religion to culturally embedded religion which Hegel described is also a progress which involves greater and greater distinction of forms of priestly elite to manage, interpret, orchestrate, and explain. The very impossibility of a direct communication of the transcendental source of spiritual identity brings the identity cultivation of religious and secular leaders closer together. For both, the identification of themselves as rising above the level of understanding found amongst their followers and subjects can not only justify normal government, but can sanction the most murderous policies of destruction of both life and culture. The actions of twenty-first-century religious leaders, such as those of Islamic State, stand in a long and destructive tradition in both secular and religious government and attempted government. When a person has identified himself or herself as a channel of divine truth or of human utopia, one road which opens is the physical destruction of all opposition, and all opponents.

Privacy in the self-identification of elites

Much discussion of identity presents it as something that is more received than created, and whilst the recipients of tradition, education, and influence are presented as human, the sources of those shaping elements are given a more shadowy presence. The conservative celebration of tradition and its radical diagnosis share a common vantage point. But even the most passive people, by their passivity, contribute to the contexts within which identities are shaped, while even tradition has to be maintained and transmitted. The poet Kathleen Jamie has chronicled the pressures imposed by older generations on aspiring youth to be 'no too cliver' and 'no *above yersel*',[13] and such traditionalists are just as much makers of the circumstances within which identity is cultivated as the most passionate actual or aspiring leader. Cultivation within received contexts can be conservative or radical, but it is still a human creation. The most vigorous contributors to this creation are, by virtue of their actions, political and religious leaders.

Elites are not only masters and mistresses of highly visible, and audible, identity cultivation, but exercise creative innovation and entrepreneurship in the identities they craft, modify, or preserve. The relevant coherence can extend beyond the merely or obviously political. Judith Herrin has argued that in Byzantium the success of three female rulers, the empresses Irene, Euphrosyne, and Theodora in the late eighth and early ninth centuries, in a society and a system of rule whose mores and perceptions were structured on male authority and dominance, was assisted by the ubiquitous presence of high-profile and high-prestige female images both in Christian iconography and in pre-Christian statuary. Constantinople was full of statues and images of female gods, female saints such as Helena (the mother of Constantine), the Virgin Mary, and female empresses. 'This striking visual presence of holy and imperial mothers also drew attention to the essential role of empresses in the construction of imperial dynasties.'[14] This context of images was one which, through the promotion of iconography, the empresses could cultivate as well as exploit. At the same time, imperial progressions, visits, and rituals, together with the founding of churches and monasteries, expressed the presence of the empresses: 'Within the urban space, it was possible to create institutions from shrines to monasteries with peculiarly female interests. These in turn preserved and reproduced the record of women's influence and authority.'[15]

But whatever rulers and leaders may do to impress their subjects and followers, there is a huge swathe of behaviour which functions principally to impress the elite itself, and to reinforce that impression in mutual support. Elites are not unique in paying attention to this dimension of identity cultivation, and are following broader patterns in beginning with themselves and those with whom they normally come into direct contact. All identity is both for the identified person and for those with whom he or she interacts, and the two dimensions are intertissued. But the elaborateness of the private-identity cultivation of those with the greatest access to and control over material, cultural, political, and spiritual resources exceeds the private cultivation of those lower down the pyramids of status, wealth, and power to an extent which places it in a different world. The very claim to be representative has the consequence of distinction and separation. Lasswell and Fox in their discussion of the role of the built environment comment that for an elite, 'physical distance and position are likely to be internalised as psychic space. The ruler who is remote and above modifies his self-image accordingly, and perceives himself as aloof and superior to other men.'[16] The greater the claim to distinction beyond association, the greater the aloofness and the extent and seclusion of the private upper world. There is a massive swathe of rituals of rule and superiority in all societies, from which ordinary people are excluded not so much by physical restriction as by living in a different social context, and neither being involved nor invited, nor even aware of what it is that they are not part of.

The participants and observers are themselves part either of the elite or of a corresponding privileged or distinguished group or association. The degree to which this exclusive cultivation of identity will outweigh the more public expression of identity can range from the almost entirely private to a presentation of identity which comes as close to identification with the public, and with public expression of that identity, as is consistent with still retaining the distance which makes it possible to talk of an elite at all.

In the National Gallery in London, the Wilton Diptych is a small item amongst hosts of larger, grander works. A portable altarpiece made for Richard II, it consists of two hinged panels painted somewhere towards the end of the fourteenth century. It is small and, by the standards of the time – and the servants available to kings, easily portable. It folds shut, like a laptop. The surfaces visible when it is closed are simple: a coat of arms on one side, a white hart on the other. On the inner surfaces the images are more elaborate and delicately detailed. On the left-hand panel, the kneeling King Richard is supported by John the Baptist, Edward the Confessor, and Saint Edmund, king and martyr. On the other side is the Virgin Mary with the infant Jesus, supported by a retinue of angels, each of them bearing on their garments the white hart which was the king's symbol.

What is it for? Kings might well carry around with them maps, treasure, and weapons. In Walerian Borowczyk's 1971 film *Blanche*, even the rosaries and crucifixes of the monks attending the king were swiftly readjusted to reveal the weapons of his clerical bodyguard.[17] But the Wilton Diptych is something else, not a concealed map nor anything to do with the material resources of government. It makes a clear religious and political statement for the king. As Lucy Freeman Sandler put it, the diptych 'served to focus Richard's own meditation, to re-enact his devotion, whether he was present or not, to proclaim to himself the certainty of his prospective welcome in Heaven, and finally, to reinforce his idea of earthly kingship under heavenly protection.'[18]

The intricate artistry of the diptych was for Richard alone, and told him, and him alone, who he was as king and successor to kings, saints, and martyrs, and as aspirant to divine protection and blessing. The cultivation of a royal identity sanctified by divine grace was a private and secluded activity which sustained the public work of kingship, but was distinct from it. This was not an eccentricity of a single English king, but a universal feature of rulers and elites of all kinds. A similar function appears to have been served by a small album of paintings on silk of the Yongzheng Emperor in early eighteenth-century China. The pictures were not for public display, but presented the emperor, to himself, in a range of guises and situations of varying fantasy, but each representing an aspect of human worth, skill, dignity, heroism, or authority.[19] The degree of the private cultivation of identity, beyond any public gaze, differs from instance to instance, as does its relation with the narrative presented to the world beyond the elite. But it is always present.

The rituals of Negara, the nineteenth-century Balinese state described by Clifford Geertz, provide an example of an exceptionally high degree of solipsistic identity cultivation by a ruling elite. There was in a very real sense more ritual than ruling, and the king's palace was a temple rather than either a residence or an office or useful building. Its arrangement of courtyards, even though it contained public spaces, emphasised the remoteness and sacredness of kingship: 'It was a theatre state in which the kings and princes were the impresarios, the priests the directors, and the peasants the supporting cast, stage crew, and audience.' But if the peasants were an audience, they were an audience who sometimes saw little more than the trailers to the main film. Their role as an audience was an incidental consequence of their principal function of auxiliaries in the drama of monarchy. 'Court ceremonialism was the driving force of court politics; and mass ritual was not a device to shore up the state, but rather the state, even in its final gasp, was a device for the enactment of mass ritual. Power served pomp, not pomp power.'[20]

That pomp and power infused the entire cycle of life and of death, which could be as elaborately marked as the mortal acts of kings. The peasantry played a necessary part in all of this, and the rituals of kingship defined ruled as well as rulers, and provided narratives for each. But the weight of the drama lay with the elite. The court life of Negara was at least as elaborate as the most extravagantly expansive fictional alternative. Mervyn Peake's *Gormenghast*[21] is a castle and a court whose every moment and movement is devoted to fulfilling escalating traditions of etiquette and ritual; but it is not a phenomenon limited to fictional fantasy, and the real world of the theatre of identity frequently outdoes the most fruitful and vivid imagination.

In imperial China, the emperors' cycle of rituals was marked both by the elaborateness and by the privacy of those rituals. The most magnificent and extended ritual sacrifice of the year was the sacrifice to Heaven, when the emperor went in procession from the Forbidden City to the Temple of Heaven, but did so along a route entirely masked from public view. The peasantry and the rest of the population beyond the pale of the imperial court were neither menial supporters nor passive spectators. They were excluded by a mixture of permanent architecture – walls and gates – and temporary screens and topiary. They could not be seen, and they could not see. The lesser annual sacrifice, to the God of Agriculture, was similarly attended by officials, servants, and courtiers, but masked and secluded from public view. At the imperial banquet in the Garden of Ten Thousand Trees, when the Qianlong Emperor received submission from the Khalkha Mongols in 1754, even the ten thousand trees were screened off from the privacy of the ceremony.[22]

The rituals of imperial China were given architectural support in the spatial seclusions of the Forbidden City, an extreme and dramatised example of an unmobilised society, where the mass of the population, though they may be a human resource for government, are not mobilised for war, public service, or public display as they are in most societies with the development of industry and the growth of towns. Societies which are unmobilised, and where the institutions of dominance are authoritarian or closed, are never closed to everyone, and to that extent the question, as with all systems, is one of degree not of kind. The Forbidden City was hardly even closed to the mass of the population of imperial China, since they were not acknowledged. The presidential palaces of Saddam Hussein, by contrast, were closed to the Iraqi population because they were acknowledged, but as subordinate to a leader whose barriers against them defined his situation in relation to theirs.

The identity-savouring and identity-nurturing rituals of imperial China were paralleled again and again in the life of imperial and monarchic courts. The splendours of Louis XIV's Versailles might serve to impress visiting representatives of other regimes, but it was the king himself who was not only at the centre of the drama, but whose identity was cultivated at every moment of every day by it, and who was the principal and most continually present audience for the theatre of royalty. Every aspect of the life of the court, and of the king's central role in it, was choreographed. There was no distinction between business and leisure, each of the activities which might in other contexts be so described and distinguished being orchestrated to exemplify the unique character of aristocracy and, at the same time, the transcendent position of the king within it. Even the masques and ballets had a role for the monarch, who by his participation expressed his superiority in every aspect of life. Norbert Elias, describing this cycle of self-definition, comments that the 'practice of etiquette is, in other words, an exhibition of court society to itself. Each participant, above all the king, has his prestige and his relative power position confirmed by others ... The immense value attached to the demonstration of prestige and the observance of etiquette does not betray an attachment to externals, but to what was vitally important to individual identity.'[23] The rituals of the court defined both elite and mass, and did so for the court, but not for the excluded people beyond the walls of the palace, in whose case it was sufficient that the court was aware of their inferiority, an inferiority which justified their not having it displayed to them, since they could be simply ignored. Elias summarises things neatly: 'It was always with people and their positions relative to each other that they were primarily concerned. In their etiquette, too, they did not come together for etiquette's sake. To enact their existence, to demonstrate their prestige, to distance themselves from lower-ranking people and have this distance recognized by the higher-ranking – all this was purpose enough in itself.'[24]

What the architecture of Versailles proclaimed within, the magnificence and privacy of the gardens proclaimed without.[25] Gardens are one instance of the created environment that can function largely or solely for the benefit of the self-identification of the privileged. The larger the palace, government building, or religious monument in a city, the more evident it is to all and the less it can be enjoyed only for the private satisfaction and reassurance of the privileged. But the larger the garden, the greater the likelihood that it will be shielded from public gaze. The small patch of the ordinary subject or citizen can be viewed from the street, from the train, from the bus. The gardens of the wealthy are not mere estates, but landscapes, and functioning for the exclusive identity cultivation of their owners. Denis Cosgrove has argued that that 'landscape constitutes a discourse through which identifiable social groups historically have framed themselves and their relations with both the land and with other human groups.'[26] But they do so in way different from that of other large human arrangements of the physical environment, since they do so behind gates and fences. Urban landscapes proclaim public identities to all. Horticultural landscapes are the proclamations of an assurance which is largely private.

The etiquette of separation reached an absurdist extreme at the court of Peter the Great in Russia. The bizarre carnivals choreographed by the tsar mocked and inverted the hierarchies of Orthodox Christianity, and created an aristocratic version of Lords of Misrule. The rituals of the Orthodox church and of its patriarchs were paralleled in grotesque form; marriage processions were conducted with riders on pigs, goats, and other animals; and drunkenness solemnly celebrated with mock noble titles.[27] It was not only behaviour which marked the court off from the population of Russia, nor behaviour from which they were excluded, but behaviour which could only have been viewed by them with a mixture of incomprehension and outrage. The cultivation of an identity which marked off the elite from the rest could not have been more extreme.

The pomp and circumstance of closed systems may itself be closed, as with Versailles, or it may be populist, as with the papacy of John Paul II or the leadership of Evita Perón. But whichever it is, it will have a distinctive extravagance, and whether the elevation of the ruler is displayed by his or her seclusion from ordinary subjects, or by his or her nobility in descending amongst the masses, the message will still be that the ruler is exceptional. So whilst the Russian and Chinese communist regimes had leaders who adopted some of the appearance of ordinary citizens, with demonstrably plain clothing, the Kremlin and the palaces of empire remained as the palaces of government. Whilst the Forbidden City of imperial China was eroded, modified, and infiltrated by the new regime after 1947, and old walls were demolished, the Forbidden City itself was not destroyed, and China's communist rulers employed a dual strategy of both seeking to emulate and transcend the urban architecture of the old regime, and incorporate its magnificence within the new order.[28]

In the Soviet Union the practices of the vanguard of the proletariat illustrated how, whatever the claims to represent the people made by rulers, the cultivation of an identity distinct from the mass can persist and flourish within an elite. The protocol governing the reception of new ambassador would not have seemed out of place in Versailles two centuries earlier. The rubric was elaborate and rigid:

> The Ambassador, together with the diplomatic personnel from the Embassy and the Soviet officials, enter the hall: the Head of the appropriate geographical Department of the Ministry of Foreign Affairs stands on the right of the Ambassador, on the left is the Head of Protocol Department.
>
> Simultaneously, the Chairman of the Praesidium of the Supreme Soviet enters through the opposite door in the hall; on his right is the Secretary of the Praesidium; on his left the Deputy Minister of Foreign Affairs. The

> Ambassador stops one or two paces short of the centre of the hall, opposite the Chairman of the Praesidium, and greets him with a slight bow. The Head of the Protocol Department presents the Ambassador to the Chairman of the Praesidium.[29]

The transition from mobilisation of the masses under the tutelage of an elite to mobilisation with democracy, or democratic aspirations, has not dulled the cultivation of elite exclusiveness, and from an early date the leaders of the new state of America made sure that, however representative they were, they were also different. When George Washington, establishing his role as President of the United States, received local dignitaries with his hat in one hand and the other hand resting on his sword, to prevent them getting above themselves by attempting to shake the president by the hand, he was making a very clear claim.[30] However much he might represent them, speak for them, fight for them, and care for them, he was both like and not like them. The president was set apart from the multitude.

Even the most apparently practical matters of comfort and convenience can, at the same time that they ease the strains of a life in office, underline the privileged character of the office bearer. When President John F. Kennedy of the United States visited the United Kingdom in 1963, a memo from Prime Minister Harold Macmillan's private secretary, Philip de Zulueta, a few weeks before the presidential arrival on 29 June, reports that one of the president's aides had accepted the offer of Macmillan's own room at Birch Grove, and would place his valet next door. However, it seems that the prime minister failed to take account of the presidential preference for a double rather than a single bed. Mr Zulueta reported that 'The only complicated arrangement for the house is that the President likes a double bed and brings his own mattress and pillows (I suppose it is for his back). They [the White House] will let us know and the Foreign Office will get one.'

Further documents reveal that Whitehall was clearly taken aback by the extent of the preparation for the president's arrival at Gatwick Airport. A Rolls-Royce was to be provided for the president's use, along with a helicopter, an ambulance, and an unspecified quantity of blood matching his type at the nearby East Grinstead hospital. The communications centre to be set up at the Grand Hotel in Brighton, twenty-five miles from Birch Grove, was to include 150 telephone lines for the press corps; 50 secure lines including permanent connections between the White House, the president's Boeing 707, the helicopter pad next to the Red Lion pub; and 5 to the president's bedroom.[31] Louis XIV could hardly have had sleeping arrangements more elaborate.

The relative privacy of the identity cultivation of elites does not make their members any less sensitive when they feel their status is not being properly sustained. This can occur in any manner of settings. A diplomat at a formal banquet in Australia turned his plate upside down in protest when he felt he was not sufficiently grandly placed at table. But, commented Lord Carrington who was high commissioner in Australia at the time, 'he was extremely greedy so he only did it for the first course.'[32]

Leaders and followers, rulers and subjects

Despite the immediate attention which is paid to the cultivation and maintenance of identity, even the most insulated elites make some demands of the mass of the population, both to express their own distinction and to nurture it by contrast with a subordinate identity amongst the rest of the population, though the extent to which they do so, and the manner in which they do so, change as rule moves from unmobilised to mobilised populations. A part of the identity of an elite is the identification of others – the led, the ruled, the followers – all those who are not part of the privileged group. To identify oneself as part of an elite is to describe others who are not so privileged, for if one's character were shared by everyone, elites would dissolve in universality. The creation of identity is, for leaders and other elites, an identification which is both self-relating and contrasted with a different identity for the mass of people. To depict a distinct governing identity is, even if only by contrast, to identify a distinct governed one. Uncontested inferiority sustains distinction, but it does so in different ways and with different degrees of attention by elites to the mass of the population. Even when a sense of distinction does not draw strength from popular acceptance or acknowledgment, it can be threatened by aspects of popular identities, a threat which will be countered both by more vigorous cultivation of elite identities, and by elite cultivation of the identities of subordinates.

Whilst all government and all leadership involve hierarchies of identity, the relation between rulers and ruled, and the character of the ruled, differs sharply between mobilised and unmobilised societies. The manner of elite-identity cultivation and the extent to which others are recruited in its promotion differ as part of the presence, extent, and nature of mobilisation. The distinction between mobilised and unmobilised societies is one of two major distinctions when considering the cultivation of elite identity, the second being the distinction within mobilised societies between democracies and various kinds of elite rule without democracy. The first distinction is between the extent of public as opposed to private identity, the second is between a passive and dominated and an active and assertive public identity. All democracies are mobilised societies, but not all mobilised societies are democracies, though the portfolio of possible features of mobilised societies is sometimes listed as flaws uniquely of democracy, as in Michael Mann's *The Dark Side of Democracy*.[33] The first feature of the modern world is not that people become democratic citizens, but that they become a direct concern of government, which deals directly with them and sees them as the foundation of both the resources and the identity of the state. Democracy may follow, but it has generally had to be wrested from the hands of those currently enjoying power. Modern societies are mobilised societies in which the mass of the population becomes possessed of a greater public identity. But this identity is not necessarily a freer or more diverse one.

In unmobilised societies, the inhabitants lack not only the identity of citizens, but even that of subjects. People are human resources, on a level with all the other resources, animal, vegetable, and mineral, at a government's disposal. Premodern governments did not mobilise the inhabitants of their territories, and dominated rather than ruled them. Thomas Bisson has argued that terms suggesting rule or government are inappropriate for societies which were simply coerced.[34] The privileged made occasional demands on the people for taxes or foot soldiers, and even the taxes and the foot soldiers could be garnered indirectly. The population was occasionally raided rather than regularly ruled. In such societies, dominating elites contribute to the identity of the mass of the population only by neglect. In such systems, it can be misleading to speak of the mass of the population as subjects, since their distance from the ruler is so great that they do not have even that restricted but at the same time identifying status. If they are ruled, it is by those far lower down the hierarchy than the king. Before populations were mobilised, the ordinary inhabitants of a territory were not only not citizens, they were hardly subjects. Feudal and other forms of rule which took cognisance only, or predominantly, of a proportionately small ruling class, also had only that class as their subjects. The lower orders were resources under the control of these political contractors, not themselves directly part of the polity. In such a society it would not necessarily cause friction or the apprehension of difficulty if the ruling elite were culturally or linguistically distinct from the mass of the population. They frequently were. A difference between mobilised and unmobilised societies is that in the latter the rulers may well tell ordinary people what they may *not* be, but will not try to control or positively to cultivate what they *are*. The populace may be kept in its place in unmobilised societies, but that requires little more than keeping them out the elite's place.

The distance from the ordinary life of the population of elite identity and its cultivation has been universal in unmobilised societies. There are two ways in which this distance is expressed: one where the seclusion of the rituals of rule constructs the separation of rulers and ruled and the qualitative superiority and difference of rulers, the other where the very representativeness or superior representativeness of the leader is both displayed to and elevated above the mass. In either case, there can be both separation from and (rare and symbolic) contact with, ordinary inhabitants. The ritual application of the royal touch to cure the king's evil by monarchs such as Louis XIV is a dramatised breach of the normal barrier which separates and insulates rulers from ordinary inhabitants, a secular epiphany. Suzanne Cawsey's account of the kings of Aragon from the thirteenth to the fifteenth centuries is of rulers who, whilst they did not necessarily present themselves to the ordinary inhabitants of the territories that they ruled, frequently and effectively did so in verbal and visual persuasion to those who were most immediately their subjects, and on whom they relied for taxes and soldiers.[35] The difference between the use and character of the Forbidden City in unmobilised China and that under communism is that in the former it was forbidden to the mass of the population because they were outside the entire world of government; it was alien to them and they to it.[36] In a mobilised China the ordinary population might not be excluded, but the even greater magnificence of the city under revolutionary transformation not only proclaimed the triumph of socialism, but provided a setting for the distinguished performance of leadership.

Rule in an unmobilised society needs to assert its identity to itself and to others, but the range of those others will be, in the normal course of the ruler's activity, limited to the wider circles of the governing elite and if the identity cultivation goes beyond this, it will be sporadic. Mobilised societies, by contrast, cultivate the identities of both elites and masses, which they take a first step in doing by putting their armies into uniform, though armies are wearing the livery of the state as servants of government, not the livery of subjects. If they are mobilised autocracies, they move on to putting everyone else in uniform as well, distinguishing organised nations by colour and insignia, plumes and braid. In mobilised societies, even if the masses are being used as infantry, unless they are directly in battle, they are clothed and plumed, not camouflaged, since as important as their role as coercers is their demonstrative expressive role as auxiliaries to the splendours and dominance of their rulers. There is every reason not to hide them with the cover of Burnham Wood or its subsequent forms of camouflage in combat dress, which fades warriors into grass and shadow. Just as an aristocracy proclaims its splendour through the livery of its servants, so the emerging mobilising state proclaims it through the livery of its troops.

The arrival of democracy is one aspect only of the arrival or mobilisation of the people; the people can appear and be mobilised before democracy appears. Hobbes's *Leviathan* has as an illustration on its title page of the sovereign as composed of his subjects, and they are the masses not simply the magnates (though they are entirely adult and entirely male). In unmobilised societies, the mass of a population is largely excluded from the regular attention of government, or from systematic involvement in the business of the state or of its rulers. Mobilised societies, by contrast, involve their population regularly and systematically in the public affairs of the state: as taxpayers, as soldiers, or as industrial and agricultural human resources. Mobilised societies include democracies, but also most other modern societies, from totalitarian regimes to theocracies. And whilst collective public identities vary by place and time, a broad distinction can be made both between the public identities of populations of mobilised and unmobilised societies, and between the identities of the rulers of the two types of society.

Mobilised nations are an accommodation between the authority of government and the redescription of subjects as the people, the nation. The population are constructed, choreographed, dressed in a way which is a part of the choreographing of the system, which presents them as members of a nation whose identity depends not on autonomous citizens or democratic action, but on membership, mobilisation, and orchestration. And as soon as the nation is described, it is also prescribed, and the prescriber, not the nation, is taking control. There may not be an exact point at which a totality of inhabitants of a territory becomes a mobilised populace, or at which the places where a mobilised populace lives become a territory, but the ends of the scale are clear enough.

Mobilisation, and democratisation as its further stage, places identity problems for government in a way which is not present, or not present in the same way, in unmobilised societies. If the mass of the population are part of a nation, then their common identity becomes relevant in a new way. Pre-mobilised societies impose cultural or religious uniformity on the governed majority, but mobilised societies have a new dimension of need, since a mobilised population is public, visible, and active. In responding to this situation governments can seek to cultivate a common identity; or exclude, expel, or kill those who do not fit the chosen image; or accept an identity which is political but contains cultural, religious, ethnic, or other diversities – a choice described by Liah Greenfeld as 'civic nationalism'[37]. The most extreme instance of the second is the ethnic cleansing of which the actions of the Nazi regime in the middle of the twentieth century were the most ruthlessly pursued. Client regimes, such as the Vichy regime in France, provided constitutional euphemisms for exclusion, removing 110,000 Algerian Jews from the category 'citizen' to the category 'subject'.[38]

There is no simple binary distinction, however, between mobilised and unmobilised societies any more than there is between religious and secular leadership and governance. There are instances of societies which would certainly be thought of as both premodern and unmobilised, where substantial sections of a population were either driven out or killed by a new ruling group in order to achieve homogeneity not merely within the elite, but across the whole population of the conquered or governed territory. There may be a material dimension to this, but there may also be one of identity, most clearly in the case of religious identity. This might, however, be more likely when the new arrivals were not simply a ruling caste who sought to remove cultural disparity, but a new community who sought land and capital. The study of medieval ethnic cleansing by Len Scales is both of rulers or conquerors purging newly acquired territories, or the territories to which they have succeeded by killing or expulsion, and of dissident groups, either popular or elite, objecting to what were seen as foreigners either capturing too much trade or unduly influencing rulers or universities.[39] If that is the case, then the conflict is not directly over identity, but over possession, with identity used as an exclusionary mark to gain or increase property or influence, and to limit by exclusion the numbers who might share in it. There is thus a difference between an attempt to sustain distinction or solidarity by enforcing a particular identity, and using or creating an identity in order to reduce the numbers of people who enjoy some material benefit. But in this case too, identity is the language of solidarity and conflict, whether an elite or an aspirant elite seeks to consolidate its own security by distancing itself from the mass of the population or by incorporating the mass of the population to its own cultural, linguistic, or most commonly religious identity. This form of identity cultivation of the population by its rulers is the major exception to the otherwise broad indifference of rulers and elites in unmobilised societies to the identity of populations within their territories. It is an instance which illustrates the limitation of both the idealised distinction between mobilised and unmobilised societies and that between religious and secular leadership. Religious orthodoxy has been enforced by secular leaders in both mobilised and unmobilised societies, and more frequently in the latter than in the former, suggesting that even the most culturally insulated identities can be unsettled if the religious practices beyond the boundaries of their estate are uncongenial or unfamiliar.

The understanding of actual instances and societies will be further removed from these ideal types in that whilst extremes of mobilisation or its absence will occur, much social life will be found at some point in between the two poles, whilst the degree of mobilisation will not be uniform across all forms of social life. People may be mobilised for war but not for religion, or vice versa. Medieval society, which might appear as unmobilised, was characterised by a high level of organisation of the religious practices of its members, whilst leaving their economic activities largely unattended, and their political ones non-existent in times of stability. Elizabeth I of England, who said that she did not wish to make windows into men's souls, was perhaps departing less radically from previous practice than appears. She insisted on public conformity to a prayer book and a liturgy that were imposed on all by secular law. What mattered was conformist behaviour.

The terms 'mobilised' and 'unmobilised' have only a limited usefulness, since they refer to degrees of involvement and exclusion which are neither neat nor uniform. Other terms, and other ways of talking of the character of a society, can be equally illuminating: the distinction between 'open' and 'closed' societies; the extent, character, scope, and power of elites; the extent of open or public politics; the existence or extent of a public sphere or of civil society; the degree of visibility or public participation or activity of the mass of the population or of those outside obvious elites or dominant groups. Even so, it is still useful to employ the distinction, not in order to fit entire societies into tight taxonomic boxes, but to consider the various features found, in different forms and with different intensities, in particular instances.

A major difference between unmobilised and mobilised populations and societies lies in the relation between the identity of elites and identity of the rest of the population. Whatever the differences in power, prestige, or material prosperity in mobilised societies, the identity of the mass of the population is an essential part of the identity of the elite. Under all other systems, the feathers of the people matter only insofar as they do not challenge those of their rulers.

Tom Nairn in his examination of the monarchy suggests that there is an organic coherence, which he calls Ukania, to the whole social and political system of the United Kingdom, so that the monarchic tip shapes and sustains the vernacular iceberg.[40] Coherence may be too strong a term, but whatever the dissonances and tensions, each social or political stratum is in part defined by the others. But though all forms of elite-identity cultivation involve a related cultivation of the identity of the rest of the population, there is a major difference between the character of this relationship in mobilised and unmobilised societies.

The trick is for an elite in a mobilised society to be neither too close to nor too distant from the identity of ordinary people. This is different from saying either that subjects reflect the character of rulers, or that rulers reflect the character of subjects. Rather it is saying that there is a symbiotic relation between the two, such that it is possible to learn a lot about the one from studying the other, and that the character of each is a matter not of autonomous identity, but of relationship. A polity is a holistic arrangement or phenomenon, and each part or dimension is as it is partly in relation to the other parts. This is the A sharp/B flat phenomenon, whereby a musical note gains meaning not in isolation, but in relation to the other notes with which it is associated. It is also an application, to a polity, of the concept of legitimation as a feature of a relationship, rather than as a one-way transfer of consent. And if it is a relationship – of law making and enforcing, and compliance, or of political activity and response – then each party to the relationship has a social identity that arises from that relationship, and that would not exist without it.

Any such judgment must be cautious and qualified. Whole societies are neither simple nor uniform. On the other hand, even in the most variegated societies, the elements take some of their character from each other. A religious sect in a secular society will differ from a sect with apparently similar theological doctrine in a religious society, a monarchist movement in a republic from one in a constitutional monarchy.

Mobilised and democratic societies are not without elites

Even unmobilised society calls for some attention from elites, both to their own appearance in the face of the population and, particularly in the character of religion, to ensuring that the population provides a congenial background to the lives of the privileged. The mobilisation of populations which accompanied both democratic and autocratic government was celebrated, in the democratic case, by a rhetoric of representation. Nor did autocracies of one kind or another renounce the powerful justification of claiming to speak for the people. In a democratic or mobilised system there is identification with the masses. But even in such systems, there is a degree of difference. The elite presents itself as representative rather than separate and different, but nonetheless representative in a distinctive way. There remains a distance between identity as association and identity as distinction. Whilst an elite might present itself to itself and to others as representing the qualities of the rest of society, it must also present that representativeness as concentrated, elevated, or in some sense different from mere reproduction of the normal or the vernacular. Were that not the case, the elite would dissolve in the mass.

There is a paradox in that the more an identity is cultivated which is different from that of the majority, the less able an elite may be to understand and hence to dominate that majority. At the same time, the dominated, whilst they will acquiesce in being dominated by those whose identity appears to be like their own but more so, are less likely to acquiesce to domination by those who appear alien. That is one of the reasons why colonialism is unstable. The key to both acquiescence and revolt is identification, as it is to electoral success.

Different systems will have different degrees of separation between leaders and led, different identities, and leadership identity sustained by different mixes of distinctiveness and representation. The degree of similarity, or of difference, between elite and mass will be a feature of the political system and, accordingly, as it differs between affinity and distance, so will the rest of the system between open, mobilised, democratic, and closed, authoritarian.

But whatever the system, an identity is in the first place that of a person or group, and one which functions to tell them, rather than others, who they are. That narrative is confirmed in the recognition of others, but nonetheless it starts with a subject, not with an observer. Once there is more than one person, personal identity, whilst it is cultivated by its subject, is entangled with the recognition, rejection, or indifference of others. Robinson Crusoe had an identity which was both confirmed and changed by the arrival of Friday. But he was not without an identity even when he was alone, and even when that solitude was ended, identity began with its subject and whilst it was affected by the presence of another, was not created by it.

This superiority is no less important if the justification is super-representativeness, and no more important if the justification is a great breach of identity between rulers and the rest of the population. In either case, rulers need to know and to celebrate their special identity. If the wider population is to have a clear role in public life, the maintenance of the distinction of elites needs special effort. Once there is a public presence of layers of the population beyond an elite, elites begin to take a new responsibility for the identity of those from whom they continue to distinguish themselves. Even if the masses are only an audience for superior persons, attention needs paying to them.

Elites cultivate their own identity, but they cultivate also that of the rest of humanity, and in each case they are energetic and resourceful. Because government, politics, and religion as societies become more mobilised involve, potentially, entire populations, the actions and identities of their elites cannot be insulated from the public presentation of the identity of everyone else, and are a part of public life to an extent which marks them off from other fragmentary, particular, or local cultures of identity.

The scenery which people, whether rulers, politicians, or some individual or group amongst the variety of less powerful subjects, construct, is a part both of how they live and of how they aspire to live. The formal order of the New Town in eighteenth-century Edinburgh was a calm and deliberate alternative to the disorder of the old town, just as Bentham's panopticon prison or proposed school was an image and expression of order, hierarchy, and deliberate rational regulation.[41] And in each case, the identity was being cultivated, or being attempted to be cultivated, by a small group for a larger swathe of the population.

The character of this cultivation will differ according to whether the population is mobilised, and according to the identity which the elite cultivates for itself. In a mobilised society, whilst the elite will still distinguish itself from the mass, there is a degree of homogeneity between the culture which the elite cultivates for itself and that which it seeks to achieve for the masses. A nationalist elite will seek linguistic and cultural homogeneity, a theocratic elite uniformity of dogma and religious practice. Each of these forms of identity can make absolute demands on the masses, the theocratic particularly so since theocratic rule not only claims divine justification, the ultimate unquestionable absolute, but seeks the application on earth and to all peoples of the divine will. But here too there will be differences between mobilised and unmobilised societies. The elite of an unmobilised society will be content with, will indeed seek, a level or mode of compliance from the masses which distinguishes it sharply from the culture of the elite: the masses must comply with the religion of the elite, but need not, indeed should not, engage with it with the sophistication, active participation, or understanding which characterises elite devotion and theological understanding. Latin will remain the secular and religious language of the distinctive few, mass will be performed behind a rood screen, the conversions of humanity will simply be the conversion of kings.

Harold Lasswell and Merritt Fox contrast autocratic separation, the Forbidden City or the Kremlin under both tsars and communism, with popular government in the United States:

> The sharpest contrast to despotism and autocracy is a well-established popular government. The official meets the citizen on a common level and the chief of state lives with an insignificant physical barrier separating him from his fellows. The White House in Washington expresses the basic relationship that connects the transitory holder of the presidential office and the rank and file of the nation. The White House is neither remote nor exalted; it has the approachability of a private home.[42]

But the White House is clearly far more 'exalted' than the average American home, and significantly less approachable. The citizens of the United States may visit and be impressed by the White House once or even several times in a lifetime, but the president can be impressed by it, and what it says about the incumbent of the presidential office, every day. As Murray Edelman puts it:

> That a man meets with his aides in the Oval Office of the White House reminds him and them and the public to whom the meeting is reported of his status and authority as President, just as it exalts the status of the aides and defines the mass public as nonparticipants who never enter the Office.[43]

Whatever message of solidarity or equality the stage of the White House may present to ordinary citizens, to the president and his aides it presents a message of political superiority and spatial exclusion.

Both superior and inferior identities are necessary for there to be an elite at all, since each defines the other. When the first fails, the elite collapses inwardly, abdicates, or dissolves. There are many accounts of the revolutions which took place in the Soviet Union and Eastern Europe from 1989. But one crucial aspect in the collapse of managerial communism was not an assault from without, but a loss of meaning and justification within. Rulers ceased to believe in themselves as rulers. One part of the disappearance of the regimes in Romania, East Germany, Poland, or Czechoslovakia was abdication by elites which no long saw themselves as marked off from their subject populations by unique insight or skill.

When the second, the identification of a mass of ordinary and subordinate, less privileged, or less talented humanity, fails, the elite is merely play-acting, since the defining others have evaporated. It is an internal instance of the crisis of identity which occurs when an enemy vanishes just as surely as when a people vanish.

A king in exile is not even half a king. The paradox of the private world of identity cultivation is that whilst it appears self-sufficient and closed within a private world, if the public world beyond is no longer there, then the private world can no longer be defined by its seclusion from it, and descends into mere fantasy. It is a fantasy performed whenever a regime collapses and its former leaders survive, in exile, privacy, or peregrination from hotel to hotel. But it is a fantasy which can be desperately sustained. R. K. Narayan recalls an evening in New York: 'Other guests for the dinner were an ex-Maharaja from India, whom everyone deliberately "highnesses" much to his delight. Royalty in exile is generally very exacting.'[44] Royal weddings are forever attended by self-proclaimed monarchs not only from monarchies which no longer exist, but from countries which no longer exist. When Prince William and Kate Middleton were married in Westminster Abbey in 2011, the guests included King Michael of Yugoslavia.

Two messages and two audiences; avoiding indifference

The published and expressed identity of an elite has two audiences, the ruler and the ruled, the elite and the subordinate. The identification of elites is partly a matter of identifying themselves to themselves, partly of identifying themselves to those whom they govern. Elites cultivate an identity which both gives meaning and justification to themselves and enables them to distinguish, both for themselves and others, their difference from the mass of humanity. Plutarch observed of Pompey that he 'sought to surround his presence with majesty and pomp, believing that he should keep his dignity free from contact and familiarity with the masses.'[45] But in so doing he was cultivating an identity not only for the included, but for the excluded.

Because the identity of elites involves a dominant relation with the mass of their fellow humans, whilst the cultivation of identity is powerfully pursued in a solipsistic manner, the recognition of an elite by others has an importance which is absent from the identity cultivation of ordinary humanity. Public indifference in open or mobilised societies is disastrous for an elite, for whom the one thing worse than being talked about is not being talked about.

So there are two audiences, and two messages: the audience of the mass outside the elite, and of the elite, and a message about the identity of the insiders, and another, complementary, message about the identity of the outsiders. Each message is relayed to both audiences, but in different tones and with different intensities.

The environments which polities construct for themselves will differ between ones with a ruling class and ones with a ruling person, the former having many statues of great men and some women, the latter having either lots of statues of the same person, for instance Atatürk or Louis XIV, or lots of statues of idealised representative persons, workers, peasants, and soldiers in their heroic Soviet apotheoses. By the end of the Napoleonic wars, St Paul's Cathedral was filling up with the memorial statues of generals and admirals.[46]

Conscripting others as supporting casts of identity; religion and politics as coercive identity cultivation

Identities are cultivated and expressed across the whole range of human creativity: speech, manufacture, consumption, movement. But because identity is constructed and cultivated not just in the external presentation of the person, but in that person's social and material setting, it is not only buildings and artefacts which are created and colonised. Other people can be seen not as the bearers of autonomous identity, but as human resources for the cultivation and creation of someone else's identity. This can take the form of an apparently benign concern for the life of others. George Bernard Shaw's analysis of philanthropy and reform described just this when he wrote that:

> the poverty of those we rob prevents our having the good life for which we sacrifice them. Rich men or aristocrats with a developed sense of life – men like Ruskin and William Morris and Kropotkin – have enormous social appetites and very fastidious personal ones. They are not content with handsome houses: they want handsome cities. They are not content with bediamoned

> wives and blooming daughters: they complain because the charwoman is badly dressed.[47]

But this desire to make the world a congenial context for one's own character can equally take the form of an attempt to compel others to have an identity either like one's own, in order to give one support, or subordinate to one's own in order to enhance one's own sense of esteem, distinctiveness, and superiority.

Whilst Shaw's fastidious reformer can seek to raise everyone else to his own culture, an aristocratic class can insist that only its own members may dress in a distinctive way. In pre-revolutionary France, only nobles with the right to be present at court might have red heels on their shoes.[48] In Renaissance Florence, sumptuary laws restricted the clothing of the lower orders and marked social difference with the visible distinctions of vestments.[49] The attempt to keep people in their place could operate within the ranks of the more fortunate just as readily as between them and the masses. Tudor sumptuary legislation could discriminate between students of law and others above the level of the common people as readily as it could mark the appropriate territories of gentry and populace.[50] Too many buttons could be a transgression of the social order resisted and suppressed by the force of the law.[51] One of the earliest contentions in the Estates General which met in France in 1789 was over the distinctive seating and dress of the different estates.[52] In less formal or overtly prescribed ways, differences of dress, speech, and manner are used in a range of political and governmental assemblies to marginalise newcomers, or women, or members of ethnic minorities.[53] Quentin Bell has observed the class dimension of clothing, though class is not the only invidious distinction:

> the history of fashionable dress is tied to the competition between classes, in the first place the emulation of the aristocracy by the bourgeoisie and then the more extended competition which results from the ability of the proletariat to compete with the middle classes ... while many political events leave fashion unaffected, those which alter the class structure do influence the course of fashion ... the schism between masculine and feminine dress takes its place naturally as part of the same process.
>
> Class and social status are joined by gender and age as identities to which distinctive clothing contributed.[54]

The point has been made precisely in relation to clothing. Thorstein Veblen in *The Theory of the Leisure Class* introduced the term 'vicarious consumption' to describe those whose flamboyant expression of their own wealth was conducted not through their own person but through their economic dependents. Quentin Bell's application of this observation in *On Human Finery* half a century later illustrated the point with the egregious abundance of useless and impeding clothing for dependent wives and children, and of archaic finery for servants.

But what each of these alternatives, of demanding that others be like oneself or demanding that they be different from and inferior to oneself, illustrates is the construction and cultivation of identity by constructing and cultivating a dramatic setting for oneself which is composed not only of material constructions and creations, but of other people. It might seem that a cultivated identity which depends upon others being identified as inferior is more oppressive of those others than one which depends on their being identified as the same. But each treatment of people as the supporting cast of identity subordinates them, and denies them their own autonomous creation and cultivation of their identity. To be compelled to shape one's identity in support of that of someone else is a denial of autonomy. In its most extreme form, this subordination of others can involve their killing. So called 'honour' murders are justified either because the victim refuses to adopt a subordinate identity or because he or she refuses to adopt an identical identity. Women are killed because they refuse to act as part of the patriarchal identity of fathers, just as they or men can be killed because they do not accept the religious practices of the killer.

This is the paradox of identification through the construction and cultivation of human and material environments. By treating the external world – human and material – as a theatre for the enactment of an individual's drama, the individuality of others can be denied. Others may be coerced to play a part in a drama not of their creation, or destroyed if they undermine the dramas of others, who may invoke their own 'honour' to justify the destruction of artefacts and the murder of people.

The enrolment, or conscription, of other people in support of one's own identification occurs with particularly authoritative justification in the case of religion. To say that a person's church requires them to act in a certain way is a different kind of statement from saying that it requires anybody else to act in that way. The second is an attempt to press-gang others as extras in the dramatic construction of self, a self which, whilst it appears to be justified by divine external authority, is itself the only location or evidence of such authority. But whilst religion may be the form most absolutely invoked for this mobilisation of others as auxiliaries in someone else's identity, political causes can make claims almost as loud and intemperate. The obliteration of one person's autonomy in the service of someone else requires the most grandiose justifications.

The salience of religious identity and of the cultivation by both religious and secular leaders of congenial and conformist settings for their own sense of identity has neither been wholly absent nor uniformly dominant. It may have had a more sustained presence in unmobilised societies as a form of ensuring that the population was quiet and orderly. But it has been a major element in public life from the end of the twentieth century.

Religious identity can be expressed and constituted in part by clothes, both to the wearer and to others. The argument at the start of the twenty-first century about headscarves in France and in Turkey, and about the jilbab and niqab in the United Kingdom, is about who people are, both for themselves and for others. It may be religious faith which expresses some particular obligation, but the form of the compliance with that obligation is social, not private or spiritual. And as with other socially constructed identities, distinctions construct an identity for each person which is not autonomous or separate, but comprehensible only in relation to the identities of others. The use of and argument about the clothes worn by female Muslims illustrates the extreme flexibility of material or evident components of identity. The same clothing can have very different significance for both wearers and audiences in mobilised and unmobilised societies, democracies and autocracies. Controversies and practices around clothing can involve the persuasion or coercion by leaders for whom the appearance of their followers or subjects becomes an important component or supporting environment for the cultivation of their own identity. It illustrates too that the distinction between political and religious leadership is an ideal type, and that religious practices can be a part of the coercive rule of government as readily as of the voluntary or socially sustained activity of subjects or citizens.

There are many ways, whose meaning is part of the circumstances in which they are used, of cultivating the distinctiveness of identity, and flamboyance is one way only. When the world is decked in finery, ascetic simplicity can be a way of standing apart from the masses. Religious dress may in its plainness, lack of adornment, and subdued colours proclaim the equality of all believers, the inequality asserted by the authority of the ascetic or the idiosyncratic choice of individuals, and in its variety proclaim hierarchy, gender division and subordination, a denial of oppressive gendered stereotypes, an assertion of individual choice or gradations of holiness, or a repudiation of extravagance which is, by its very evident severity, extravagant. It may be an assertion of religion or a secular assertion of identity.

Coerced identity is more a feature of religious than of secular leadership. This may be in part another aspect of the difference between political and religious proselytising. Religious faith has been seen by those who possess it as a desirable dimension of life which should be communicated to, and if necessary imposed on, as many people as possible. That is not uniformly the case with political faiths, and democracy, for instance, is more frequently regarded as a good, like material sources, which its possessors have no burning desire to share with others, and which they may actively prevent or hinder others from enjoying if it is not consistent with their own perceived well-being.

This feature of religious faith co-exists with a distinction which can allow religious elites to dismiss or exclude much of a population from the fullness of religious experience, either as laity restricted on the concealing side of a rood screen, or as beyond the finer points of theological understanding. Such a faith will seek external compliance, and see secular law as an appropriate way of achieving it. Bede's record of the progress of Christianity in the British Isles is a record of the conversion of kings and lords – the rest of the population was assumed to follow.

The manner of presentation to the crowd indicates something of the rulers' conception of his or her subjects. But, in addition, it is not just formal legitimation claims that constitute the legitimation activities of rulers. Everything they do can have a legitimating dimension. Messages about legitimating identities are being conveyed all the time. Plumage is an indicator of some part of self-image, some conception of legitimating narratives. It is not an infallible indicator of all aspects of a regime or government, but it is to be seen both as something which will be in a coherent relationship with other aspects, and also a contributory dimension of the whole. Ferdinand Mount has argued eloquently for the importance of the most visible and audible aspects of government: 'The myths and rituals which a regime has allowed or, more usually, encouraged to grow up around itself often reveal something very significant about the real nature of that regime – the essentially populist, good-humoured, consensual nature of Macmillan's Toryism, the aristocratic, activist liberalism of the Kennedys, the autocracy of de Gaulle.'[55] And they are not simply clues to some underlying or undeclared reality. They are a substantial part of that reality. George W. Bush was a president who enjoyed dressing up as if he were a fighter pilot in ways which did not involve his actually going to war. This was not a clue to the identity of the president, it was part of that identity.

Two bodies: the person and the personage

Religion is one human activity where the tensions of identification are most evident. The other is government and politics. The distance in religion between the human and the divine, supernatural, or metaphysical is paralleled in the secular world by the distance between the public identity and the biological person, what Kantorowicz has termed the political body and the natural body.[56] In both cases it is the material, visible, tangible, and audible actions and artefacts which constitute identity, in the case of religion of the faithful in the absence of any possible direct manifestation of the divine or the supernatural, in the case of government, of rulers, presidents, leaders, and princes, despite the mere corporeal presence around which identity clusters. The deep social gap which separates the naked ape from the created person has frequently been used for comic effect. The distinction between the public person and the private bearer of the public identity is visually caught in Thackeray's cartoon of Louis XIV. The reference of the cartoon is to Hyacinthe Rigaud's grand formal portrait of the king, heavy with royal regalia and posed before a setting of theatrical grandeur. A carved column is draped with a huge and heavy red and gilt curtain, whilst the king's spreading robe, embossed with gold fleurs-de-lys, comes to rest on a stool bearing his crown. A massive sword hangs from his side, and from amongst all this material display Louis gazes with tolerant condescension (figure 5) Thackeray's visual comment consists of three drawings – one of a set of robes; one of a small, bald, and elderly man; and the third of the two combined to create Louis – with the caption: 'You see at once, that majesty is made out of the wig, the high-heeled shoes, and cloak ... Thus do barbers and cobblers make the gods we worship' (figure 6).

The relation between biological and social persons was recognised by politicians as different as Joseph Stalin and Arthur Balfour. When Stalin's adopted son replied to a reprimand over exploiting his father's name that he was a Stalin too, Stalin is reported to have replied: 'You're not Stalin and I'm not Stalin. Stalin is Soviet power. Stalin is what he is in the newspapers and the portraits, not you, no not even me.'[57] Discussing his career possibilities with Margot Asquith, Balfour observed, with rather more qualifications than Stalin, 'I do not think you quite realize what a small fraction of what we call personality can really be said to depend upon the person. Personality, as you use the word, really means the power of striking the popular imagination: and this is in every case as much due to favourable accident as to inherent capacities.'[58] But the significance of these apparent breaches between bald king and regalia, private Stalin and public Stalin, and house-party Balfour and parliamentary Balfour, is not that the first is 'real' whilst the second is a mask or a mere display. Either there are two identities, or there are levels of identity, or different degrees or intensities of identity. One is no more, and no less, real than the other. There may have been moments when King Louis, not the cartoon image but the monarch, was without his regalia. But they were the smaller part of his life. Whatever the human individual did, whether with or without regalia, as a person he existed in exactly the same way as any other person, through what he wore, where he wore it, and how he acted. That the clothing, the scenery, and the actions were not everywhere the same does not alter their constituting role in who the person was, whether that identity was single or plural. So with Stalin, the public father of the nation might have differed

5 Royal splendour

6 What makes the king

from the private father or the domestically located ruler, but they were all real cultivated people. In no case did the mere physical organism to which the name Louis or Stalin attached constitute the whole or only person.

Thackeray's cartoon makes a point which was well appreciated by those who celebrated and maintained monarchy in medieval Europe, and was recognised in funerary and monumental art. The clothes might express the king, but they expressed at the same time something that was more than the mortal body who wore them. The king, as Kantorowicz put it, had two bodies, one political and one natural, and each real and each an existence of which the mundane world needed to take account.[59] Nor were secular rulers the only ones with more than one identity; the church's rulers could be equally segmented, and the distinction was expressed in the ritual and statuary of funerals, where the separation of the mortal body from the continuing role of public person was portrayed by two effigies: one corruptible and passing, the other formal and continuing. The tomb in Canterbury Cathedral of Archbishop Chichele contains two life-sized carved figures, the first of the prelate in full episcopal regalia, the second of an emaciated cadaver (figure 7). They are two identities born by a single biological person, the dead priest and the living, because having lived, bishop. When Frederick William I of Prussia is reported as having replied to the cleric telling him that naked we come into this world and naked we depart from it that no, he would die in his uniform, he was missing the point of

7 Two bodies

kingship. Even if the king did indeed die in his uniform, there was, at the point of death, a separation. The mortal king was entombed, the uniform continued, and the museums of royal Europe were endowed with the clothing which expressed the continuation of the office of monarch long after the death of any particular incumbent. Politics, like religion, is frequently conducted by metonymy, and crown imperial can, like the Stalin who is distinct from the natural Stalin, both hover about and transcend a mere temporary person.

The gap between the ordinary human and the extraordinary role is potentially greatest in hierarchies, whether secular and sacred. The king's two bodies, like the prelate's, were a feature of circumstances where the mantle of sovereignty was almost too heavy for an ordinary mortal to bear. In monarchies and empires, as in papacies, new names indicate the several dimensions of identity of new incumbents, a more comprehensive expression of a perception which still, in the United Kingdom, gives the sovereign an official birthday which is different from and unrelated to the chronological birthday of the incumbent. But what the Chichele tomb expresses is the understanding that both bodies are real.

Tension between association and distinction in open societies

The tension between representativeness and superiority appears in every aspect of governing identity. It is most striking in language, as language is the most active medium of recognition. A governing elite may seek to impose or cultivate a language on those whom it dominates to characterise them as its special subjects, or to reserve a language for its own particular use in order to characterise its difference from ordinary people. It is language, as W. J. M. Mackenzie has pointed out, which is the fundamental and essential characteristic and condition of collective identity.[60] Whichever it is, the cultivation of the identity of the elite has as a necessary aspect a narrative about the identity of the mass of ordinary people. If the elite bans or persecutes the use of the language of a group or caste or community whom it wishes to assimilate under its control or influence, it uses language as a missionary tool. If the elite, conversely, sets itself apart from the mass by its use of cultivated French, or ecclesiastical Latin, or European English, then language becomes a mark of both superiority and subordination. The Norman French who seized power in England in 1066 felt no desire or need to amend their language or culture to that of those whom they now ruled, or to transform the language or culture of their subjects. The practice of the British Empire in India, by contrast, illustrates a very different, if complex and uncertain, relation between a ruling and a ruled culture.

In mobilised societies rulers must be sufficiently like those whom they govern not to appear alien, but unlike them sufficiently to be justified in being in command. They need, in order to maintain their position, to create a public identity with which the mass of people can associate or which they can accept as at one and the same time familiar and superior, unless that mass is so unmobilised as to be of no significance. Ernest Jones observed that a ruler 'just as a hero, can strike the imagination of the world in one of two ways. Either he presents some feature, or performs some deed, so far beyond the range of average people as to appear to be a creature belonging to another world ... Or, on the contrary, he may capture the imagination by presenting to us, as it were on a screen, a magnified and idealised picture of the most homely and familiar attributes.'[61] One way of claiming the distinction which marks a person or group off from the mass is precisely to claim that, whilst representative of everyone else, they are by the intensity of their representative character, special, and above the crowd. This paradoxical claim can arise in all kinds of mobilised regime, not only those with claims to be democratic. Adolf Hitler is reported as having said of the daunting vistas of the Reich Chancellery, 'I stand here as representative of the German people. And whenever I receive anyone in the Chancellery, it is not the private individual Adolf Hitler who receives him, but the Leader of the German nation – and therefore it is not I who receive him, but Germany through me.'[62] The apparent obliteration of the self as a mere representative is at the same time the elevation of the self as embodying the whole people. Not just *l'état*, but nation and folk as well, *c'est moi*. Hitler's remark would have resonated with Vitruvius who, dedicating his treatise on architecture to Augustus, praised his patron by whose beneficence 'the majesty of the Empire' had been 'expressed through the eminent dignity of its public buildings.'[63]

The intense identity culture at the top of social, political, and religious hierarchies presents in dramatic form the tensions present in all identity cultivation. This is particularly so in mobilised societies where the need to create solidarity with the population conflicts with the desire to cultivate an exceptional identity. In the case of government and rulers, this tension is not only a feature of identity dissonance, but a potential source of governmental failure. The greater the uniqueness of a ruling elite and its heightened sense of worth, the greater the potential for a fatal rupture of the relations necessary for effective government.

Notes

1 Henry Bettenson (ed.), *Documents of the Christian Church* (London: Oxford University Press, 1959), p. 282.
2 Bernard Bosanquet, *The Philosophical Theory of the State* (London: Macmillan, 1965), pp. 216–17.
3 Bede, *A History of the English Church and People*, translated by Leo Sherley-Price (Harmondsworth, UK: Penguin, 1955), p. 189.
4 Diarmaid MacCulloch, *Christianity: The First Three Thousand Years* (London: Allen Lane, 2009), p. 540.
5 *The Bible, Authorized King James Version* (Oxford: Oxford University Press, 2008), John, 1:1.
6 Rowan Williams, 'The Formation of Christendom', *New Left Review*, 170 (July–August 1988), 122.
7 Michael Savage, '"Living goddess" has deity stripped after US trip', *Independent*, 4 July 2007, pp. 28–9.
8 J. M. Barrie, *Peter Pan* (Oxford: Oxford University Press, 2006), p. 173.
9 James Joyce, *Ulysses* (London: Bodley Head, 1962), p. 8.
10 Charles Taylor, *Hegel* (Cambridge: Cambridge University Press, 1975), pp. 63–4.
11 Quoted in Jonathan Willis, '"By These Means the Sacred Discourses Sink More Deeply into the Minds of Men": Music and Education in Elizabethan England', *History*, 94:315 (2009), 294.
12 Jan Cienski, 'Cross proves catalyst for Polish church crisis', *Financial Times*, 14 September 2010, www.ft.com/cms/s/0/8cfd1fec-c004–11df-9628–00144feab49a.html (accessed 29 September 2010).
13 Kathleen Jamie, 'The Queen of Sheba', in *Mr and Mrs Scotland Are Dead: Poems 1980–1994* (Tarset, UK: Bloodaxe, 2004), p. 112.
14 Judith Herrin, *Women in Purple: Rulers of Medieval Byzantium* (Princeton, Princeton University Press, 2004), pp. 240–57.

15 Herrin, *Women in Purple*, p. 245.
16 Harold D. Lasswell and Merritt B. Fox, *The Signature of Power: Buildings, Communication, and Policy* (New Brunswick, NJ: Transaction Books, 1979), pp. 15–16.
17 Walerian Borowczyk, *Blanche* [film] (Abel & Charlton, Télépresse Films, 1971).
18 Lucy Freeman Sandler, 'The Wilton Diptych and Images of Devotion in Illuminated Manuscripts', in Gillian Gordon, Lisa Monnas, and Caroline Elam (eds), *The Regal Image of Richard II and the Wilton Diptych* (London: Harvey Miller, 1998), p. 154.
19 Regina Krahl, 'The Yongzheng Emperor: Art Collector and Patron', in Evelyn S. Rawski and Jessica Rawson (eds), *China: The Three Emperors 1662–1795* (London: Royal Academy of Arts, 2006), pp. 242–3; Craig Clunas, 'At the Royal Academy', *London Review of Books*, 27:23 (2005), 22.
20 Clifford Geertz, *Negara: The Theatre State in Nineteenth-Century Bali* (Princeton: Princeton University Press, 1980), p. 13.
21 Mervyn Peake, *Gormenghast* (London: Eyre and Spotiswood, 1950).
22 Rawski and Rawson (eds), *China*.
23 Norbert Elias, *The Court Society*, translated by Edmund Jephcott (Oxford: Blackwell, 1983), p. 101.
24 Elias, *The Court Society*, p. 100.
25 Ian Thompson, *The Sun King's Garden: Louis XIV, André Le Nôtre and the Creation of the Gardens of Versailles* (London: Bloomsbury, 2007).
26 Denis Cosgrove, *Social Formation and Symbolic Landscape* (Madison, WI, and London: University of Wisconsin Press, 1998).
27 Zitser, *The Transfigured Kingdom*.
28 Geremie Barmé, *The Forbidden City* (London: Profile Books, 2008).
29 Thomas M. Franck, *The Power of Legitimacy Among Nations* (New York: Oxford University Press, 1990), pp. 107–8.
30 James Morone, 'The Triumph of Plunder', *London Review of Books*, 26:18 (2004).
31 Cahal Milmo, 'Why the FO had to buy a double bed for Kennedy', *Independent*, 27 February 2002, p. 11.
32 Chris Bowlby, 'Ambassador, you are really spoiling us', *BBC News*, 10 October 2006, http://news.bbc.co.uk/1/hi/magazine/6034687.stm (accessed 8 November 2016).
33 Michael Mann, *The Dark Side of Democracy: Explaining Ethnic Cleansing* (Cambridge: Cambridge University Press, 2005).
34 Thomas N. Bisson, *The Crisis of the Twelfth Century: Power, Lordship, and the Origins of European Government* (Princeton: Princeton University Press, 2009).
35 Suzanne F. Cawsey, *Kingship and Propaganda: Royal Eloquence and the Crown of Aragon, c. 1200–1450* (Oxford: Oxford University Press, 2002).
36 Barmé, *The Forbidden City*.
37 Liah Greenfeld, *Nationalism: Five Roads to Modernity* (Cambridge, MA, and London: Harvard University Press, 1992).
38 Patrick Weil, *How to Be French: Nationality in the Making since 1789*, translated by Catherine Porter (Durham, NC: Duke University Press, 2009), p. 87.

39 Len Scales, 'Bread, Cheese and Genocide: Imagining the Destruction of Peoples in Medieval Western Europe', *History*, 92:307 (2007), 284–300.
40 Tom Nairn, *The Enchanted Glass: Britain and its Monarchy* (London: Radius, 1988), p. 93.
41 Markus, *Order in Space and Society*.
42 Lasswell and Fox, *The Signature of Power*, p. 16.
43 Edelman, 'Space', 2.
44 R. K. Narayan, *My Dateless Diary: An American Journey* (New Delhi: Penguin Books India, 1988), p. 40.
45 Beacham, *Power into Pageantry*, p. 50.
46 Holger Hoock, 'Nelson Entombed: The Military and Naval Pantheon in St Paul's Cathedral', in David Cannadine (ed.), *Admiral Lord Nelson: Context and Legacy* (Basingstoke, UK: Palgrave Macmillan, 2005), pp. 117–18.
47 George Bernard Shaw, 'First Aid to Critics', in *Major Barbara* (London: Constable, 1926), p. 158.
48 Philip Mansel, *Dressed to Rule: Royal and Court Costumes from Louis XIV to Elizabeth II* (New Haven, CT: Yale University Press, 2005), p. 15.
49 Carole Collier Frick, *Dressing Renaissance Florence: Families, Fortunes, and Fine Clothing* (Baltimore, MD: Johns Hopkins University Press, 2002).
50 Watt, *Dress, Law and Naked Truth*.
51 Tim Parks, 'A Most Delicate Invention', *London Review of Books*, 33:18 (2011), 22.
52 Wrigley, *The Politics of Appearance*, pp. 59–62.
53 N. Puwar, *Space Invaders* (London: Berg, 2004).
54 Bell, *On Human Finery*, p. 155.
55 Mount, *The Theatre of Politics*, p. 9.
56 Ernst H. Kantorowicz, *The King's Two Bodies* (Princeton: Princeton University Press, 1957).
57 Montefiore, *Stalin*, p. 4.
58 Nancy Ellenberger, *Balfour's World: Aristocracy and Political Culture at the Fin de Siècle* (London: Boydell, 2015), p. 2.
59 Kantorowicz, *The King's Two Bodies*.
60 W. J. M. Mackenzie, *Political Identity* (Harmondsworth, UK: Penguin, 1978), p. 111 ff.
61 McKibbin, *Classes and Cultures*, pp. 13–14.
62 Goodsell, *Social Meaning*, p. 4.
63 Beacham, *Power into Pageantry*, p. 130.

4

French Revolution: Liberty and Democracy

The oddity of democracy

In the third year of the French Revolution Louis XVI, having put his signature to a new constitution, was shown in a variety of popular prints with a cap of liberty on his head (figure 8). It may have been an uncongenial identity for the king, but it graphically presented the unique paradox and oddity of democracy. The head of state was one of the people and a subject like everyone else, and, by inversion, the subjects were also sovereign. Louis XVI was not a typical inhabitant of France, but this image symbolised the duality of democracy and the unique duality of its population, where government by the people existed together with government of the people, where the people had two aspects to their identity, both as sovereign and as subjects.

For much of the twentieth century, whilst few aspiring politicians would have questioned the desirability of democracy, however much they might have sought to evade, undermine, or destroy it in practice, this formal or merely compliant accord obscured rather than addressed the problems of democratic government and politics. For there to be government, by the people or by anyone else, there has to be someone to be governed. Even 'self-government' by an individual depends on there being a divided self, the rebellious id and the controlling super-ego. Though democracy is government by the people it is also government of the people, who are simultaneously sovereign and subjects, and in any population larger than a household, there will be institutions and persons who manage the collective business of society, enforce its rules, and formulate and administer its policies. When the people is everyone, or at least all adults, in order for there to be government, the people have at one and the same time to be sovereign and ruled, like plays in which one actor takes many parts. The oddity of democracy is that government by the people means that the same group who are sovereign are, at the same time, the subjects. There is a continuing tension between democracy as rule by the people and

8 Citizen ruler

democracy as rule of and for the people. All other forms of government start with the rulers. Long before the rights of man or of woman, let alone universal human rights, right was something claimed by the few against the many. '*Dieu et mon droit*', which still stands under the coat of arms of the monarchy of the United Kingdom, is a claim to territory and to domination, an assertion of divine sanction for royal exercise of power over a population. Democracy, by contrast, makes sense only with a demos whose people, whilst they are governed, are also sovereign and possessed of precisely that right which was formerly claimed as a royal monopoly. So the obverse of the identity of the elite in hierarchies is the identity of the demos in democracies.

The dual role of a democratic population creates unavoidable tensions and contradictions of identity, and has called forth many proposals for dealing with or explaining them. Two solutions to the problem of reconciling the people, the demos, as both sovereign and ruled are represented in different ways in the accounts of Joseph Schumpeter and George Bernard Shaw. For the first identity of democratic citizens, as members of the sovereign demos, there needs to be equality; for the second identity, as ruled citizens, a distinction is necessary between providers and provided, those whose principal occupation is to govern, and the remaining majority for whom government is carried on but who are subject to its legislation and administration. This distinction is presented theoretically by Schumpeter, and graphically by Shaw. Schumpeter described as democratic elitism a set of arrangements and practices which were elitist because small groups governed, and democratic because these governing groups were chosen by democratic competition, and as a result of choices between alternative governing identities presented to, rather than constructed by, the electorate.[1] Shaw's more picturesque metaphor preceded this account by some years. Government, he suggested, was like the theatre, and the people were the audience. They did not write the play, but they could applaud, boo, or walk out, and the success of the theatre depended, therefore, upon both the presentational skills of the dramatist and the players, and the support of the audience.[2]

In a democracy the people are still governed, but they are at the same time the government, or at least the owners or shareholders, and this gives them a potentially unique relationship with governing officials and institutions. Schumpeter goes some of the way to describe this relationship, but Shaw's metaphor is fuller and more illuminating: Schumpeter's version is closer to people as customers, in which relation only buying or not buying of favoured and desired or uncongenial and unwanted human goods occurs, though even there it does not take the economic analogy further and see the demos not only as a customer but as an employer. Shaw's metaphor covers not only the commercial, self-contained, and completed action of buying a ticket, but the sustained and open-ended action of cheering, booing, and throwing rotten tomatoes. If people's identity goes no further than being customers, only money talks; if they are an audience of citizens, the people talk, and talk in many voices, in many ways, and on many occasions. But a duality remains, since as subjects, people are not the equal of the personnel of government; as the sovereign demos, they are.

The implication of each of these accounts is that the population of a democracy has some kind of ownership of government, or that government acts on behalf of a demos, or that government acts subject to the cheers or boos of the populace. Whichever version is accepted, the population of a democracy stands in a very different relationship to the persons and institutions of government from the relationship of a population to any other form of political arrangement in either mobilised or unmobilised populations. There is no necessity for unthinking or unavoidable deference to the institutions or persons of government, for they are agents of the population, and the title 'public servant', with emphasis on the noun, describes a unique feature of this relationship. A mobilised society, if it is no more than that, is an attempt by government to achieve predictability. But if the society is also a democracy, one of its characteristics is unpredictability. The population of a democracy is governed, and some of its number have the task of carrying out that government. But at the same time the people rule, and in their political actions behave with a freedom and an unpredictability which marks them off from the merely mobilised. They may not even go to the play, or visit the theatre at all, but spend their time and energy in quite different ways.

Any relationship contributes to the identity of the parties to it, and the identity of the population of a democracy is in that way constituted as independent and critical. There is a broad range of activities and potential activities which constitute such a demos and which, even if some of them are found amongst the populations of other kinds of system, are not carried out in the same way there. In a monarchy, rights are rights of government. In a democracy they are rights against and over government. The character of a democratic population is correspondingly unique, and an essential part of the polity in a way that the character of the population of no other system is.

Democracy depends not only on good government or good governors, but on the political role of a demos of active citizens

Identity can be cultivated in solitude, by hermits or by castaways; Robinson Crusoe did not lack visible character. But the cultivation is most sustained and elaborate when it is conducted in the presence of other people, and in engagement with them. Flourishing identity cultivation is a public activity, and in the comprehensive public activity of governing and being governed, it flourishes vigorously. But the extent to which the mass of people is actively engaged in the cultivation of political identity differs with the character of the polity under which the people live. Not all forms of human government have much place for the majority of those whom they govern, and conversely the more open and democratic a polity, the greater the likelihood of broad engagement in public political identification. The distinction between being somebody and being nobody is one that fades as more and more of a population achieves public status as opposed to public subordination or private exclusion or marginalisation. Once the rulers and the ruled are one, identity cultivation enters a new dimension.

Rulers pay great attention to their own distinctive identity. They do so in all political systems, but in democracies they do so in a unique way. Democracy is marked off from all other systems of government and politics by the fact that rulers and subjects are the same people. In mobilised societies, the identity cultivation of rulers can no longer ignore, or pay only sporadic attention to, the identity of the mass of the population. Once that popular majority has achieved democratic status, the continuous and public cultivation of identity becomes something in which both rulers and ruled play an active part, a part made unique by the novelty of the ruled being also the rulers and the political employers of those who exercise governmental power.

The paradox of people who are both sovereign and ruled is the root of a series of oddities and tensions within all democracies, tensions which can never be wholly resolved. Whilst the people both rule and are ruled, for them to be ruled there are institutions, officials, and governors as in any other system of government, who are distinct from the rest of the population, and who cultivate an identity which constitutes that distinction. And because the people, the demos, are the source of authority, they at one and the same time rule in the most general sense, and frequently and constructively conflict with the actions, policies, and ambitions of rulers in particular matters and in the day-to-day conduct of their lives. The demos is ruled, but the people's response to that rule is unpredictable, takes many forms, and is an essential component of their democratic status just as much as is their choice of government through voting and all the activities which surround and sustain a system of free election. There are tensions within democracy between the cultivation of the good citizen as sovereign and the cultivation of the good citizen as subject, supporter, and contributor. But that is not necessarily an undesirable thing. Clockwork depends on tension to tell us the time and the string which restrains a kite also enables it to fly; release the tension and the kite falls.

Schumpeter's account of democracy is of occasional or regular choices by the electorate between competing political elites, but with implied quiescence in the long times between those exercises of choice, a periodic Hobbesian contract agreeing to be ruled. It is an account which has been followed by and has sustained a view of voting as a rational choice much like the purchase of food or consumer goods. But there is more to voting than this. In voting, the population of a democracy is acting out its sovereign identity, an action independent of any calculation of the likely further consequences of its choice, of parties successful or policies implemented. Voting is much more than a rational purchase, as the civil rights movement in the United States dramatically demonstrated, when to cast a vote, whether or not that vote influenced a final result, was an assertion of citizen right and citizen identity.[3] Every ballot cast is a component of the democratic identity of the voter and of the whole polity. Were voting no more than a calculated pursuit of material advantage, or of any advantage at all consequent on the victory of a particular candidate or party, there would be many circumstances where a rational citizen would not bother to leave the house to put a marked slip in a box. That citizens none the less do so is illustration of how much more there is than this to the ballot. Citizens act out their identity in voting, as they do in their use of the streets; in their use of universal provision of public services; in demonstrations, petitions, protests, and free association with each other. In their role as active citizens whose agent government is, the people of a democracy will not curtail their political activities once they have cast a vote. They will organise, demonstrate, argue, agitate, lobby, protest, and act not just as Schumpeter's choosers between elites or even as Shaw's audience restricted to the theatre, but as continual critics, connoisseurs, and auditors of public life in the streets, in public places, and at any time.

Democracy, if it is to be an active debate over the work of government and not merely a homogeneous and occasional consent to rule, is characterised by uncertainty and unpredictability, and unpredictability expressed not just in narrowly or conventionally political activity, but in the whole range of actions which characterise public or social identity. The necessary unpredictability of democracy requires an absence of uniformity with a presence of accepted and practised rules and restraints. The boundaries between the two are always and necessarily fluid. Is a law against blasphemy an imposition of religious uniformity, or the acceptance of rules of public discussion? There is no universal and simple answer. It depends how blasphemy is understood to begin with. Is a ban on the wearing of distinctive religious clothing by pupils in schools an assertion of the fact that all citizens are equal and that there are no special distinctions or social credit points, or is it an interference with the right of every citizen to dress as she pleases? The uncertainty of the answer, and the absence of a single, authoritative, imposed, and universal orthodoxy, is what makes for the constant uncertainty of a democratic society, but is also the mark of its necessary freedom and vitality. It is also a mark of this freedom that not only can there be many and conflicting opinions, but that any single opinion can be changed, as the French feminist Christine Delphy has described in relation to the debate in France and elsewhere over headscarves worn by female Muslims, where discussion has been marked by sophisticated shifts from criticising the covering of heads as an oppressive threat to a secular society and gender equality, to supporting scarves as a free choice of women.[4] The dependence of any material dimension of identity for meaning on cultivated context and significance enables Gary Watt to argue that throughout 'its long history, the veil or mask worn by females has challenged and disconcerted predominantly male authority'.[5]

The duality of the people as rulers and the people as ruled means that there is a distinction between a democratic society and a democratic state. Each is a necessary component of the whole, and for the whole to thrive, each must have a degree of both autonomy and continuity. That is evident in the case of a democratic state, less so in the case of a democratic society. But a democratic society requires something not only greater than but distinct from regular and free elections. Whilst the people may be sovereign, the business of making and operating laws and policies is done by a minority. A democratic polity thus requires both an active citizenry and an active but representative and responsive government and administration. They are two aspects of a single but complex political and social phenomenon, and the one can, to that extent, be read off from the other.

A way of telling one kind of political system from another, and gaining an initial clue about what one is confronting, is provided by the character played by Bernard Miles in the 1948 Boulting brothers' film, *The Guinea Pig*, who charms his son's supercilious public-school teacher by telling him that from his own army experience he had learned to tell the calibre of the officers from the quality of the soldiers, and so he knew what the man would be like before meeting him, having already been impressed by his pupils.[6] The same applies in politics; it is possible to tell a lot about one segment of a group by the conduct of another segment. It will frequently, even normally, not be necessary to look at both ordinary people and the formal machinery of government: in mobilised societies, the one will reveal a lot about the other, and a great deal about the form of government can be induced from the actions of ordinary subjects. A polity is all of a piece, which is very different from being homogeneous. English boarding schools, whatever their other virtues, may be mobilised societies but are certainly not democracies, and Miles's parent with military experience knew a well-run regiment when he saw one simply by meeting the troops.

It is possible to read off one aspect of a democratic society from another because to say that a society is democratic and mobilised is to identify a feature which is not conveyed at all by titles such as 'oligarchy', 'despotism', 'dictatorship', or 'theocracy'. All these other words describe who it is that rules. It is possible to give an account of any one of them without giving an account of ordinary people, the inhabitants of the land. Nothing follows, from the nature of these systems of government, about the character of the subjects, which can vary widely. If, on the other hand, they can be described also as mobilised, and even more so if they can be described as a democracy, then the nature of rule and the nature of the ruled are inextricably engaged with one another. In that sense there is as much difference between a mobilised theocracy and a premodern theocracy as between a theocracy and a military dictatorship, and an equally great difference between a constitutional monarchy in a society which is mobilised but not democratic and a constitutional monarchy with a democratic population. It may not always be possible to tell from studying ordinary people whether they live in a theocracy or a military dictatorship. But if they are in mobilised states, there will be much to be learned about the character of their government from the lives of ordinary men and women. And democracy is distinct again, since while all the other forms of government can exist in either mobilised or unmobilised societies, democracy is, by its very nature, mobilised.

The identity of a democratic society: acting out citizen identity

The roles of sovereign citizens as proprietors or clients of government go far beyond conventional democratic politics, and can extend in a quite different direction, apparently away from politics altogether and towards indifference to it. The first role is the action of well-behaved mobilised democrats, the second of badly behaved democrats, who nonetheless exhibit a form of behaviour which is essential for the health, vitality, and survival of democracy. A democratic citizenry is identified not only by its self-assertive approach to government, but by its frequently behaving towards government and politics exactly as it pleases.

Oscar Wilde's alleged complaint that the trouble with socialism was that it did interfere with one's evenings so dreadfully might appear to be a dismissal of democracy and the demands which meetings and all the other participations in public affairs made on one's time, but it is, on the contrary, an assertion of it. The democratic citizen may be well advised to pay attention to public affairs, but is under absolutely no obligation to do so, any more than a potential theatre audience is obliged to go to the theatre, or a browser in a bookshop obliged to buy. The populations of mobilised autocracies may be required to attend parades, but the populations of democracies may do as they wish, when they wish, how they wish. Writing shortly after the end of the Second World War, Quintin Hogg delivered what seemed a witty put-down to active democrats when he wrote that conservatives 'do not believe that political struggle is the most important thing in life. In this they differ from Communists, Socialists, Nazis, Fascists, Social Creditors and most members of the British Labour Party. The simplest among them prefer fox-hunting – the wisest religion.'[7] But the typical conservative was not, as Hogg supposed, preferring old authority to new radicalism, but making the kinds of choices which are only fully available to a democratic populace.

The word 'democracy' can be used too loosely, to apply to anything from an election to a decision on what to have for breakfast, replacing Stalin's 'socialism in one country' with 'socialism in one coffee bar'. But it is difficult to have a society where in their formal, constitutional, legal, and political relations people are equal, but in their economic or social ones they are not. A flourishing democratic polity requires a flourishing democratic society, what David Owen has termed a 'common consciousness'.[8] It is for this reason that John Dryzek has argued that because 'movements for democratization almost always originate in insurgency in civil society rather than the state, a flourishing oppositional civil society is the key to further democratization'.[9] The deference described in di Lampedusa's *The Leopard*, where the newly enfranchised electors wait to see how the prince is going to vote before exercising their own democratic right to decide, vitiates the formal democracy of institutions and laws.[10] Deference is different from respect, and while the unpredictable freedoms of a democratic society require the latter, they preclude the former. The politician, not as prominent as he thought himself to be, who arriving at a theatre in a university town without a ticket and being denied admission by the student on the door and demanding, 'Do you know who I am?', was met with the call to the foyer 'Is there a doctor in the house? There's someone here who doesn't know who he is,' was being met with humour but without deference. It was an application of the historian and socialist R. H. Tawney's advice that it was the mark of an egalitarian society that you could tell anyone to go to hell, and they would not be under the slightest obligation to do so.[11]

A democratic culture is not only broad, varied, and unpredictable, but difficult to define within a narrow definition of politics. This is well illustrated in Tom Paulin's inclusion of quietist or anti-political poems in his anthology of political verse, for instance Derek Mahon's 'A Disused Shed in County Wexford', with its allusive use of snails to suggest lessons about civic freedom.[12] The relevance of snails is not immediately obvious, but the unpredictability and loose frontiers of democracy involve just such surprising flexibility.

The defining political character of democracy is the equality of all persons. But that equality extends beyond the most obviously political aspects of identity to the whole social identity of the population; an identity which, while not immediately political, is an essential component of the freedom and equality on which a more conventional conception of democracy places value.

The defining messages about public life can often be conveyed by many more means than simple words. The importance of how you look – the sight, the sound, the movements, all combine to compose the public person. And all of this is conveyed, not by a constitutional document or a treatise on law or a political manifesto, but by appearance and behaviour, by voice and clothing. A democratic people has a character which is not derived from laws or constitutions, but which is in symbiotic relationship with them.

Just as democracy is characterised by a tension between a sovereign people and a ruling elite, so it is further characterised by the contrary demands of democratic solidarity and individual freedom, the stress between association and distinction. When a mobilised society becomes a democracy, the tension between the solidarity and equality of action, which characterises mobilisation and defines in one way the demos, and the equality of individual choice which characterises democracy begins. Both ends of the spectrum can be played at the same time: liberty caps were a part of the people's liberty during the French Revolution, and to wear one was part of one's identity as belonging to a free people. At the same time, not to wear one, and more particularly to display expense or extravagance in dress, was taken as a mark of treason or subversion, in which case one's freedom was curtailed or attacked by those who saw democratic freedom as a feature of the population as a homogeneous whole, not as the sum of the freedoms of its individual members. The sentiment of aversion to the visible extravagances of wealth expressed in Robert Burn's 'A Man's a Man for a' That', which became a political theme song for many Chartists,[13] received often more brutal application in France. The 'man o' independent mind' only 'looks and laughs' at 'yon birkie, ca'd a lord' with his 'ribband, star, and a' that' in Scotland,[14] but visible aristocratic splendours were not always and everywhere safe from everything but mockery. Yet if the term democracy is to have a distinctive meaning when applied not to the government of a territory but to its inhabitants, the actions and identities of those inhabitants can be prescribed only by themselves, and by all and each of them, not simply by a majority. So, to the tension of identity and status between a sovereign people and its rulers is added the tension of identity between a sovereign people as possessed of a collective identity and a sovereign people whose sovereignty is constituted by the self-government and self-identification of each of its members. The paradoxical tension in identity between association and distinction is nowhere more clearly expressed.

Clothing and physical appearance are the first evidence of identity, before an opinion is expressed, an accent heard, or a manner of behaviour observed. A class-divided society can be identified by the appearance of its members without any other evidence. One mark of a democratic society may be a democracy of appearance, dress, and the public presentation of persons. Citizenship has frequently been seen to be appropriately expressed not only by the proprietorial behaviour of those who own their own polity, but by forms of dress, whether Mao jackets or liberty caps, which made citizens as distinguished, or as undistinguished, as those who managed public matters on their behalf. In a society which is divided by class or caste, the aspiration to equality has a sartorial dimension. The desire for simplicity and a refusal to flaunt one's identity at the expense of others is an ancient and venerable tradition: take no heed for what you shall eat or what you shall wear, consider the lilies of the field.[15] Monasticism and Puritanism alike attempt to reduce clothing to a functional level, but cannot avoid at the same time using it to proclaim both an egalitarian and ascetic message and the distinctiveness of the wearer. John Moore, visiting Paris in 1789, observed that 'in a short time a little black cloak on a brown thread-bare coat became respectable; and afterwards, when the cloaks were laid aside ... a great plainness or rather shabiness of dress was ... considered as a presumption of patriotism.'[16] Democracy as the rule of all entails the abolition of visible distinctions between categories of persons: Mirabeau, at the start of the meeting of the Estates General in France in 1789, objected to the enforced distinctions of dress between the three estates. Yet it was not long into a revolution which set out to abolish inequality, that new distinctions were being insisted on, created, and introduced.[17] Identity has both an associative and a distinguishing dimension, and in a society with a substantial degree of equality, differences of dress will contribute to individual identities both by departing from egalitarian similarities and by employing them in heightened or exaggerated form, aspiring both to identity by association and distinction by exemplary forms of common or shared characteristics, seeking simultaneously both equality and superiority. The challenging of the uniformities of caste and class by the paradoxical varieties of democratic equality has provided a continual issue for both theorists and practitioners. Equality could go, in the eyes of some, too far, and it was not long before the revolution was planning ways of acceptable distinction, between officials and ordinary citizens, between national representatives and mere articulate adults. By 1798, deputies had a coat of national blue, a tricolour belt, a scarlet cloak, and a velvet hat with a tricolour cockade.[18]

The American Revolution followed the French in its choice of homespun-appearance in clothing in, 'conscious opposition to British corruption and luxury', and the direct domestic preparation of cloth and garment 'through a chain of tasks mobilizing the entire family, rehearsed the republican credo of propertied independence. When yeomen then donned the coarse products of their home industry they embodied an equally republican frugality.'[19] The cultivation of the simple and egalitarian in clothing applied both domestically and abroad in the formal presence of the new nation. James Buchanan, American ambassador to London, was in 1854 unable to attend the State Opening of Parliament because he declined, in line with American practice, to wear ceremonial dress. He wrote home to the Secretary of State that 'A minister of the United States should ... wear something more in character with our democratic institutions than a coat covered with embroidery and gold lace.'[20] Half a century later, in a photograph of the court of Edward VII in 1903, the US ambassador still stands out, by wearing a mere formal black suit.[21]

The trade unionist and Labour MP Will Thorne, in the early years of the twentieth century, when invited to dinner with Lady Astor and the Prince of Wales, replied that he would come only if he could wear his 'everyday clothes.'[22] In a democracy, if the workers were to dine with aristocracy and monarchy, they would not do so by wearing the marks of privilege. It was a similar sense of democratic solidarity expressed in 'everyday clothes' which led the historian R. H. Tawney to wear for many years after he had ceased serving in the army the sergeant's jacket which had marked him off as a common soldier rather than an officer during the First World War.[23] The use of clothing to cultivate solidarity with the ordinary citizen can, too, involve an identity which rejects a location low down in a social or economic hierarchy. 'Zoot suits' adopted by American workers have been understood as sartorial compliance with capitalism, but they can equally be understood as a rejection of the subordinate status of waged employee.[24] But the common dress of democracy can be a perilous trap for the politician who too obviously attempts an uncharacteristic ordinariness. Shortly after succeeding John Major as leader of the Conservative Party in 1997, William Hague appeared in public wearing a baseball cap, and was met with widespread derision as much amongst his own supporters as amongst political opponents.[25]

Whilst rulers or leaders may wish to establish distinctions between citizens and officials, there is a contrary belief that all people should be, and should appear to be, equal. Hence eccentric, flamboyant, or unsettling action, appearance, or behaviour can be stigmatised. Once again, the tension inherent in the democratic aspiration obtrudes. If democracy is rule by *the people*, and the demos is seen as culturally, socially, homogeneous, then rule by *people* is debarred, since individual citizens are expected or constrained to conform to a common identity. If on the other hand rule by *the people* not only allows but is characterised by varieties of identity, then rulers or leaders cannot establish or publish a representative identity, and any identity they do publish will distinguish them from large numbers of their fellow citizens. This dilemma emerged early on in the French Revolution, when an attempt was made to ban distinctive religious garb at the same time as freedom of dress was being applauded.[26] This might seem to say that in theory democracy is impossible. But even if it does not work in theory, it works in practice, and does so as an element in a polity with other elements, with which, when the modus vivendi works, it conflicts, jars, compromises, and accommodates.

The visibility of a sovereign democracy has been located in streets, in dress, in the courtesies of everyday life. Arriving in Barcelona in 1936, George Orwell reported that 'Waiters and shop-walkers looked you in the face and treated you as an equal. Servile and even ceremonial terms of speech had temporarily disappeared.'[27] From a different political direction, Herbert Morrison, reflecting on his experience of London politics and the change from horse-drawn to petrol-powered buses, commented that:

> the old horse-driver in his front seat on the top of his vehicle would chat and joke with City clerks and stockbrokers – the seats near him being a privilege place. He rode in distinguished company. From what I learned in my youth I would say that the bulk of horse-bus drivers voted Tory. With the motor-bus driver it was different. His vehicle was a new-fangled device appealing to the young and forward-looking. There was a call for a sense of adventure. The drivers were isolated from the passengers. The bulk of the motor-bus drivers, as a consequence of their different way of life, voted Labour, and by the 1920s a few of them communist.[28]

Morrison could have added to this account that the origin of the name of this form of transport was the Latin 'omnibus', meaning for everyone. The freedom to move wherever one wishes and a suspicion of any apparent restrictions on this freedom have been a continual feature of democratic self-assertion. In Britain, the Kinder Scout trespass of 1932, when 400 protestors attempted to walk on land in the Derbyshire peaks closed off as grouse moors, was a mixture of new democratic assertion of rights of public access with claims to traditional rights which had been eroded or subverted.[29] In the United States the road plans of Robert Moses in New York were criticised for being designed to restrict bus access and hence keep the black and the poor out of Jones Beach Park.[30] This claim has been disputed, but public access, and the identity of those who enjoy it, persists as a contested element in the politics of identity. In the public provision of health and education, services available equally to all members of a population express an egalitarianism which is conversely rejected in selective availability and different levels of access or quality according to status or ability to pay.

In the spaces within which people move, and the buildings they use and inhabit, equality or hierarchy can be found. Collegiate inward-facing seating, as in the British House of Commons or the choirs and chancels of older churches, contrasts with the arrangement of meetings where officers, leaders, or representatives are raised on platforms facing the rest of the assembly or community who are, as mere spectators, spatially separate. The palaces of presidents and monarchs are met in democratic Glasgow by the public tea rooms and galleries of the People's Palace.

Neither the conflict between the sovereign identity of the people and the governing identity of their rulers, nor that between the collective identity of the sovereign people and the sovereign identity of each individual, is readily, if ever, resolvable. An ultimately unsuccessful solution to the first, with implications for the second, is to present either the state or the ruler as the highest form of the identity of the subject/citizen, so that in exercising authority over the citizens, the ruler/state is not in conflict with their self-creating authority, but developing it to its fullest extent. This was Rousseau's account of the General Will. But such a solution denies variety or individuality, and proposes a comprehensive and orthodox common identity. Even if it does not do this, but locates individuals in categories which constrain their equal freedom, the result is what Anthony Appiah has termed the Medusa syndrome, whereby individual identity is smothered and ossified by the categories into which people are slotted by others.[31]

The individual diversity which democratic equality entails draws attention to the second paradox of democracy. If a democratic society is a society of equals, its solidarity must rest on some set of common values or characteristics. But the more precisely those values and characteristics are specified, the greater the numbers of individuals and groups who will not match the pattern. On the one hand is the argument, as put by David Miller, that 'if we aspire to a form of democratic politics which extends beyond the machinations of a few elected representatives, then a shared nationality is an essential precondition.'[32] On the other hand is the argument that if the people are sovereign, then each individual has a share in that sovereignty and a role and a right to cultivate his or her own, rather than a common, identity. One proposed solution is a political identity for the sovereign population but a cultural, religious, and social identity for its individual members. This has been described as civic nationalism by Liah Greenfeld, and as a common national narrative and civil contract by the former chief rabbi of the United Kingdom, Jonathan Sacks; the intention being that it will provide a container but not a constrainer for diversity, at the same time as cultivating the sovereign identity of the whole people in matters of common concern.[33] Such a solution differs from proposals for multiculturalism, which does no more than replace the Medusa gaze of a uniform demos with the Medusa gazes of a variety of community leaders or representatives.

Democratic audit: satire

In democratic or open societies, the leadership is open to constant scrutiny and criticism, and also to praise and commendation. Its continuation in office depends not on universal and unqualified approval, but on free election, and the certainty that however firm its hold on office, it is on approval until the next vote. But whilst the mandate to govern is not revocable from day to day, and a government with a working majority can expect to survive hostile scrutiny, the sovereign people exercise their sovereignty not only by the irregular and occasional act of voting, but by all the actions which they take from day to day, in assessing, commenting on, and passing judgment on the conduct of government. Criticism, protest, condemnation, and satire are essential aspects of the popular sovereignty which justifies the existence of democratic government. And such free voicing of criticism, enquiry, and dissent is necessarily both variegated and changing. There is no one unfaltering voice of the people, but a medley of voices and views. And in such exercise of continuous sovereignty, nothing is off limits: any aspect of the public order and its inhabitants may be praised or pilloried, often with passion and frequently with magnificent disrespect. No part of the state, head of state, official religion, armed forces, politicians, administration, or bureaucracy is or can be immune.

Caveat emptor is a respectable principle in commerce. It applies equally in political life, and the very rhetorical switch which transforms citizens into customers rebounds to assert the right to choose, ignore, praise, or ridicule. Distrust is not only a recurring but an inherent feature of democracies and open societies. Democratic distrust can be vigorously expressed, and ridicule is no more than its vigorous form, as Vivienne Hart has argued in *Distrust and Democracy*, addressing the fears of those who thought that when citizens, voters, became discontented and disillusioned this was bad for democracy, and that a healthy state depended on rulers, politicians, leaders, being held, if not in awe, then at least in respect bordering on deference.[34]

In such a view satire is dangerous, and subversive of the respect that is necessary to make government and orderly public life possible. This was the argument of those North American conservatives who in the 1970s argued that there could be too much citizen participation, and that an obedient citizenry was to be sought rather than an active one. Samuel Huntington in 1975 argued that:

> [the] essence of the democratic surge of the 1960s was a general challenge to existing systems of authority, public and private. In one form or another, this challenge manifested itself in the family, the university, business, public and private associations, politics, the governmental bureaucracy, and the military services. People no longer felt the same compulsion to obey those whom they had previously considered superior to themselves in age, rank, status, expertise, character, or talents. Within most organizations, discipline eased and differences in status became blurred. Each group claimed its right to participate equally – and perhaps more than equally – in the decisions which affected itself.[35]

Democracy could only be saved, it seemed, if there was a lot less of it, and distinction carried an elite of citizens to heights where they were scarcely visible to their distant but inferior associates.

The different view, which Hart presented with great clarity, is that distrust is an expression of a gap between citizens' expectations of what democratic politics requires, and their perception of how it is in fact being conducted, between the expected and actual identities of rulers. Respect has to be earned, it is not a perk of office. Whilst total alienation may lead to the collapse of social order and good government, and a total disregard for all conventions and rules would dissolve society, unqualified respect and total deference will corrupt a political order in the other direction, and allow very bad government indeed. Those who see themselves as both commanding and enjoying an existing order can sometimes have difficulty distinguishing between criticism and a lack of deference, and insurrection and revolution. One or many critical or satirical voices may not be comfortable, but they do not call the entire basis of rule into question. Such actions by the people may be critical and sceptical, but they are not subversive or revolutionary. It may even be the case that there is only one thing worse than being talked about, and that is not being talked about. In a democracy, government may be able to live with only a certain degree of indifference, and require at least a minimum of public presence, in however hostile a gaze.

The urge to assess and scrutinise is a response to the otherwise stultifying demotion of the sovereign people to the position of mere subjects. The democratic citizen acts in a range of ways which constitute his or her role as sovereign. But at the same time the regular and daily business of rule is carried out by specialists, officials and politicians of various kinds, for whom there is a continual momentum to distinguish themselves from ordinary citizens, and cultivate a unique and monopolistic governing identity. In this relationship the citizen is subject, not sovereign, but as a democratic subject he or she is nonetheless assertive, sceptical, and unpredictable. The citizen will argue, advise, criticise, complain, and protest, and employ all the forms of opposition which are both made possible by democracy and are a corrective feature of it.

There is a range of dramatic actions where citizens may express a sceptical distance from those in positions of formal authority: carnival and the various forms of festivals of misrule, in which conventional authority is inverted; satire and the heckling of politicians; derisive or humorous election candidatures, such as those of the Monster Raving Loony Party in the United Kingdom. Each of these says to government, in effect, we are keeping an eye on you, and we won't necessarily accept without question what you tell us, or approve without enquiry what you do or propose to do, or the seriousness with which you take yourself. The citizen will not only criticise, assess, complain, and protest, but will also laugh. The refusal to take seriously the actions of public servants, and the willingness to subject them to satirical review, provides a powerful auditing tool for democrats. Satire draws attention to real or alleged incongruities of identity: the evangelist who preaches morality but takes bribes, the politician who assumes grand and heroic postures but is unimaginative and prosaic, the aristocrats who disdain their fellow humans but are uncouth and ignorant themselves. Satire is about identity, the relationship between its layers, and the incongruities and absurdities of its composition. It is most effective when most widely published, and is therefore a feature of democratic and open societies. In closed or autocratic societies, it has to be disseminated covertly and often at great risk.

The freedom to laugh in public about public matters is a freedom of democratic societies. Laughter may not be the most obviously fearsome weapon in the hands of governments or citizens, but it is one which political leaders seem to dislike to a surprising degree. This raises the question of why public figures are so sensitive to satire, and whether there are public figures who are not. In 1954 the two Houses of Parliament of the United Kingdom commissioned Graham Sutherland to produce a portrait of the by then aging prime minister, Winston Churchill. The image of Churchill was not a grand or heroic one, but a picture of an elderly and slightly grumpy-looking man slumped in a chair. The identity portrayed is not one of a charismatic leader in either war or peace. Churchill so disliked the painting that it was destroyed once it was in his possession, on the orders of his wife, Clementine. The powerful can be surprisingly thin-skinned. A man who had been through the Boer War as a reporter, and two world wars as a minister, was wounded by a picture.

In 1991 after the first Gulf War, northern, Kurdish, Iraq was effectively an independent region. One of the fruits of this independence was a broadcasting system free from the control of Baghdad and its ruler, Saddam Hussein. An embellishment of that freedom was a satirical film about the Iraqi dictator, written and directed by the comedian Mahir Hassan Rashid. It was not long before a CD of the programme arrived in Baghdad, and the alleged response of Saddam Hussein was to send a team of assassins north to eliminate the entire cast. They were not successful, though the actor/comedian who played Saddam Hussein then had six attempts on his life in the next four years, and went into hiding.[36] Paintings may not always be safe under democracy, but in general painters are. So are writers. In 2014 Hilary Mantel published a short story which imagined the assassination, in 1983, of the prime minister and Conservative leader Margaret Thatcher.[37] There was some criticism from those who regarded such a speculation as in bad taste, a criticism which became louder when the BBC broadcast the tale as part of their *Book at Bedtime* series the following year. Mantel was accused of producing a 'sick' product of a 'sick mind', and the interesting claim was made that if the BBC 'really was independent it would avoid doing things that were provocative'.[38] But statements of dismay and disapproval were the extent of the reaction. Meanwhile, Sony Pictures in the United States was about to release a satire which imagined a plot to assassinate the North Korean leader Kim Jong-un. The government of North Korea responded with accusations of an act of war, and made loud if unenacted threats of 'merciless' retaliation.[39] Satire might not threaten the power of autocrats, but it can damage their self-esteem whether or not their subjects have access to it. The knowledge that you are being laughed at is enough, and the desire or need of rulers for the cultivation of grand and noble identities can trump all other calculations of power or advantage.

If satire can be so disconcerting to despots who apparently dominate their population without any need to obtain its assent, it is not surprising that in democracies laughter can be an even more powerful weapon in the hands of the opponents or critics of rulers. The freedom to laugh is an important privilege of democratic societies, and an important component of their power. The workings of that power are given fictional examination in Umberto Eco's *The Name of the Rose*. The novel revolves around a mystery in a library, and it emerges that at the centre of things is a book that is both sought by some and closely guarded by others. When the secret is finally revealed, it is that those who guarded the secret were afraid of laugher. The thing which the monk Jorge, the defender of the status quo, most feared and set out to suppress was Aristotle on humour. Laughter may not be the most obviously fearsome weapon in the hands of citizens, but it is one which, like the mouse proverbially alarming the elephant, unsettles the complacence of power.

Being in either coercive physical or legitimate democratic control seems never to be enough, and rulers, at least in mobilised societies, fear the voice of the small boy who cries out that the emperor's clothes are not as substantial as claimed. To suggest this is an extension into an account of identity of Weber's argument that the fortunate 'is seldom satisfied with the fact of being fortunate. Beyond this, he needs to know that he has a *right* to his good fortune.'[40] The need to cultivate and defend a comprehensive identity which celebrates and justifies one's status is hugely powerful. Satire undermines identity by ridiculing its inconsistencies, limitations, or pretensions; it not only says that the emperor has no clothes, but that it is possible to laugh at the ones that he does have. The cartoonist Low's regular characterisation of the Labour and then national government minister the railway trade unionist Jimmy Thomas, who had a predilection for the high life, as 'The Rt Hon Dress Suit MP', was not unkind, but was certainly effective, and concentrated on the alleged social ambitions of a man who in his own presentation of himself was a straightforward and blunt trade-union politician (figure 9).

9 Dress-suit MP

In autocracies, satire undermines how rulers see themselves. In democracies it undermines both the self-esteem of elites and the deference of citizens. That is why rulers of all kinds react so violently, not only to the laughter, but to the fact that someone doesn't take them seriously, or rather is seen and heard not to take them seriously, and to be out of their control. It is not just what the small boy says, but the fact that he can say it.

A part of the discomfort that satire can cause governments may lie in the disparity between the vernacular language of satire and the official language of government. Satire is vernacular politics rather than elite politics. This does not mean that it is 'the true voice of the people'. But it can be another voice, the vulgar, untutored voice of the small boy or the peasant. It means, too, that it can be sometimes offensive, tasteless, and not always successfully funny. Satire against Queen Victoria and Albert in the nineteenth century, or the elitist snobberies to be found in *Private Eye* in the twentieth, can be crude and offensive. Such unpredictability and freedom from the constraints of good taste is the price to be paid for Internet sites such as the *Onion* from the United States, and magazines and newspapers such as *Private Eye* in Britain or the *Portadown News* from Northern Ireland, which was so effective, or offensive, according to your tastes, that it managed to enrage both unionists and nationalists. W. C. Fields remarked that no one who hated children and dogs could be all bad. One might say equally that no one who manages to infuriate both Ian Paisley and Gerry Adams can be wholly without merit.

Rulers dislike satire because it can call them to account, and does so not in their own terms or on their own ground, but by means of one of the few political devices which they are unable effectively to use themselves. Satire both illuminates and excludes them. Because satire comes from below, and attacks precisely the things that are settled, established, dignified, and in control, it is necessarily subversive. When it is not, when it is attempted from above, it can too easily appear tasteless or triumphalist. Political leaders can be witty and amusing, particularly at each other's expense but also, amongst the most skilled, at their own expense. In the United Kingdom, Tony Blair told a audience which greeted him with applause to calm down because he hadn't gone yet; Margaret Thatcher joked about a film poster announcing 'The Return of the Mummy'; Neil Kinnock appeared as a nuisance political canvasser in a 1984 pop video for a song by Tracy Ullman. But on a larger stage, government is not good at humour, and frequently lacks the light touch or the imaginative vulgarity which fuels vernacular satire. Official cartoons are solemn or vindictive, and when political parties satirise or stigmatise, they are more often vituperative or fanatical than amusing. British government cartoon posters of the First World War, or Nazi propaganda in the years leading up to and during the second, were unpleasant, but not usually funny. But the further they move towards artistic responsibility, and the more stages there are between them and their official patrons, the more amusing and undeferential cartoons are capable of being. The heavy hand of official humour – 'Chemical Ali' or 'Doctor Germ' – lacks the easy zing of 'the toxic Texan' or 'Blairforce One', and the denunciations of their opponents by totalitarian regimes, as traitors, running dogs of capitalist imperialism, or subverters of the nation's heritage, almost always lack any style or wit. Since the essence of satire is to deflate those persons and institutions who take themselves over-seriously or with great gravitas, gravitas is not the best place from which to generate or direct it. A 'real' or 'grass-roots' satire can do it without the malice which seems to sit more easily with 'official' satire. The difference between rulers and the ruled can be the difference between satire and demonisation.

But rigid distinctions are usually too simple. If there is a scale, with the solemnity of 'official' humour at one end and the lightness of 'vernacular' humour at the other, there is too a distinction between the humour associated with closed systems and that associated with open ones. Britain during the First World War could produce the cartoons of Bruce Bairnsfather who, despite his semi-official status, could present the life of the ordinary infantry soldier in humorous rather than heroic terms.[41] In the Second World War, posters warning that 'careless talk costs lives' could, as well as taking the dramatic form of lurking spies and deadly gossip, portray the Nazi leadership, Hitler and Goering, as cartoon characters sitting on a bus eavesdropping on the gossip of two passengers.

Political humour and satire, despite their frequent capacity to disconcert, are still instruments of limited effect. 'Take the toys from the boys' was effective feminist deflation of military gravitas in the campaign against the siting of cruise missiles in the United Kingdom. But when John Humphrys, interviewing Tony Blair on the *Today Programme*, suggested that if the military threat from a Middle-Eastern nation were ever again used by the government as a reason for the UK to commit its troops abroad, everyone would laugh, the prime minister was disconcerted but no more. George Orwell was equally optimistic when he predicted that fascism with goose-stepping militia could never succeed in Britain, 'because the people in the street would laugh.'[42] If Humphrys and Orwell were right, it was a real check, but laughter has a short memory.

Even open societies limit speech by laws of libel and slander, but there is a frontier here which the smugglers of political information can sometimes cross to the advantage of citizens. Satire can enable things to be said which cannot be said. It enables messages to be passed in code which could not be passed directly. *Private Eye* was able to communicate information about what became the Profumo scandal before anything could be said in the more mainstream media, writing, for those who could read the code, about the antics of 'gay, fun-loving Miss Gaye Funloving.'[43]

There is something of the relation between overdrafts and creditworthiness in the prevalence of satire: the only people who can get them are those who don't need them. Humour is only an effective weapon against regimes and governments which, whilst they do not like it, do not find it intolerable, or are constrained by their espousal of freedom and democracy not to try to prevent it. Satire is an instrument of democracy, and one which will work only in democracies. So, paradoxically, whilst it may be a defence against bad government and an incitement to good government, it works best where government is already at the good end of the scale, and hardly works at all where it is most needed. There is, therefore, for those who seek satire as the secret weapon of democrats, a problem, in that satire is most effective in regimes against whom it is least necessary. Satire is a resource of citizens, rather than of those who are deprived of citizenship. Its presence is in part a symptom as much as a cause of open and intelligent politics.

Doubt is cast on the political relevance of satire by those who claim that it is not serious politics. This was the objection of some on the left to George Bernard Shaw, that by laughing at evils, people accept and come to tolerate them. In this view satire functions in a similar way to sour grapes, as a sufficient response to what is feared, despised, or disagreed with, and laughter necessarily not only ridicules, but trivialises. Satire can also be seen as an alternative to conflict. The late nineteenth-, early twentieth-century German social theorist George Simmel claimed that some degree of discord could be a source of stability in society, the lords of misrule being a way of expressing resentments whilst making their causes acceptable – lords of misrule being the alternative to alternative lords, and rebellion.[44]

So can satire be a diversion, a kind of bread and circuses to keep the intellectuals happy? It can certainly be an alternative to wounding attacks. In the House of Commons, William Hague as Conservative leader was consistently witty and often devastatingly satirical at the expense of the prime minister, Tony Blair. But this did not markedly help the party in opposition in either hampering or embarrassing the government, or in advancing their own electoral fortunes. It may be that, to be effective, satire has to come from outside the circle of the powerful, otherwise it appears to ordinary citizens little more than a private fight.

John Stuart Mill argued that 'The amount of eccentricity in a society has generally been proportional to the amount of genius, mental vigour, and moral courage which it contained,'[45] a concise advocacy of creative distinction. The point applies equally to sceptics and satirists. One mark of the position of a state on the scale from despotism to openness and democracy, and of the corresponding degree of popular sovereignty, is the absence or presence of open satire, and the response of rulers to ridicule, as is their attitude towards free expression in general. Secret satire can exist in oppressive regimes, but its very secrecy is an indication of the lack of freedom. Conversely, one mark of the character of a body of subjects or citizens is the authority with which its members say and do whatever they please. There are many reasons to be sceptical about the effects of the World Wide Web, but even so the number of Internet cafés in a country is probably a better rough guide to the reality of its freedoms than are the formal clauses in its constitution.[46]

Satire has been described as the canary down the mineshaft of political power. The problem with this metaphor is that if there is gas down there, the canary is dead. Laughing at a government to test its liberality can be a dangerous exercise in political testing, since the satirist may end up just like the canary, if not gassed, then at least caged. Even within democracies, would-be autocrats of one kind or another will assume that violence is justified in responding to their critics. The choices for the sceptical citizen at the two extremes of the spectrum are clear enough. No one would hesitate to publish satires of their rulers in Europe or North America. It would be unwise in China or Zimbabwe. But it is precisely where the atmosphere needs to be tested, and where there is an unstable mix of democracy and autocracy, liberty and control, in twenty-first century Turkey or Iran, that whilst the test may be of the greatest value, the danger to the brave canary is greatest. Wherever there is a conflict between the desire to laugh and the belief that one's own identity is privileged and must not be challenged or ridiculed, the satirist and the citizen are in danger. In France in 2015 that conflict, between aspirant authoritarians and a free press, led to murder. We may not think of comedians or cartoonists as the front-line troops in the war for liberal democracy and popular sovereignty. But they can often be the forward patrols who test the terrain, with all the dangers that entails. They deserve support and gratitude, as well as just laughter.

To be able to laugh at others and at oneself requires a level of critical reflection and awareness of identity which is not achieved if life is guided entirely by habit and deference. Unpredictability is a characteristic of democracy. Just as Mill gauged cultural vigour by the numbers of eccentrics, so the extent of a democratic society and the existence and vitality of a demos can be gauged by the extent of unpredictability and variety of identities. This raises a paradox, since if a vigorously democratic demos must expect not simply variety but eccentricity, troublemaking, and bloody-mindedness, one of the characteristics which some of its members may well display will be a disinclination to engage in politics at all, but to pursue whatever private activities they choose. A single public identity is the last thing that a healthy demos will exhibit.

Satire provides one of many audits of government in a democracy. In that sense it is, whilst a feature of democracy, a road test on its healthy operation rather than a constituent part of its everyday life. That everyday life is composed of the multifarious details of public life, including what Ferdinand Mount has described as the 'myths and rituals which a regime has allowed or, more usually, encouraged to grow up around itself'.[47] A prime minister on a bicycle is different from one in a limousine, just as a citizen who is treated with courtesy by a public servant is different from one who is patronised or ignored. In a society where the rulers are also the ruled, the servants the masters, it is as true as elsewhere that if you have seen the servants, you do not need to see the master.

Carnival and masking, the lords of misrule: the people's last resort before revolution

When laughter is dangerous, it can be presented in a form so outrageous that, as a brief departure from the manners and conventions of daily life, it can, at one level, be dismissed as a brief but temporary excess, a reversal of the normal but not, by that very fact, a threat. That is the character of carnival and of the various festivals in medieval and later Europe, where lords of misrule of one kind or another parodied the normal hierarchies of church or state, and the normal identities of rulers and ruled, if only for a day. Carnival can be threatening if erupting from below, or effective at diverting threats if inspired from above, since it visibly subverts existing identities, and the more carefully they have been cultivated, the more elaborately they are subverted. The inverted order of carnival sets up boy bishops, not boy cobblers.

In Coventry in 1480, traditional rituals and practices were employed by groups of citizens in an extreme way in order to defend what they saw as their established rights against the claims and actions of the prior of St Mary's. Their actions neither sustained the order nor challenged it, but engaged in politics within its general landscape by pushing its practices close to their limits, in one case by blocking the entrance to the priory with dung and rubbish.[48] The limits had been pushed further in Norwich in 1443, when traditional Shrove Tuesday processions were anticipated many weeks early as a means of protesting against a ruling by the Earl of Suffolk in a dispute between the city and the abbot of St Benet's Hulme over water mills.[49] But such a form of cocking a snook at authority can be unstable; either it is so bizarre but so harmless that it does indeed serve to contain resentment and justify the continuation of the existing order of things, or the resentment which it briefly masks is so intense that, as in Romans in southern France at the end of the sixteenth century, it becomes the vehicle and springboard for rebellion. In Romans in 1579, the Feast of St Blais, the patron saint of drapers, provided the occasion for an armed parade. There was, too, a *reynage*, the election of a 'king' of the celebrations. This may not have inverted the existing social and political order, but it provided a brief parody version of it. But in 1579 the assembled craftsmen, ploughmen, and other citizens elected not just a king of misrule, but a long-term leader for their political campaign of grievances against taxation and privilege. In 1580 at carnival, the chosen popular leader, Paumier, regularly went around dressed as the Candlemas Bear, a symbol also associated with St Blais, bringing together both political and religious authority, and a parody of both. The events of February 1580, culminating in a coup and massacre by the old elite of the town against the leaders and members of the popular movement, was also conducted through the organisation of carnival, feasting, processions, and dancing, the latter providing the context within which the organisation and the carrying out of the attack on the popular forces took place.[50] In Romans, the authorities used carnival, a carnival of their own, as a mask for something much more bloody. But this was unusual. It was in France too, over two centuries later, that fear of what carnival and misrule might be about to become led once again to repression. In revolutionary France, the authorities banned the wearing of masks and carnival cross-dressing as concealing counter-revolutionary or royalist intent.[51] Carnival may be the last resort of an excluded population, a feature of a society not only far from democratic but only partially mobilised, but it may also be the last resort of a dominant class to avoid revolution and allow discontent to evaporate into popular circuses.

The problem of professional rulers and the tension between sovereign democrats and their agents

Active citizens will not be indifferent to the identity of their leaders and in a democracy, and in a particular manner, the expressed identity of rulers and leaders is crucial, since citizens, whether they see rulers as leaders or as instruments, will expect to see in them a fuller expression of their own identity. The permanent tension within democracy means that the people are the players, and therefore expect those who are full-time players to be like them, whilst at the same they expect them to be exceptional versions of themselves, themselves as they might be, themselves transformed and elevated, yet still in touch with their roots. It is always an impossible paradox. The logic of liberal representative democracy is that its leaders will be superordinary, though Ian Buruma has suggested that the limitations this can place on ambitious self-presenters causes democratic leaders to strut on the world stage because they cannot strut at home.[52] A monarch or a theocrat has no constraints in publicly proclaiming his or her superiority, special insight into divine law, high breeding, or outstanding qualities of understanding and leadership. Democratic leaders must in one sense believe themselves to be superior, but in a system which even formally and occasionally is described as government by the people, there are strong incentives for them to describe themselves as pretty ordinary guys or gals. There are striking instances of this even in the modification of monarchies, which, far from being their transformation or abolition, are adaptations to democratic expectations in nations from the United Kingdom to Japan.[53] When Marie Antoinette dressed as a peasant at the Petite Trianon, it was for the entertainment of herself and her courtiers. When democratic leaders do it, it is to entertain and to entice their citizen subjects.

Conclusions

In democratic states there is a confusion and a tension between the equality which all people share as rulers, and the distinction which exists between the same people in their identity as ordinary subjects of the state and the specialised groups who carry out the day-to-day business of government. There is a continuing tension between democracy as government by the people, which means that the people rule, and democracy as government for the people, a tension which economic liberals have attempted to resolve by replacing or overlaying it with a consumer sovereignty in which the people are the customers but not the shopkeepers.

If the people are both rulers and ruled, then in some aspects of their lives they must be subordinate to others, officers or servants of the state. The pull towards association and equality on the one hand is met by the pull towards distinction and authority on the other. This is evident in every aspect of life in societies which claim to be democratic. On the one hand there can be an advocacy of democratic and egalitarian plumage, on the other a continual striving for distinction. Mao jackets and the universal title 'comrade' arrive to cultivate equality and solidarity, and the egalitarian title is rapidly qualified by the suffix 'chairman', 'general', or 'manager'. The French Revolution of 1789 was wracked by just such stresses, apparently about little more than clothing, but in fact about the whole character of a democratic society and state, and part of the ambivalence of people as simultaneously rulers and subjects. In universities that seek the common identity of teachers and scholars, 'professor' is the title for all, but is simultaneously qualified by the prefixes 'full', 'associate', or 'foundation'.

The greater the degree of democracy, the more it matters what feathers the demos wears, as well as what leaders wear. The identity of the citizen is an essential component of a democratic society. But government in whatever form attempts to acquire, patronise, regulate, and customise appearances and ritual for purposes which it leads and guides. The cultivation of all the aspects and dimensions of identity is a vital dimension of the ordering and management of political life, and a recurring aspiration of political leadership. In revolutionary France, a society compelled to include the masses, and hence to abolish the distinctiveness of a class of rulers, reintroduced order and predictability by constructing or cultivating other distinctions of both office and gender.[54] In seventeenth-century revolutionary England, the rebellion against royal autocracy transmuted into the repression of leveller and digger egalitarianism.

Being governed is being subject to rules and hence to uniformity and solidarity. Governing, on the other hand, is or can be dynamic and unpredictable. This is why the term democracy refers to a form of life which is different from that of all other regimes. Since the people are not only governed, but the governors, they too are unpredictable and dynamic. It is, though with difficulty, possible to imagine a state with civil society and a free, variegated, and unpredictable populace which is nonetheless not a democracy. It might be argued that empires can be like this, but in fact if empires are a form of pluralist government of governments, then the population is not free from particular rulers, but is simply not directly subject to the overall imperial sovereign. Alternatively, civil society in a homogeneous centralised empire will be intolerant of local civil society.

The tension in identity between association and equality, and distinction and inequality, is reproduced in the paradox of the push and pull between the perennial ambitions of government and the continual impetus to political inequality, and the continual assertion of democratic identity, the continual stress between the urge to govern and the democratic temperament, between the stubborn, sometimes bloody-minded, sometimes brave and enduring insistence from within the people of their sovereignty, and the sustained, relentless impetus of rulers, governors, elites, and managers, to preside, and to preside with presiding identities. Within the sovereign identity of the demos there is a further paradox, a never-resolvable stress between the desire for solidarity and homogeneous identity, and a forever renewed resistance to the freezing stare of Medusa and an insistence that if the people are sovereign, then each one of them has an inalienable right to cultivate his or her own identity, and to resist either the inclusion or the exclusion which is an unavoidable feature of the bear hug of one great all-enveloping national character. The tensions and paradoxes of democratic identity are inherent and inescapable. And they are crowned by the over-arching paradox that they are the source both of democracy's instability, and of its vitality and survival.

Notes

1 Joseph A. Schumpeter, *Capitalism, Socialism, and Democracy*, 5th ed. (London: George Allen and Unwin, 1976), pp. 269–83.
2 George Bernard Shaw, *Ruskin's Politics* (London: Ruskin Centenary Council, 1921), p. 15.
3 Barker, *Legitimating Identities*, pp. 112–15.
4 Christine Delphy, interview with Andrea Catherwood, *BBC4 Woman's Hour*, 19 February 2016, www.bbc.co.uk/programmes/b070hscm (accessed 18 May 2016).
5 Watt, *Dress, Law and Naked Truth.*
6 Boutling and Boulting, *The Guinea Pig.*
7 Quintin Hogg, *The Case for Conservatism* (West Drayton, UK: Penguin, 1947), p. 10.
8 David Owen, 'Self-Government and "Democracy as Reflexive Co-operation": Reflections on Honneth's Social and Political Ideal', in van den Brink and Owen, *Recognition and Power*, p. 294.
9 John S. Dryzek, *Deliberative Democracy and Beyond: Liberals, Critics, Contestations* (Oxford: Oxford University Press, 2000), pp. 113–14.
10 Giuseppe Tomasi di Lampedusa, *The Leopard* (London: Vintage, 2007), pp. 78–82.
11 Ross Terrill, *R. H. Tawney and His Times: Socialism as Fellowship* (Cambridge, MA: Harvard University Press, 1973), p. 133.
12 Tom Paulin (ed.), *The Faber Book of Political Verse* (London: Faber and Faber, 1986), pp. 444–6.
13 Kate Bowan and Paul A. Pickering, '"Songs for the Millions": Chartist Music and Popular Aural Tradition', *Labour History Review*, 74:1 (2009), 55.
14 *The Poetical Works of Robert Burns*, edited by J. Logie Robertson (Oxford: Oxford University Press, 1921), p. 328.
15 *The Bible, Authorized King James Version* (Oxford: Oxford University Press, 2008), Matthew 6:29–31.
16 Quoted in Hunt, *Politics, Culture and Class*, p. 75.
17 Wrigley, *The Politics of Appearance*, p. 62.
18 Hunt, *Politics, Culture and Class*, pp. 79–80.
19 Michael Zakim, *Ready-Made Democracy: A History of Men's Dress in the American Republic, 1760–1860* (Chicago and London: University of Chicago Press, 2003), p. 1.
20 Zakim, *Ready-Made Democracy*, pp. 213–14.
21 Mansel, *Dressed to Rule*, illustration 47, p. 140.
22 Will Thorne, *My Life's Battles* (London: George Newnes, 1925), p. 211
23 Terrill, *R. H. Tawney*, pp. 79, 234.

24 Jeffrey Wright, 'Capitalism and Working-Class Acquiescence', *Socialist History*, 36 (2010), 99.
25 Harriet Walker, 'If the cap fits, wear it. But not if your name is William Hague', *Independent*, 24 August 2010, www.independent.co.uk/news/people/news/if-the-cap-fits-wear-it-but-not-if-your-name-is-william-hague-2061171.html (accessed 18 March 2016).
26 Wrigley, *The Politics of Appearance*, pp. 63–4.
27 George Orwell, *Homage to Catalonia* (London: Penguin, 1962), p. 8.
28 Herbert Morrison, *Herbert Morrison: An Autobiography* (London: Odhams, 1960), p. 139.
29 Mike Squires, 'The Mass Trespass of Kinder Scout: How Breaking the Law Achieved Change', *Socialist History Society Newsletter*, New Series, 1:1 (2012), 1–3; Ben Harker, '"The Manchester Rambler": Ewan MacColl and the 1932 Mass Trespass', *History Workshop Journal*, 59:1 (2005), 219–28.
30 Langdon Winner, 'Do Artifacts Have Politics?', *Daedalus*, 109:1 (1980), 121–36; but see Bernward Joerges, 'Do Politics Have Artefacts?', *Social Studies of Science*, 29:3 (1999), 411–31.
31 Appiah, *The Ethics of Identity*, pp. 105–10.
32 David Miller, 'Reflections on British National Identity', *New Community*, 21:2 (1995), 157.
33 Greenfeld, *Nationalism*; Jonathan Sacks, *The Home We Build Together: Recreating Society* (London: Continuum, 2007).
34 Vivien Hart, *Distrust and Democracy: Political Distrust in Britain and America* (Cambridge: Cambridge University Press, 1978).
35 Samuel P. Huntington, 'The United States', in Michel Crozier, Samuel P. Huntington, and Joji Watanuki, *The Crisis of Democracy: Report on the Governability of Democracies to the Trilateral Commission* (New York: New York University Press, 1975), pp. 74–5.
36 Luke Harding, 'The joke's on Saddam', *Guardian, G2*, 14 March 2003, p. 5.
37 Hilary Mantel, *The Assassination of Margaret Thatcher: Stories* (London: Henry Holt, 2014).
38 Jon Stone, 'Tory grandees angry as BBC chooses Hilary Mantel's "The Assassination of Margaret Thatcher" for Book at Bedtime', *Independent*, 14 December 2014, www.independent.co.uk/news/uk/politics/tory-grandees-angry-at-bbc-for-serialising-thatcher-assassination-book-9923514.html (accessed 21 February 2017).
39 BBC News, 'Sony hack: North Korea threatens US as row deepens', *BBC News*, 22 December 2014, www.bbc.co.uk/news/world-asia-30573040 (accessed 8 November 2016); BBC News, 'North Korea threatens war on US over Kim Jong-un movie', BBC News, 26 June 2014, www.bbc.co.uk/news/world-asia-28014069 (accessed 8 November 2016).
40 Max Weber, 'The Social Psychology of the World Religions', in Gerth and Mills, *From Max Weber*, p. 271.
41 Tonie Holt and Valmai Holt, *In Search of a Better 'Ole: The Life, the Works and the Collectables of Bruce Bairnsfather* (Barnsley, UK: Pen & Sword Books/Leo Cooper, 2001).

42 Orwell, 'The Lion and the Unicorn', p. 81.
43 Wayland Young, *The Profumo Affair: Aspects of Conservatism* (Harmondsworth, UK: Penguin Books,1963), pp. 14–15.
44 Georg Simmel, *Conflict* and *The Web of Group-Affiliations*, translated by Kurt H. Wolff and Reinhard Bendix (New York: Free Press, 1964), p. 15.
45 John Stuart Mill, 'On Liberty', in *Three Essays* (Oxford: Oxford University Press, 1975), p. 83.
46 BBC News, 'Global net censorship "growing"', *BBC News*, 18 May 2007, http://news.bbc.co.uk/1/hi/technology/6665945.stm (accessed 19 May 2007).
47 Mount, *The Theatre of Politics*, p. 9.
48 Chris Humphrey, *The Politics of Carnival: Festive Misrule in Medieval England* (Manchester: Manchester University Press, 2001), pp. 83–95.
49 Humphrey, *The Politics of Carnival*, pp. 63–78.
50 Emmanuel Le Roy Ladurie, *Carnival: A People's Uprising at Romans 1579–1580*, translated by Mary Feeney (London: Scolar, 1979).
51 Hunt, *Politics, Culture and Class*, pp. 66–7.
52 Ian Buruma, 'The Indiscreet Charm of Tyranny', *New York Review of Books*, 52:8 (2005), 37.
53 Ruoff, *The People's Emperor*.
54 Melzer and Norberg, 'Introduction', p. 9.

5

Reformation and Revolutions

Why revolutions are so sartorially perilous

In Robert Wise's 1962 film *Two for the Seesaw*, Shirley MacLaine reassures besuited middle-class lawyer Robert Mitchum, arriving at a Greenwich Village flat, 'Take off your hat, and no one will know you've come to the wrong party.'[1] The colour of a pair of socks or the style of a shirt in settled times are matters of social recognition or at the worst mundane snobbery. In unsettled times, they can be matters of physical safety or even survival. When people are most uncertain or insecure in their identities, normally trivial items or actions can become evidence of friend or foe, and justification for alliance or attack. Because the costumes and scenery with which humans construct and cultivate their identities constitute their social existence, different costumes and scenery, different identities, have the capacity to disconcert or antagonise, and to be the soil of conflict, just as readily as they can construct, cultivate, and confirm social existence and security. Even if other people are not treated as auxiliaries to a person's identity, those people's recognition of that identity plays an important role in the confidence with which its many elements are worn by its possessor. Conversely, the very existence of a different identity can seem to challenge the validity of the life constructed by the observer by calling into question its uniqueness, or by valuing a different form of life, and the apparently smallest and least significant of differences can be taken as evidence of an existential challenge. In Tehran in 2007, men and women were accused of attempting a 'soft revolution' against the regime, having been arrested for haircuts which were deemed to flout Islamic dress codes.[2] For young men in England in the 1950s, simply to wear a Teddy-boy jacket and haircut, or in the 1960s to ride a motorbike in a leather jacket or a moped with a short haircut, could be seen, however calm and law-abiding their behaviour, as announcing a threat to decent and orderly society.[3]

A heightened sensitivity to the smallest digressions is not the only response to challenges to familiar identities. A despondent conviction that nothing can be done and that attempts either to change things or to resist change will be both futile and onerous can seek security in acquiescence. As the headmaster played by John Cleese in Christopher Morahan's film *Clockwise* put it, 'It's not the despair, Laura. I can stand the despair. It's the hope.'[4] The burden and uncertainty of change or resistance can lead to defensive passivity. But when change is either actively promoted or fiercely resisted, all the dimensions of identity achieve prominence, and every aspect of identity becomes part of the politics of transition and revolution or of the defence of identities which until that point had been tacit, unobtrusive, and mundane. Human plumage, like the quills of the porcupine or the hair of the cat, is flaunted and flared not in moments of calm but in moments of crisis, and personality and identity are most attended to in times of transition. In the controversies within the Christian church in England in 603, the simple failure of Archbishop Augustine of Canterbury to rise to greet the bishops of the Celtic church was enough to indicate to them the invalidity of his entire theological and organisational claims.[5] When in 1670 the archbishop of Mexico failed to lower the train of his robe in the presence of the viceroy, the gesture was deemed to threaten and was intended to threaten viceregal authority and that of the Spanish colonial regime.[6] In 2012 the reported burning of copies of the Koran by United States troops led to riots and death in Afghanistan.[7] During the French Revolution the allegation that royalist troops had trampled on tricolour cockades was a sufficient occasion for protest marches from their republican opponents.[8] Protest marches were not the only possible consequence of the choice and treatment of clothing. The wrong cut or the wrong colour could be enough to prove treason or counter-revolution. Every aspect of human clothing, conduct, and culture from the colour of a garment to the shape of a shoe could be seen as both a sign and a component of an allied or an alien loyalty, and be the occasion for solidarity or hostility, fraternity or assault.[9] In revolutionary France, a police agent warned of the need to 'survey carefully all those who seek to distinguish themselves from others; these are not true republicans.'[10] Comte Horace de Viel-Castel commented that 'the crime of *lèse-costume*, if one can so describe it, was a crime expiated on the scaffold', while Abbé Grégoire in a report to the Convention complained of the stigmatising of what he termed proper clothing and even 'cleanliness and decency' as 'counter-revolutionary crimes.'[11] And just as familiarity and similarity with associates can become a mark of security and solidarity, so the distinction within a group or nation of exceptional status or more intense representativeness can become an indication of hostility or threat. When the call is for '*les aristocrates à la lanterne!*' the tension which is always there between association and distinction becomes deadly, and it becomes perilous to mark yourself out as a distinguished or exceptional representative of the nation.

In China in the twentieth century, periods of revolution and instability were marked by the stigmatising of supposed enemies identified by their dress. Young red guards attacked in the street people whose dress infringed political etiquette, treating clothing as both a sign and an active pursuit of counter-revolution.[12] The meaning of appearance is fluent and flexible, arising not from material qualities but from social narrative and perception. As the narratives changed, dress could be condemned as insufficiently modern, insufficiently Chinese, or revealing a bourgeois and counter-revolutionary deviation.[13] But the flexibility of the significance of dress did not diminish the potential violence of its consequences. Whilst it may be possible to get away with no more than condescension or humour by going to a funeral in brown boots, small pieces of fabric can be the bearers of overwhelming significance.[14] In the United States in the twenty-first century, the possibility that opponents of the Bush administration's foreign policy might burn the national flag caused such outrage that a law to make flag-burning a specific crime was in June 2006 defeated in the Senate by only one vote.[15] It was not the first time the Stars and Stripes had been prominent in the politics of protest and outrage. In Boston in 1976 its use as a weapon against a black lawyer by a white opponent of bussing as means of educational desegregation, caught on camera by Stanley Forman, concentrated and intensified political passions.[16] To attack a fellow citizen with a pole was assault; to attack him with a flagpole to which the nation's flag was attached was secular sacrilege.

An even more powerful component of identity in times of conflict, uncertainty, and transition is the one which is the most unavoidably public and social: language. Whilst it is possible to talk to no one but oneself, language – unlike clothing, architecture, or eating – normally requires more than one person, one to speak and one to listen and understand, and the listener needs to be present or able to hear before the speaker begins. For language to do its job of confirming association, there has to be comprehension between the speaker and at least one other person. This privileges language as a dimension of shared identity, making it uniquely dependent on recognition by others. The identity function of language may also be quite the opposite where the language of the elite is privileged, where the mass of people do not understand it and thereby have their inferiority or cultural subordination cultivated and sustained. Failure to understand in this instance is as important as ability to understand in the other. In each case, others beyond the speaker, who can be assumed to hear either directly or indirectly, are necessary.

Because language has a special place as a component of identity, its denial can be the occasion for the most resolute and violent political action. The uprising within Pakistan which resulted in the creation of the new state of Bangladesh was fuelled by the attempt of the government in the west to establish Urdu as the national language, and the resistance of those in the east whose identity was vitally sustained by their use of Bengali. One of the celebratory days of Bengali assertion was the 'Language Day', commemorating 21 February 1952 when four students were shot in Dhaka during a protest over the promotion of Urdu.[17]

How a person speaks is frequently even more vital to their security in unsettled times than how they dress. The origin of the term 'shibboleth' illustrates the potential importance of vocabulary and pronunciation. The Book of Judges recounts that in fighting between the tribes of Gilead and Ephraim, fleeing Ephraimites tried to pass themselves off as members of the tribe of Gilead, so were asked to pronounce 'shibboleth'. Those who could only manage 'sibboleth' were killed as enemies posing as friends.[18] A similar turnpike for murder or survival occurred in England during the peasant uprising of 1381, when those who said 'case and brode' instead of 'bread and cheese' were allegedly killed as foreign Flemings.[19] In the Dominican Republic in 1937, the pronunciation of names was equally fatal in the so-called 'parsley massacres', when President Trujillo's policy of clearing the frontier areas of Haitians by both expulsion and killing was pursued by his troops with requests aimed to detect whether or not a Spanish 'r' was used in the words *perejil* (parsley) or *tijera* (scissors).[20] Saying serviette rather than napkin was never so perilous.

The distinction between private and public is particularly fluid and uncertain in revolutions

Identity is cultivated both by association with others and by distinction from others. It is thus impossible to separate a threat to a collective identity from one to the identity of an individual, or to exclude individual identities from the assertion of new or altered collective ones. 'Honour', 'repute', or 'reputation' is far more than a matter of personal vanity, and continually expands to enrol others in the identity of the individual, or recruit the individual to the identity of the collective. When new identities are being attempted or old ones attacked, one aspect of the fluidity involved is uncertainty as to the boundaries between public and private, or even of the meaningfulness of the two terms. When transformation is hoped for or feared, every aspect of identity becomes potentially contested, and the apparently smallest component of personal identity can be taken as a litmus test proclaiming the identity of the whole person or group. This leakage of meanings was a cause of continual uncertainty during the revolution in France, and the distinction between personal insult and political challenge dissolved as every aspect of individual life could constitute membership of a greater political grouping.[21] The choice of playing cards or the design of a plate could reveal loyalty or treason.[22]

The unsocial individual who acts without any reference to the values or conventions of the society which he or she inhabits is in peaceful and confident times treated with a range of reactions from suspicion to satire. A whole school of humour depends on just that judgment. But what is a matter for no more than tolerance or derision in stable times can be responded to with a passionate perception of deviance or danger in times of uncertainty or transition. Whilst alternative identities, however unobtrusively or privately they are displayed, provide threats to moral or religious reformers who seek to recruit all members of their society as auxiliaries to their own identities, they are even more threatening to the most ambitious of all cultivators of auxiliaries – governments and those who seek governmental power for religious or cultural strategies. The more ambitious the attempted transformation, the more intrusive the policing of every aspect of behaviour, whether in a public space or in the seclusion, but no longer the privacy, of the household. Books read, songs sung, jokes told, can all be treated as symptoms of dangerous opposition. It is precisely because a Bolshevik after 1917 believed so passionately that the world is secular and material, and because that belief was part of who he or she was, that religion was suppressed and oppressed in the new Soviet Union. It might have seemed a more practical and altogether easier route, if simple power were all there was to it, for the new regime to recruit Orthodox Christianity to its retinue of support, or simply ignore it. But that would have been inconceivable. A Marxist materialist could not take seriously the claims of religion any more than an Orthodox Christian could treat the doctrines of Bolshevism as much more than a cover for materialism and the greed for goods and power. To allow an alternative set of assumptions about the nature of the world and its human inhabitants, assumptions which were visibly and audibly nurtured in the religious worship of Orthodox Christians, would have been to admit that communism and dialectical materialism were no more than possible options amongst many ways of living. At the other end of the twentieth century, the rulers of communist China harassed and suppressed the Falun Gong movement not because it actively opposed the communist identity, but because it ignored it. It is not only ambitious socialites for whom there is only one thing worse than being talked about, and that is not being talked about. For ambitious states, being ignored is one of the most humiliating forms of opposition, and one of the most damaging threats to the confidence with which they cultivate their identities.

Four responses and strategies in circumstances of transition

The greatest attention is paid to the costumes, culture, and scenery of public life when change is being attempted, accommodated, or resisted. A settled and uncontested identity does not need robust expression; a hoped-for one does, and like a resisted or resented one is the occasion for attempts both at creation and assertion and at undermining and destruction. In times of actual or attempted transition and change of identities, four principal strategies can be detected: the introduction of new forms of identity or the adoption by individuals or groups of different identities – new plumage; the attempt to destroy or discredit current practice as one part of the creation of new identities – plucking the old plumage; the attempt to effect change by presenting new identities as continuous with or reassertions or developments or fulfilments of old or existing manners and customs, which manners and customs may be real or invented, reclassifying or redefining, arguing that the old was always pointing in the newly desired direction – grafting the new onto the old; and the assertion or reassertion of existing customs and ways of life – defending. These four ideal types, creation, destruction, grafting, and defending, provide the span within which the most robust assertions of public identity occur. The mingling of these ideal types will in the actual world be a means of cultivating change, or adapting to change by domesticating it, or of resisting change or subverting or avoiding it.

Creation

When an attempt is made to create a new world either by rulers or by revolt against rulers, every aspect of human identity finds a place on the revolutionary agenda. Whilst attempted transformation from above differs in many ways from insurrection from below, each seeks to create new identities, and may do so across the whole range of human culture. There are both destructive and creative dimensions to such campaigns. In their extreme form, they involve the attempt to completely replace one way of life with another by replacing one set and kind of people with another. This, though gradually and selectively, was what England attempted in Ireland after 1652, following Cromwell's seizing control of the country at the conclusion of a dozen years of rebellion and unrest. The Down Survey of land, its ownership, use, and inhabitants which William Petty organised in Ireland after 1652 was to be the basis of a transformation by selective resettlement of human life in the island. Each year, 10,000 Irish women of marriageable age were to be exchanged with the same number from England. The latter would raise families of English culture or household economy – food, clothing, manner of life – the former would be widely distributed and absorbed in English culture.[23] But the attempted Anglicisation of Ireland was one instance only of a history of ambitions to transform identity, ranging from compulsory changes in religion, or dress, or language, through expulsion and colonisation, to mass killing. Attempts to destroy peoples, both by the killing or expulsion of their members, or by destroying their government, their language, or their cultural practices, occur throughout human history. English ambitions in Ireland had many precedents, and the killing of Danes in Britain in 1002 or the expulsion of Jews in 1290 exemplified a recurring desire for familiarity, uniformity, and the elimination of difference.[24]

The revolutionary regime in France changed not only the divisions of the calendar and the names which described them, but the titles of professions and the names of tasks. Lawyers who had been *procureurs* and *avocats* under the monarchy were rebranded as *hommes de loi* under the new order.[25] The French Revolution was not unique in this respect. Twentieth-century communist revolutions in Russia and China, which claimed to have introduced socialist equality, entitled all their members as comrade, though hierarchy continued to flourish as the egalitarian title became an adjective in front of 'general', 'chairman', or 'leader'. Nor were revolutions original in their use of language, clothing, or the other attributes of visible and audible identity. In 1892 the imperial government of China argued that political and administrative reform required not only the adoption of Western ways of conducting public business but the adoption of Western dress, a policy which was subsequently spelled out in detail with distinctive etiquette for morning and evening wear.[26]

Just as people and jobs can be given a new identity with a new name, so can places. Colonists arriving in unfamiliar lands will seek the reconstruction of their homeland by old names, or rituals of home architecture, cooking, or festivals: New Amsterdam, New Hampshire, New York. Threat or attack strengthens this reconstruction, and transforms the smallest details into icons of identity. In the colonial conflict with the indigenous people of New England at the end of the seventeenth century,

> English possessions were, in a sense, what was at stake in the war, for these – the clothes they wore, the houses they lived in, and the things they owned – were a good part of what differentiated the English from the Indians. These were not simply material differences, they were cultural, for every English frock coat was stitched with threads of civility, each thatched roof rested

> on a foundation of property rights, and every cupboard housed a universe of ideas.[27]

The ambitions of rulers have again and again been to transform their populations, to change, as Peter the Great sought to change in Russia, their people from 'beasts into human beings.'[28] When Kemal Atatürk began the construction of modern Turkey, the creation of a new nation involved a comprehensive revision of identity, and clothing and headgear were not excluded from the agenda; the wearing of the fez was forbidden by law. New regimes could be introduced and sustained by new identities, religious as well as secular. The emperor Constantine constructed his unique identity by the adoption of a new religion, and in consequence the Christian church became the official religious body of the Roman Empire.

New worlds can be built from the human inside with the clothing, language, and habits of new identity, and from the outside with new towns and cities, new secular and religious public buildings. New building is a manner of stating a new, revised, or ascendant identity. Pippin, father of Charlemagne, inaugurated a massive programme of cathedral and church building, the import of saintly remains and relics, and new or elaborated ceremonies and anointings. It was a use of ecclesiastical scenery and liturgy which was to be frequently repeated, and discussing the later church building of eleventh-century Europe, Diarmaid MacCulloch commented that 'each new church was a reform in stone.'[29]

Utopia has always been well inhabited by architects, and the plans for improved or transformed humanity have again and again been drafted in street plans and elevated homes and public buildings, and allocations and distributions of space which embodied and embedded social hierarchies and distinctions. As Thomas Markus has argued:

> A characteristic feature of utopian town and building plans is the high degree of zoning, classification and functional definition. Each person, group and activity has its specifically defined and fixed location. These locations represent the classification system of the society and its activities which the designer assumes in his or her universal scheme. The most evident expressions of this drive to perfect order can be seen in organisations or institutions where there is the largest gap between controllers and the controlled. Institutions for the physically or mentally sick, for the criminal, and for the young, hospitals, asylums, prisons, workhouses and schools display all the features of elaborate classification.[30]

When the industrialist Titus Salt wanted his Yorkshire mill to be not just the centre of a thriving economy, but of a wholesome and reformed populace, he built the modestly entitled Saltaire on the River Aire with orderly clear streets, and buildings for the promotion of learning, religion, and health. Political leaders ambitious for the character of their new nations, or the new character of their nations, have constructed new capital cities and frequently done so in new places: Washington in the new nation of the United States, Canberra in Australia, Ankara in Turkey, Brasilia in Brazil, St Petersburg in tzarist Russia, Astana in Kazakhstan, or Naypyidaw in Burma/Myanmar.[31] Just as those who seek a new or an improved society can build grand cities for improved humanity, so those who want only to remedy the flaws which mar existing humanity look to the arrangement of urban spaces to design out crime.[32]

Existing and new components of identity can be used both by and against elites

The subordination of others as auxiliaries or extras in the drama of one's own identity has as its obverse the cultivation and assertion of identity as resistance to domination or oppression, and the efforts by all manner of religious and political movements, sects, and parties to create new worlds by means of language, dress, music, and every aspect of human behaviour and creativity in place of societies whose character or controllers they repudiate or wish to transcend.

When people who have lived under coercive rule demonstrate against it, they are cultivating a different identity as active citizens, democrats, members of an oppressed nation, religion, or ethnic group. What happens is similar to the transformation of identity in war as described by Hegel. Whatever conception or perception of external circumstances there may be, there is also, and of equal importance, a conception of identity which is formed and shaped in relation to those circumstances, and in particular in relation to the conception of others who constitute the social, human, dimension of those circumstances. People who see themselves as both part of and an expression or instance of a national insurgency are not the same people as they were when they saw themselves as isolated, albeit in no sense unique, underlings in a tightly controlling autocracy. '*Aux armes, citoyens*' is not only a call to citizens, it is a call which creates citizens. Language as the creation and cultivation of identity was dramatically depicted in Arnold Wesker's 1958 play *Roots*, where in beginning to talk as a radical, a person becomes a radical.[33] Whilst subjects can become citizens through speaking out, nationalists can oppose alien rule or the remnants of alien rule by renaming their land and its cities. Bombay becomes Mumbai, Madras becomes Chennai, and Calcutta reverts to its earlier, indigenous pre-anglicised title of Kolkata.

Attempts to create a different public order will frequently be pursued through movements which themselves cultivate new public identities for their members, followers, or supporters. Music is but one of the ways in which new identities can be cultivated, or existing ones enhanced or strengthened.[34] For many English Protestants in the reign of Edward VI, music in church was initially regarded with suspicion because of an association with the Catholic mass, for what a people will not do can be as important a part of their identity as what they will.[35] In nineteenth-century Britain, Chartists paraded in their thousands with music, banners, and song. Processions, rallies, concerts, and feasts were a collective and identity-sustaining activity, acting for political movements as marching music acted for military formations; playing musical instruments was widespread, and singing involved everyone.[36] The cultivation of new identities in movements seeking new political and social orders could display many of the same features as religion, with a sense of transformational goals and values and resources beyond the limitations of an inadequate or flawed present, providing the faithful with a sense of transcendent collective personality which gave individuals a perception of both belonging and meaning. For members of the Communist Party in the first half of the twentieth century, the collective mission of creating a new social and political order, and the separation from society as it existed which pursuing that goal provided, gave a sense of identity in a common purpose analogous to that which a believer gained from a church or religious crusade.[37] On the right of the political spectrum, fascist movements both presented themselves as the true expression of their nation's culture and destiny, distinction within association, and created extensive and elaborate rituals, regalia, and activities as components of a new, distinctive, and radically separate identity. So on the one hand the British Union of Fascists could attempt to incorporate the rituals of Armistice Day into its own public image by holding fascist commemorations complete with wreaths, dipped colours, and bugle calls, or the rituals of familiar Christianity with 'fascist baptism', whilst on the other hand uniforms, invocation of new dawns, and denunciation of existing society laid claim to a new and radical identity.[38]

The careful use of clothing can be a way of asserting particular identity against a homogenising imperial state or a dominant group or class, as readily as it can be the instrument of a state, class, or group which wishes to recruit more effectively the loyalties of those whom it treats as subordinates. Identity is attributed to appearance, not inherent in it, and clothing shares in this flexibility. In 1960s Britain a characteristic outer garment of the radical young, much seen on demonstrations by the Campaign for Nuclear Disarmament, was the duffle coat. The same garment, in the recent past, had been the characteristic outdoor wear of military figures in films celebrating Britain's heroic moments in the Second World War.

A similar fluidity in the significance of clothing occurs in religious identity. In medieval and Catholic Europe, simple dress was part of the identity of monks, friars, and nuns, and if there was colour, it was often black or brown. The Protestant reaction in and after the European Reformation distanced itself from what it saw as the excesses of the Catholic church by adopting its own version of the very visual signs of Catholic monasticism: simple clothes, absence of colour, preference for black. Similarly, in eighteenth-century Britain, the equality of all the faithful was promoted by religious leaders through an advocacy of simple clothing for all, a sartorial politics common to Quakers and Methodists.[39] The materials of identity have ever been flexible, deriving meaning from the contexts in which they are employed.

Destruction

Change can be attempted by destruction as well as by creation, and one tactic amongst many is the obliteration of aspects of identity which are depicted as hostile, antisocial, treacherous, or alien. There is a metaphor for an important element in the understanding of identity in the stories of witchcraft's harming real people through dolls which represent them, and the idea that somehow the 'real' person is contained in a manufactured object. In at least one fictional account of witchcraft, the physical survival of a person depends on, is indeed embedded in, a series of manufactured objects. The seven horcruxes in J. K. Rowling's Harry Potter series of books contain the physical life of the opponent, and their destruction destroys him. But this is not only fantasy. The conduct of individual and national self-assertion, where it involves the destruction of the social existence of an enemy, involves precisely this destruction of the material embodiments of the enemy's life. This is the stuff of fairy stories, but it reflects something far more real about human identity.

The Nazis, in destroying the physical structure of Jewish culture in Poland, planned to remove selected artefacts to museums, thus simultaneously preserving a record but, by so doing, denying the real continuing existence of those whom they sought to destroy by assigning the remaining fragmentary components of the material and artistic dimension of identity to an exhibition of the past.

There was nothing new in such identity warfare conducted by the destruction of culture. The Reformation in Europe was conducted in part through image breaking, the destruction of objects. Nor was such politics confined to specifically religious zealots. During the revolutionary conflicts of eighteenth-century France, a resurgence of the cult in Toulouse of Notre-Dame-la-Noire, the Black Madonna, was countered by secular opponents burning the revered statue.[40] Iconoclasm is not restricted to societies thought of as religious, nor is it foreign to societies thought of as secular. Flags and the images of leaders and presidents can accumulate reverence similar to that accorded to sacred images, and can correspondingly be vulnerable to equally extreme hostility. The toppling and smashing of Saddam Hussein's statue after the invasion of Iraq in 2003 was treated by the press and television as a transformative act, evidence of a new political culture and an end to the old regime. The destruction two years earlier by the Taleban regime in Afghanistan of the 1500-year-old statues of the Buddha in the Bamiyan valley and of a Palmyra temple by Isis in Syria in 2015 were accorded similar status by the image breakers, acts which both symbolised and constituted the Islamic orthodoxy of the country and the removal of anything which contributed to an alternative and hence hostile human life. Statues and monuments have always been vulnerable to the ambitions of those who want to establish or consolidate new orders, though not always by means of destruction. The government of Germany had plans in 1940 for Nelson's Column, after a successful invasion, to be transported triumphantly to Berlin.[41] Statues are destroyed, or captured, not only as symbols but as constituent parts of cultures which are alien to their destroyers.

Detainees at the United States' prison camp at Guantanamo Bay allege that when interrogators were attempting to extract information, they defaced copies of the Koran in a prisoner's presence.[42] This was not conventional torture, though physical coercion and torture were used as well. But it was threat to the identity of the prisoner. Children who chant 'Sticks and stones may break my bones, but words will never hurt me' describe an indifference to the potential threat to identity that is bold rather than realistic. Insults and taunts may be shrugged off, but threats to an existing identity, to the very essence of what makes people who they are, can be as fearsome as threats to their physical security and survival. Guantanamo's Koran occupied the same family as Orlando's housekeeper's wedding ring. Similarly, books are burnt not just to prevent their being read, but symbolically to destroy the culture which they express. Archives, libraries, and museums, as well as churches and mosques, will be targets for the destruction or scattering of identity. A charge made against the actions of Israel in its military conflict with Palestinians in Nablus, and after the establishment of the state of Israel, was that records of identity had deliberately been destroyed in order to obliterate historical evidence of the identity of the Palestinian nation.[43]

The revival of real, imagined, or repackaged pasts is not only a presentation of positive narratives, but also of the remembrance of defining hostilities and an attempt to pursue, or repursue, old enemies. Among the features of a revived Scottish nationalism at the end of the twentieth century was a renewed interest in the highland clearances which had depopulated large parts of northern and western Scotland to the profit of the aristocracy. One focus of this political retargeting was a memorial to:

> one of the traditional villains of this tragedy, the first Duke of Sutherland. In 1994, an unsuccessful campaign was waged to remove the statue of the Duke from the place it has occupied on a 100-ft pillar on Ben Bhraggie, near Golspie. Comparisons were made with the removal of statues in the former Soviet Empire, but opinions were divided, and there were those who wished to retain the statue precisely because it served 'to remind the people of the iniquities that took place and of the continuing absurdity of how land is held and who has power over it.'[44]

Those seeking to create an identity frequently put a great deal of effort into destroying the physical context of other identities. From Carthage to Armenia, from Palestine to Tibet, the conquerors destroyed the physical constructions and contexts of those whose present, future, and past they sought to remove and deny. The more evident the material expression of a conquered or colonised group, class, religion, or culture, the more likely the physical destruction of that expression by the conqueror.[45] Heinrich Himmler commented on the destruction of Warsaw, begun with the initial invasion in 1939 and accelerated with the 1944 rising, that 'Warsaw, the capital city, the brain, the intelligence of this Polish nation, will have been obliterated.'[46] During the civil wars in the territories of the former Yugoslavia, churches and mosques were destroyed, not as military targets but as cultural ones, as constituents of the identity of opponents.[47]

The dimensions of identity during conflict and transition extend to the entire constructed human environment. But the more substantial the artefacts, the more difficult is swift change or new construction. Cockades and shirts can be changed – statues, monuments, and buildings are rather less malleable; destruction is easier and swifter as an assertion of dominance by conquerors, colonists, or new regimes. Just as buildings can convey messages, so can their demolition and the depiction of their destruction be a means of destroying one identity and asserting another. Robert Bevan's account of the demolition of buildings in sectarian and national conflicts is appropriately named *The Destruction of Memory*. The Twin Towers of the World Trade Center in New York, destroyed in a terrorist attack in 2001, served both for attackers and attacked as an expression and a constituent part of US economic, and global economic, power and prestige.[48] In Paris in 1871, the communards demolished the Vendôme column with the statue of Napoleon on top of it, an action far more readily possible than the construction of an alternative polity and society.[49] The human effort devoted to such destruction is inexplicable in narrowly utilitarian terms.

But as part of the bitter conflicts of identity it provides a destructive product at a price the destroyers of identity are happy to pay.

The most powerful elements of an identity reside in the physical presence of the person, and after the artefacts have been destroyed, the destruction of the body is the final counter-assertion. The execution of kings and presidents has an identity-denying or identity-destroying function far outweighing any merely utilitarian military or political strategy. The killing of symbolic opponents, whether witches or opposition journalists, serves to dramatise a victory of one identity over another, just as it dramatises heroic defiance and murderous oppression. But whilst the symbolic killing of leaders may be part of a limited destruction of human life in the search to establish new identities, the killing can be far more extensive, seeking change not by altering the identity of a people, but by obliterating it.

Grafting and excavation

New identities can be formed either by recycling old ones, or by presenting innovation as continuity with overlooked precedents or by the discovery or rediscovery of traditional customs and practices. The presentation of continuity is a strategy which can serve several purposes. It may be a means of lubricating the mechanisms of change, or a partly cosmetic exercise by the agents or initiators of change.

The presentation of continuity in order to facilitate change is an ancient strategy. Ever since Pope Gregory the Great, the Christian church has known how to introduce new religion on old foundations. Gregory had advised Augustine, whom he had sent to establish Rome's jurisdiction in England through the archiepiscopate of Canterbury, to graft his teaching and his worship onto the existing beliefs and practices of his potential flock, building new churches on old pre-Christian sacred sites, not in order to obliterate those sites but to secure continuity with existing religious loyalties. The Christian church when it began proselytising in South America, followed the same practice.[50] Both clergy and laity in Reformation and post-Reformation Europe employed similar devices of continuity with sacred sites in nature, although the cultivation of continuity between new Protestantism and old Catholic popular pieties was as much an unrationalised search for the securities of old habit in ameliorating engagement with new doctrines as a deliberate justificatory tactic.[51] It was not without ancient precedents. The historical books of the Old Testament record discovery after discovery of old and neglected tablets in the temple whenever a secular or a religious leader wanted to reform religious observance. The church in Europe throughout the Middle Ages employed similar devices, manufacturing ancient doctrinal and devotional identities as sanction for new ecclesiastical practices with a series of forged papal, royal, and imperial decrees. *The Protocols of the Elders of Zion* was no more than one of the more unpleasant additions to an ancient practice, paralleled in the narratives of cultural nationalism by the alleged ancient poems of Ossian, fabricated in eighteenth-century Scotland by their supposed discoverer, James MacPherson.[52]

Nationalist assertion in places where the nation is not the state and the government is culturally different from the culture which nationalists seek to create is frequently composed in part of a distinctiveness in dress, and an attempt to spread, develop, recover, or rediscover distinct nationalist forms of clothing. In Hungary in the nineteenth and early twentieth centuries, there was an attention to early or original Magyar forms of appearance and decoration, and the incorporation of designs and motifs from a supposed Magyar origin into the fabric, literally, of everyday life.[53] Iconic images from folk art became embedded in a national identity cultivated in costumes, in architecture, and even in confectionary.[54]

As well as nationalist assertion within an existing state, political assertion which does not challenge the national identity can involve contests over the scenery of public life. In Britain during the nineteenth century there was what has been referred to as 'statue mania',[55] and whilst the first surge of creation and placing was of establishment figures, dissident identities also laid claim to their own environment with the installation of statues to radical leaders. After the death in 1855 of the Chartist leader Feargus O'Connor, statues were erected in a number of British towns, in what Paul Pickering has described as 'part and parcel of the Chartists' assertion of their rights as citizens'.[56]

Nor has the identity significance of food ever been neglected. Creative eating can be used as a means of sustaining, restoring, or introducing particular social arrangements. Sir Benjamin Heywood described the Christmas dinner held in Manchester in 1835 as designed to promote social solidarity across classes:

> for the purpose of receiving and preserving, with the hearty old holiday customs of our forefathers, the social and joyous feelings with which they were accompanied; that our kindly and benevolent sympathies might be awakened, and that with us, as with our forefathers on these occasions, there might be hospitality in the hall, and charity in the heart.[57]

Defence: assertion, reassertion, and discovery in times of stress and uncertainty

Celebrants of settled order have frequently been aware that changes in the visible and external character of men and women can be corrosive of existing ranks, conventions, and culture. At the end of the sixteenth century in England, Philip Stubbes complained that:

> it is very hard to knowe, who is noble, who is worshipfull, who is a gentleman, who is not: for you will have those, which are neither of the nobylitie gentilitie nor yeomanry, no, nor yet anie Magistrat or Officer in the common welth, go daylie in silkes, velvets, satens, damasks, taffeties and such like, notwithstanding that they be both base by byrthe, meane by estate, & servyle by calling.[58]

In the eighteenth century, Daniel Defoe deplored the poor dressing, or trying to dress, above their station.[59] Even more disconcerting than simple boundary challenging by those lower down the social and political hierarchy is novelty, variety, and unpredictability. A Chinese journalist in 1912 complained that 'Chinese are wearing foreign clothes, while foreigners wear Chinese clothes; men are adorned like women and women like men; prostitutes imitate girl students, and girl students look like prostitutes.'[60] For just as cultivated character is expressive of one order of social life, it can be also a challenge, a defiance, or an abandoning of that order. The minutiae of tangible, visible, and audible character are never so carefully marked as when they appear challenged or in flux. In twentieth-century Bhutan, one way of attempting to preserve what was seen as a distinctive way of life was to insist, both by social pressure and by public law, on a distinctive Bhutanese form of dress.

The defence of language, and a corresponding hostility to what are seen as foreign influences on or imports into spoken and written identity, becomes more energetic and more conservative when identity is believed to be threatened. A contributor to *Le Monde* warned readers in 1979 'Beware! If the French language recedes all we who speak it are threatened in our identity and being.'[61]

At times of social or national stress or uncertainty, the construction of the public stage can be used to reassure by asserting or reasserting public identities. The commemoration of the dead is also a sanctification of the living, and the memorials to those killed in war can be statements about what is hoped for as well as about what has been lost. The Slav architect Dušan Jurkovič designed thirty-seven cemeteries for the dead of the First World War. Describing one of them, Anthony Alofsin writes that 'a square with a polygon forming a truncated arrow, is outlined by a perimeter fence made of a pair of massive logs laid flat over rough rubble. On top of the logs sits [*sic*] cross members and a double-layered roof characteristic of Slovak folk architecture. Jurkovič applied the same roof treatment to the entry gate.'[62]

The mixture of innovation and tradition as the form in which new or adjusted identities are crafted can be pursued by the most seemingly traditional of regimes. The presentation of continuity can also be a way not of facilitating change but of surviving it. In Japan following military defeat, American occupation, and the imposition by the occupying power of constitutional change, the imperial family, whilst not being able formally to resist the alterations to its legal status, nonetheless acted in order on the one hand to maintain the regard and respect in which it was held, and on the other to find new and additional ways of nourishing that regard. The emperor began making public visits and tours, and the media began to present aspects of the life of the imperial family which expressed their ordinariness as well as their imperial status. Kenneth Ruoff comments that 'Traditionally the monarchy had been described as being "above the clouds." In the post-war era, the palace worked hard to bring it, if not to ground level, then at least to an altitude where it could be seen from the ground.'[63]

Deception is another defensive identity response, of or near the last resort, to challenges to existing practice. If the challenge is overwhelming, if resistance to it by asserting existing identities appears futile, then acceptance of new practices whilst covertly continuing old ones is sometimes resorted to. Jacobites in England might raise their glasses to toast the king whilst holding them over vessels containing water, so that the toast was, though only to those who knew the secret, 'The King, over the water.' In Spain after the Catholic monarchy began its imposition of religious uniformity in the fourteenth century, there were Jewish and Muslim communities who adopted Catholic worship for the public gaze, whilst at the same time continuing covertly their own religious practices. The extent of this covert and overt religious observance by *conversos*, Marranos, and Moriscos may not have been as great as the Inquisition supposed, but it clearly occurred.[64]

Identity, like fashion, is both disseminated and monopolised by minorities

Revolutions are carried through by minorities either from above or from outside or below, and are attempts to construct the character of public life in a way which sustains the cultivated identities of the revolutionaries. The constraints within which identity is cultivated, if they were the only elements in that cultivation, would prevent any change to an existing order. Alternative or altered identities will sometimes seem unrealistic or utopian, but they are advanced and replace, in various degrees, those of their opponents, which is why Michael Rosen argues that there is a necessary recognition of the role of the visionary, the passionate, or even the deluded in making possible mass participation in circumstances where despair seemed ubiquitous.[65] The plumage and scenery of change or resistance are constructed and cultivated, not spontaneously generated; even spontaneous combustion needs a detonator. This view of change was prefaced by Pareto in his image of circulating elites and by Lenin in his image of the vanguard party. The essence of all such arguments, which is most clearly expressed by Rosen, is that choice is possible even if it is made against apparent obstacles and restraints, and in defiance of what might seem rational. This does not set aside the force of circumstance and convention, but insists that it is one element only, even if it is commonly the most powerful. But it also insists that whilst identities may be shaped by the circumstances in which groups and persons exist, those circumstances are themselves the results of human action.

In mobilised societies, one aspect of the identity of any elite is likely to be its claim to be representative of the wider population. In transition the initiative may be taken by a few, but its success can depend on at least its acceptance by the many. Just as an excessive distance between the identity through association of a population and the distinction which elites cultivate within the context of that association can lead to a range of stresses from indifference to insurrection, so a successful replacement of one order by another involves the cultivation of an alternative which can be both distinctive in its leadership and recognisable and desirable amongst its associates and potential associates.

In all cultivations of identity, whether sustaining or challenging existing orders, none of the evidence for a particular identity is inherent, and any artefact or human production can be given radically different interpretations and significance. The examples of Trobriand cricket and Aztec Christianity illustrate the dependence of artefacts and all the creative activities of humanity on humanly derived significance. This dependence is not limited to inanimate objects, but extends to human action itself. Language may embed meanings and values, but its status can shift and mutate according to the aspirations of those who use it. In pre-revolutionary France, French was the language of the elite, and marked them off from the many who lived through their own languages and dialects. With the revolution, conversely, French became the language of enlightenment, rationality, and radical progress, and was actively promoted, just as Basque, Breton, and other minority languages and dialects were actively discouraged. In the twentieth century, Breton suffered after the Second World War by being associated with the Vichy regime, whilst by the century's end it had moved from right to left to become associated with radical decentralised democracy and popular choice against centralised conservatism.[66]

There is a tension between the effectiveness of habitual identity and the lure of novelty. Transformations of public identity of a whole nation or society are neither easy nor straightforward, and there is a substantial capacity of old identities and characteristics embedded in habit to survive the most vigorous and sustained efforts at change, and to re-emerge, like streams in limestone reappearing miles further on from their last visible surface presence. Trobriand cricket is a neat example of the resistance of existing identities to innovation, and their ability to absorb and recharacterise it. The conquistadores from Spain who thought that they were importing Christian monotheism into the culture of their Aztec subjects failed to notice that the European deity was simply being added to the existing indigenous ones, a divine fraternity which was to survive into the twenty-first century.[67] This is at the same time an illustration of why it is perilous to dismiss actions which people treat as important as frivolous, whimsical, or unimportant. Anything from the pronunciation of a single word to the way in which a shirt is closed at the neck can, especially in times of uncertainty or transition, be a matter of solid significance for those involved and therefore of essential significance for those who wish to understand what is going on. However triumphant the establishment of new worlds and new identities may seem, there is a ubiquitous recessive persistence of old ones. Catholicism in Ireland and Orthodoxy in Russia each survived the efforts of determined governments to replace them in the identity of their nations. Government can transform, and *cuis regio, eius religio* [whose realm, his religion] worked across Europe in the years of Reformation and Counter-Reformation, but English rule in Ireland bypassed or dispossessed the indigenous ruling class without replacing it with a settled and unalienated alternative. If tradition is simply persecuted or undermined, there is no control over the identities which will replace it or which will respond to the persecution. And if the leaders of change seek to identify themselves as leaders of a nation, or faith, or culture whilst at the same time, by the claim of leadership, distancing themselves from ordinary humanity, they both illustrate the ambivalence of identity cultivation and its constant tension between association and separation, and render potentially insecure their own control of it. The complexity of change and resistance makes universal patterns or predictions fragile, and whilst it is never the case that anything and everything is possible, nor is it the case that everything is determined and predictable.

Notes

1 Robert Wise, *Two for the Seesaw* [film] (Beverley Hills: United Artists, 1962).

2 Robert Tait, 'Iranian police give barbers the chop to enforce Islamic dress code', *Guardian*, 25 August 2007, p. 28.

3 Paul Rock and Stanley Cohen, 'The Teddy Boy', in Vernon Bogdanor and Robert Skidelsky (eds), *The Age of Affluence 1951–64* (London: Macmillan, 1970), pp. 288–320.

4 Christopher Morahan, *Clockwise* [film], screenplay by Michael Frayn (London: Studio Canal, 1986).
5 Bede, *A History of the English Church*, pp. 99–101.
6 Alejandro Cañeque, *The King's Living Image: The Culture and Politics of Viceregal Power in Colonial Mexico* (London: Routledge, 2004), p. 122.
7 Agence France-Presse, 'Obama forced to apologise to Karzai for Koran burnings in Afghanistan', *The Australian*, 24 February 2012, www.theaustralian.com.au/news/world/obama-forced-to-apologise-to-karzai-for-koran-burnings-in-afghanistan/story-e6frg6so-1226280166800 (accessed 25 January 2015).
8 Hunt, *Politics, Culture and Class*, p. 58.
9 Hunt, *Politics, Culture and Class*, p. 53.
10 Wrigley, *The Politics of Appearance*, pp. 85–6.
11 Quoted in Wrigley, *The Politics of Appearance*, pp. 1, 81.
12 Finnane, *Changing Clothes*, pp. 228, 230, 239–40.
13 Finnane, *Changing Clothes*, p. 257.
14 R. P. Weston and Bert Lee, 'Brahn Boots', *All Poetry*, https://allpoetry.com/Brahn-Boots [originally published 1940] (accessed 21 February 2017).
15 Charles Babington, 'Senate rejects flag desecration amendment', *Washington Post*, 28 June 2006, www.washingtonpost.com/wp-dyn/content/article/2006/06/27/AR2006062701056.html (accessed 21 February 2017).
16 Louis Masur, *The Soiling of Old Glory: The Story of a Photograph That Shocked America* (London: Bloomsbury, 2008).
17 Alyssa Ayres, *Speaking Like a State: Language and Nationalism in Pakistan* (Cambridge: Cambridge University Press, 2009), p. 45.
18 *The Bible, Authorized King James Version* (Oxford: Oxford University Press, 2008), Judges 12:5–6.
19 Scales, 'Bread, Cheese and Genocide', 284.
20 Richard Lee Turits, 'A World Destroyed, A Nation Imposed: The 1937 Haitian Massacre in the Dominican Republic', *Hispanic American Historical Review*, 82:3 (2002), 616.
21 Charles Walton, *Policing Public Opinion in the French Revolution: The Culture of Calumny and the Problem of Free Speech* (Oxford: Oxford University Press, 2009); Lynn Hunt, 'A Touchy Lot', *London Review of Books*, 32:5 (2010), 9–12.
22 Hunt, *Politics, Culture and Class*, p. 53.
23 Ted McCormick, *William Petty and the Ambitions of Political Arithmetic* (Oxford: Oxford University Press, 2009).
24 Scales, 'Bread, Cheese and Genocide', 300.
25 Hunt, *Politics, Culture and Class*, p. 20.
26 Finnane, *Changing Clothes*, pp. 69–73.
27 Jill Lepore, *The Name of War: King Philip's War and the Origins of American Identity* (New York: Random House, 1999), p. 79.
28 B. H. Sumner, *Survey of Russian History* (London: Methuen, 1961), p. 88.
29 MacCulloch, *Christianity*, p. 365.
30 Thomas A. Markus, *Visions of Perfection: Architecture and Utopian Thought* (Glasgow: Third Eye Centre, 1985), pp. 15–16.

31 Rowan Moore, 'The space station of the steppes,' *Observer, New Review*, 8 August 2010, www.theguardian.com/world/2010/aug/08/astana-kazakhstan-space-station-steppes (accessed 21 February 2017).
32 Davis, 'Designing Out Crime.'
33 Arnold Wesker, *Roots* (Harmondsworth, UK: Penguin, 1959).
34 Marcello Sorce Keller, 'Why Is Music So Ideological, and Why Do Totalitarian States Take It So Seriously? A Personal View from History and the Social Sciences,' *Journal of Musicological Research*, 26:2 (2007), 91–122.
35 Jonathan Willis, *Church Music and Protestantism in Post-Reformation England: Discourses, Sites and Identities* (Aldershot, UK: Ashgate, 2010).
36 Bowan and Pickering, 'Songs for the Millions,' 44–63.
37 Linehan, 'Communist Activism'; Thomas Linehan, *Communism in Britain, 1920–39: From the Cradle to the Grave* (Manchester: Manchester University Press, 2007).
38 Craig Morgan, 'Crisis, Patriotism and the Growth of Fascism: The British Union of Fascists in the Midlands, 1932–34,' *Socialist History*, 41 (2012), 63; Thomas Linehan, 'Space Matters: Spatialising British Fascism,' *Socialist History*, 41 (2012), 11.
39 John Styles, *The Dress of the People: Everyday Fashion in Eighteenth-Century England* (New Haven, CT: Yale University Press, 2007).
40 Hunt, *Politics, Culture and Class*, p. 66.
41 Mace, *Trafalgar Square*, p. 17.
42 Dan Eggen and Josh White, 'Inmates alleged Koran abuse,' *Washington Post*, 26 May 2005, www.washingtonpost.com/wp-dyn/content/article/2005/05/25/AR2005052501395.html (accessed 9 August 2010).
43 Gale Courey Toensing, 'First destroy the archives,' *Counter Punch*, 31 July 2006, www.counterpunch.org/toensing07272006.html (accessed 5 June 2011); Noga Kadman, *Erased from Space and Consciousness: Israel and the Depopulated Palestinian Villages of 1948* (Bloomington, IN: Indiana University Press, 2015).
44 Pickering and Tyrell, 'The Public Memorial,' p. 16.
45 Bevan, *The Destruction of Memory*, p. 28; Toensing, 'First Destroy the Archives.'
46 Quoted in Bevan, *The Destruction of Memory*, p. 97.
47 Bevan, *The Destruction of Memory*, pp. 42–3.
48 Sudjic, *The Edifice Complex*, pp. 12–13.
49 Maurice Agulhon, 'Politics, Images, and Symbols in Post-Revolutionary France,' in Sean Wilentz (ed.), *Rites of Power: Symbolism, Ritual and Politics since the Middle Ages* (Philadelphia: University of Pennsylvania Press, 1985).
50 Bede, *A History of the English Church*, pp. 86–7; MacCulloch, *Christianity*, p. 698.
51 Alexandra Walsham, *Reformation of the Landscape*.
52 Margaret Drabble (ed.), *The Oxford Companion to English Literature* (Oxford: Oxford University Press, 1985), pp. 604–5.
53 Alofsin, *When Buildings Speak*, pp. 129–30.
54 Alofsin, *When Buildings Speak*, p. 130.
55 Pickering and Tyrell, *Contested Sites*.

56 Paul A. Pickering, 'The Chartist Rites of Passage: Commemorating Feargus O'Connor', in Pickering and Tyrell, *Contested Sites*, p. 103.
57 Quoted in Hunt, *Building Jerusalem*, p. 98.
58 Quoted in Jones and Stallybrass, *Renaissance Clothing*, p. 5.
59 Styles, *The Dress of the People*.
60 Quoted in Finnane, *Changing Clothes*, p. 99.
61 Quoted in Maryon McDonald, *'We Are Not French': Language, Culture and Identity in Brittany* (London: Routledge, 1989), p. 6.
62 Alofsin, *When Buildings Speak*, p. 164.
63 Ruoff, *The People's Emperor*, pp. 204–5.
64 MacCulloch, *Christianity*; Yirmiyahu Yovel, *The Other Within. The Marranos: Split Identity and Emerging Modernity* (Princeton, NJ: Princeton University Press, 2009).
65 Michael Rosen, *On Voluntary Servitude: False Consciousness and the Theory of Ideology* (Cambridge: Polity, 1996), pp. 262, 272.
66 McDonald, *'We Are Not French'*.
67 Jenni Hyde, 'Culture Shock: The Arrival of the Conquistadores in Aztec Mexico', *The Historian*, 104 (winter 2009), 6–12.

6

Plumage and British Identity

The variety of British identity

In 1951 the poet Laurie Lee wrote a commentary for the Lion and the Unicorn Pavilion at the Festival of Britain. The intimation of the pavilion's presentation was of a homogeneous British character, but Lee's Britain was diverse not monolithic, characterised by its variety rather than by some pervasive essence, and he observed that 'the British do not simply leave the development of language to the professionals of literature', and that the 'Cockney has added a local vocabulary to the national one; and every British county has contributed a proverb, or a telling phrase'.[1] It was not so much a case of the British language as of the languages of Britain. It needed a poet to make the sensible empirical point that the only meaning that can be given to the phrase 'the British people' is an account of the identities of all the people who live in Britain at the time to which the statement refers. Vocabulary and accent are not homogeneous, but are particular to place and not only to geographical but also to social location and character. And just as language changes from one part of the population to another, so it does from one time to another. Shaw's complaint that the 'English have no respect for their language, and will not teach their children to speak it' rests on a misapplication of a correct observation.[2] There is no single or one-dimensional English language, and even less so a single British one, but a rich collection of ways of speaking that, whilst in their totality constituting language in the British Isles, no more have a single version which is, could be, or should be used by everyone than a meal can be reduced to a single ingredient or an orchestra to a single instrument.

What applies to language applies to every other aspect of identities within the British Isles. Time is important because not only will the answer be different at different times, but so will the meaning or even accuracy of the term 'Britain' and the titles of the governed territory, from England at the beginning of the modern period, to the Kingdom of Great Britain in the eighteenth century, United Kingdom of Great Britain and Ireland in the nineteenth century, and United Kingdom of Great Britain and Northern Ireland in the twentieth, each title referring to greater or lesser proportions of the islands of Britain, and to different combinations of those territories. During 400 years the geographical distribution of government within the British Isles has shifted many times, from two kingdoms with a single monarch under James I and VI after 1603, through a union of Scotland and England in 1707, and between the Scottish–English kingdom with a Welsh appendix and Ireland in 1800, to a territorial redistribution of government with the establishment of a new state in Ireland in 1921. The geographical extent of the various governed territories has grown and contracted, so that over three centuries a state centred on London has moved from England, Wales, and Ireland, to England, Wales, Ireland, and Scotland, to England, Wales, Scotland, and Northern Ireland. Nor have the shifts, expansions, and contractions been limited to the islands of Britain. Kings thought of as English have governed territories in continental France, and kings thought of as French have governed what is now thought of as England. Very shortly after John had confirmed what is frequently presented as the quintessentially English Magna Carta, in Latin, London and substantial sections of eastern England were under the control of Louis of France. So I do not apologise for telling a story from an early twentieth-century perspective; there is no fixed territorial foundation or vantage point, but nor is there a possibility of narrating from nowhere. I hope to avoid making any imperial claim for 'England' in so doing and, on the contrary, question the idea of a single homogenous English, let alone British, identity. That is not the only story that could be told, but any story has to be told from a vantage point, and the choice is just as contingent on circumstance as are the shifting combinations of governed territory about which, from one particular perspective, the story is told.

The fluid borders of hard territory are not the only shifting strands of the story. To talk of 'the people' is itself to use language which has meaning at one time but not at another, and to mean something quite different from the world alluded to if the adjective 'common' is added. The title which Bede gave to his history in the early eighth century is normally translated as 'A History of the English Church and People'. But *Historia ecclesiastica gentis Anglorum* could as readily be translated as 'A History of the Church and People of England', which has very different implications. A nation and a people are a perception of a relatively late time in the life of the British islands, and a perception of a nation which was equally represented by all its adult inhabitants an even later phenomenon, and one which was always a direction taken, rather than a point arrived at. A tomb to 'A British Warrior Unknown by Name or Rank' which was dedicated in Westminster Abbey in 1920 would have been puzzling or incomprehensible to the generation which celebrated heroism by means of grand memorials to military leaders in the wars against Napoleon. Even as part of an undifferentiated military mass, the common soldier had to wait for acknowledgment until after the end of the Crimean War in 1856, when regimental memorials first appeared in St Paul's Cathedral alongside the memorials which admitted only officers to the rank of hero.[3] It is not that a word or a concept – nation, people -changes, or that the terms used to describe an unchanging human phenomenon alter, but that different concepts, terms, and perceptions are the currency of discussion at different times, and different human phenomena, people differently perceived, categorised, and evaluated, are similarly described at different times. The concepts and perceptions, and the people to whom those concepts and perceptions refer, are historically specific, and relate to specific worlds of understanding and meaning. Identity is a human cultivation, and meaning and narrative are not only accounts of identity, but components of it. Whilst there are continuities, they are continuities within flux, growth, and decay. An unchanging character of an unchanging nation is a feature of narrative, not of the phenomenon to which the narrative allegedly refers. Tradition, as Eric Hobsbawm has argued, is invented.[4] Such a narrative may characterise a time, a place, and a people, but it is the narrative, not the alleged object of the narrative, which is real, and present, and which is also a moment in a pattern of understanding which is always changing. The narratives of national character and national history are themselves components of identity, and frequently contribute a dimension of homogeneity and continuity which is lacking in the shifting world to which the imagined descriptions attempt to refer and which they claim merely to reflect.

Even if presenting an account of 'Britishness' were a simple matter of declaring who, legally, is British, and how nationality is in law determined, there would be changes over time, a history of frequent uncertainty, ambiguity, and disagreement. Not only has legal status moved from subject to citizen, but the conditions to be met for each status have been matters of contest and amendment. Women were not fully citizens in the basic sense of all having the right to vote until 1928, while simple legal equality between males and females in other aspects of public identity continued slowly to be approached throughout the twentieth century. Citizenship even in law was not necessarily blind to either parenthood or gender, and until the passage of the 1981 British Nationality Act, women, unlike men, did not enjoy the right to transfer their citizenship to children born outside the UK.[5] Even then, there was an unsuccessful move by MPs working with Enoch Powell to distinguish between men and women when determining rights to citizenship.[6] And beyond the law are perceptions which are brought to bear when the law is formed and when its rulings are contested, of 'ways of life', 'national values', 'culture', 'origin', and 'ethnicity'. The alleged gasp of astonishment in the dining room of the Savoy Hotel when the results of the 1945 general election were coming through – 'But this is terrible – *they've* elected a Labour Government, and *the country* will never stand for that'[7] – may be apocryphal, but neatly illustrates the familiar specificity and insularity of perceptions of 'us', 'ordinary people', or 'the country'. As greater and greater layers of the population became in one way or another part of a public social space, the distinctiveness, peculiarity, and separateness of remaining realms of exclusivity – imperial governance, and espionage in all its dimensions both at home and abroad – became more and more pronounced. In the case of parts of the government such as MI5 and MI6, these two worlds could be strikingly insulated from one another not only by the assumption that how one lives is how everyone else lives, but by the filtering and insulating screens of secrecy. 'Pig sticking', which was listed as a pastime by a surprising number of MI5 officers between the wars, was not a characteristic or common British weekend hobby.[8] Different stories are not alternative interpretations of a single and independent historical reality, but are themselves different components of different realities, each of which is a dimension of something larger than itself.

While the character of the governed territories has mutated since the dual crown linked Scotland and England in 1603, so did the identities of the governed people, with a slow extension first of mobilisation and then of democratisation. Whilst not a transformation, or a disappearance of caste, class, or hierarchy, there was a slow shift in the relative weights of family origin as against other aspects of identity, and a narrowing, though not a vanishing, of the distances between various rungs in the social ladder and of the privileged and penalising differentiations of gender. If distinctions, exclusions, and privileges remained, they nonetheless increasingly, if unsteadily, did so within a common forum, rather than in a society rigidly even if not impermeably divided between the classes and the masses. At every stage, clothing, manners, speech, diet, and religion have been part of those identities. And so also are the accounts, claims, and challenges about these components of identity. A selective account of 'Englishness' by a right-wing movement such as the English Defence League, or a moral condemnation of social mores by a puritanical zealot, does not provide an accurate account of the world its advocates inhabit. But they do form a part of that world, and their ideology is a component of the shifting and variegated whole, of which a comprehensive account must take note. In seeking to give a dominant account of the world in which they live, such accounts do something very different: they add further evidence of that world's complexity. Challenges to an account of Britishness as no more, and no less, than the sum of everything and only at any one particular time serve only to sustain such an account by attacking it and providing immediate evidence of diversity. The retort that there is an essential Britishness, or Englishness, the essence of which is then delineated in terms of religion, taste for cricket, diet, household ethics and conventions, or skin colour, serves only to provide one more example of the contingency of any account of the world, British, English, or anywhere else, and the absence of a single homogeneous uniformity.

Whatever conclusions are reached about the identity of the population of the British Isles or parts of that territory, they will account for identities, and varieties of identity, which are continually shifting, changing, and argued about. Even if the territory and the population can stay still for a moment, the variety of terms to describe them refuse to settle in to a single agreed title, as Krishan Kumar has minutely demonstrated.[9] Those identities are composed of both private and public actions, the latter comprising both organised and spontaneous or informal actions and events with a more or less ritual dimension. The twentieth century saw numerous public celebrations of national identity, but many of them were semi-unofficial or completely unofficial, or possessed of an identity-cultivating role which was not a part of the actions of planners of the event: the Oxford and Cambridge Boat Race, Wimbledon, the Last Night of the Proms, but also the growing crowds receiving the coffins at Wootton Bassett of returning British dead from the war in Afghanistan, or throwing flowers at the funeral cortege of Diana Princess of Wales.[10]

The history of the population within the changing borders of the political communities of the British Isles is of continuous conflict and shifting relations between a democratic identity and a ruler's identity, with the latter slowly and unevenly distinguishing itself increasingly by its exceptional exemplification of the associative identity shared with those whom the ruler aspires to lead. It will illustrate the dual nature of identity cultivation, whereby on the one hand distinctiveness from other countries or nations is cultivated, whilst on the other the distinctiveness of groups, classes, or strata within the UK is formed by adopting or adapting foreign or other practices. And in all of this, identity is crafted and cultivated by what is done as much as by what is said, and with reference both to tradition, or how things are, and to rights, justice, and claims of how things should be. So a state and a political society about which it is frequently claimed that, unlike its continental neighbours, it enjoys stability and continuity, is at the same time characterised by continual fluidity, adaptation, innovation, and shifting variety.

The broader assumption on which an account of shifting national identity rests, and which is sustained by the plurality of identities both temporally and geographically in the islands of Britain, is that national identity can never be fractal, with each individual reproducing an instance of a universal character. The identity of a nation or a whole society can never be reproduced in that of any one of its members. The identity of the inhabitants of any governed area is, whether there is overall harmony or cacophony, still orchestral rather than fractal, though it will be fractured by fractal claims, both radical and conservative, about what a national identity should be. The description of any individual or group as 'British' or 'English', unless it is a description of legal status, can never be more than its locating as one component part of a whole, even though its character may have features which the observer believes to distinguish everyone, or most people, or a dominant group. Descriptions of English or British character can never be more than guides to aspects of identity which may be found in the islands of Britain. It is always possible to describe the character of a whole population because such a description is orchestral; it is never possible to describe the character of all the people who live in the islands of Britain because such personal identity is never fractal. The abbreviation of differences and the dramatic ordering and simplification which any description or narrative involves, can give an impression of a single English character. But even when religious uniformity was managed by coercive law, not each and every person could be fitted to a single template, whilst the islands of Britain throughout their history have been the recipients of invaders and immigrants from continental Europe to sustain and contribute to the varieties of faith, class, and culture.

Subjects, citizens, and human resources

Social bonds and group identities will not always and in all places sit neatly within the borders claimed by governments, and may either divide the inhabitants of a territory or sustain bonds across territorial state boundaries. When they have corresponded to territorial boundaries in the islands of Britain it has been in part because the sea has provided a permanent and enduring frontier which has enclosed human communities and made difficult, though not impossible, the generation of such communities across political boundaries, though even the sea has not prevented just such refusals to be accommodated within governmental boundaries, a refusal which has divided the island of Ireland.

Whilst the identity of government and governors is one part only of the identity of an entire population, it is government which, through its command of territory, sets the context within which it is possible to speak of a people, a society, or a population. The relationships between rulers and people are a major ingredient of who those people, and those rulers, are. Governments create nations, rather than vice versa.

Identity is never restricted to an individual, and if there is not a desire to secure others to share an identity's components, there will be a contrary desire to ensure that other identities, either by subordination or appropriate contrast, sustain an individual person's identity. In either case the identity of an individual is sustained by the auxiliary identities of others. When one of the parties to that engagement is an elite, dominant, or governing person or group, the identity of the other party will again and again need to be asserted, worked for, and cultivated in order to resist or limit domination. And whilst elites may circulate, the very exceptionalness which legitimates an elite in a democratic society fortifies the distance between elites and the populations within and beyond which their identity is cultivated. For leaders, the dilemma is as ever whether to see where the people are going in order to lead them, or to see where they ought to be going in order to direct them. For the people the problem is how to cultivate the identity they wish for against elites who are constituted by their advantages in material, social, and political resources and whose identity agendas, whilst they may correspond, so far as their distinguished version of identity permits, with the aspirations and aversions of the rest of the population, cannot be relied upon to do so.

Within the shifting territorial boundaries of the islands of Britain, a series of transformations have moved the population from one divided between an aristocracy or lordship and a subordinate mass, through a population increasingly mobilised and included in the interests of both economic and military ambitions, to one which, in its formal political life, was steadily more democratic. The move to mobilisation and then democratisation presented choices to governing or dominant elites. Once a substantial section of the population had a public and political status, there was a new and enhanced need to define who, legally, they were. Once citizenship became a dimension of adulthood, questions about, for instance, the status of prisoners or of those in receipt of public relief, which had not existed before, required answers. Prisoners or the poor, in an unmobilised society, needed no further designation. But as either recipients of public benefits, or objects of punishment or restraint, those who had previously been occasional and anonymous subjects became active ingredients of a mobilised society whose status was both public and recorded. Once they were part of a mobilised society, and even more once they were part of a democratised one, individuals had, or had potentially, legal and constitutional identities which required clarification in the light of other accounts of who citizens were. Individuals were increasingly both human resources and active and hence unpredictable participants in the life of the political community, so that the multifaceted debate over the political rights of prisoners was one of many which continued unresolved into the twenty-first century.

The move through mobilisation towards democracy was neither neat nor harmonious, unimpeded, or steady. The public and legal identity of persons living in those parts of the British Isles governed by the Crown was in the first place simply a distinction between those who were and those who were not subjects. National identity as distinct from subject identity was a further step, and citizenship a step further still. It was not until 1914 with the British Nationality and Status of Aliens Act that the statutory definition of nationality was set out. But the measure was passed not in order to either accord or recognise an element of the identity of adult inhabitants of the country, but to enable aliens to be defined with the approach of war. It was not so much a declaration of who was British, as a declaration of who was not, though its wording and effect was to proclaim both. The qualifications and entitlement to citizenship were still being clarified at the end of the century when, for the first time, tests of familiarity with various aspects of British life were incorporated in the tests of fitness for admission to the body of citizens.

Civil society as a public dimension of life outside the household or the workplace but below government can be seen not so much as changing, as coming into existence. But while a progression from people as human resources to people as subjects and then as citizens can be sketched, no changes are either simple or incremental and irreversible. People, insofar as they had a public identity as distinct from a private or economic one, were to begin with identified by the person of whom they were subjects, and their public identity was an aspect of the identity of royal government. Identity in relation to a nation or a territory came later, and citizenship, in relation to a political community of equal persons, later still. A population is mobilised to make it a more effective human resource, and the treatment of persons as resources does not disappear with their emergence as democratic citizens. It may even develop in new forms, and by the end of the twentieth century both public and commercial organisations felt no sense of irony in renaming their personnel departments 'human resources'. It is not only prophets who care for their people as shepherds care for their sheep.

A society generated by the mobilisation of a population, and a civil society, have been ones in which varieties of identity which previously had been obscured or private gained greater and greater public presence. These identities could either be suppressed in an active policy of cultural uniformity, or accepted as an aspect of a society which, whilst it might be equal in its political laws and to that extent uniform, was in its culture varied, many faceted, and unequal. The unsteady progression through mobilisation towards democracy involved both proliferations and erosions of visible and evident difference. Conspicuous consumption ceased being the defining feature of a relatively small segment of the population and became, if not democratised, then popularised. And whilst more and more people had access to clothes and goods which those selling them declared were the marks of great distinction, the signs of wealth, privilege, or good fortune became increasingly subtle, as the heel colours of royalty had been in previous centuries. When the poor no longer go barefoot, the mere possession of shoes is no longer sufficient to proclaim superiority, and brand names, stitching, colours, and the smallest detail of construction become the heralds of identity. The styles and manners which are part of the public identity of an elite continue as one model for wider and wider circles of consumers in an increasingly popular – though not necessarily or incrementally democratic – society. But there is a contrary development, in that the more segments of a population develop their identities as part of public society, the more possibilities there are for plural or multicultural identities, which may be simple alternatives to prevailing identities or, like punk in the 1970s, a deliberate eschewing of expensive or dominant style. There was a movement from a horizontally diverse to a vertically diverse society, a development with several possible consequences. One possible consequence is that resentments arising from dissatisfied emulation which previously would have been against 'society' or 'the system' will now be more parochial, and will be felt against a community or subculture. This in its turn can make resentment either more or less likely to lead to violence, insurrection, rebellion, or unrest. Witch-hunts were local, parochial, neighbourhood events, as were the 'paedophile' vigilante episodes of the twenty-first century.

At the beginning of the eighteenth century, most people would recognise someone with whom they were not in daily or frequent contact solely by their clothing, equipment, and bearing. By the middle of the twentieth century, photography, cinema, and television meant that the face was as important, and the proclamation of rank or profession by clothing was of declining relevance. Whilst the privileged and the powerful still proclaimed and cultivated their status by clothing and cars, much presentation became a statement of allegiance or membership, rather than of what Veblen called the invidious distinction of superior wealth.

As a mobilised society became more democratic and the formal distance between elite and mass became both smaller and less mined with obstacles, the identity of rulers shifted in engagement with the shifting identities of the ruled and the growth of a culture of citizenship. The changing public presentation of the people was complemented by a shift in that of monarchy, military, judiciary, legislature, church, and executive. The identity of government from London moved from monarchy to constitutional monarchy to representative government. As each element changed, the balance between them changed also. The components of the polity were very different in 2010 from those in 1700. Not only were there different components which were not present before, but even when there was continuity, the character of a component, and its relation to other components, had changed.

The economic, social, and legal subordination of women meant that what appeared to be the creation of a public society of adults was initially a society of males, and this exclusion was only slowly and incompletely altered. The place of women in public life (as opposed simply to activities outside the household) and the development of a distinct, independent, or autonomous female dimension to the public sphere in deportment, dress, and speech grew more slowly than those of men. Under the 1914 nationality act, whilst men conferred their nationality when they married, women lost theirs. A man with British nationality conferred it on a non-British wife. A woman who married a non-British male forfeited her British nationality. Although women had consistently been engaged in the movements and campaigns which had slowly and with difficulty and delay grown mobilisation into citizenship, the acknowledgment of gender equality lagged behind the pursuit and cultivation of democracy, and whatever their contribution to democratic advance, the gains to women themselves were consistently less substantial. Those who sought a fractal account of the identity of the inhabitants of the British Isles could still speak of the typical Englishman.

Rulers and elites, political, governmental, and social: the monarchy – Tudors to Windsors

The relations between privileged and unprivileged, rulers and ruled, government and subjects, have moved from an unmobilised population with a ruling monarchy and aristocracy to a mobilised population moving in a democratic direction. In this process the governing functions of monarchy have steadily shifted to career politicians and administrators. But whilst monarchy is no longer a central component of government, its changing character illustrates the wavering path through and beyond mere mobilisation. Paradoxically for an institution whose defining claim is that it is not representative, but autonomously authoritative, '*Dieu et mon droit*', the narrative of monarchy represents, or at least draws attention to, the narrative of the nation. As the population became more mobilised, and slowly democratised, so too the identity of the governing elite mutated as upper and lower levels of public life became more engaged with each other. By the time that Ireland had been added to the legal state of Great Britain in 1800, government in the British Isles had already moved away from rule by monarchy in a constitutional frame towards parliamentary negotiation and ministerial collaboration or coexistence with a monarch who, whilst still exercising power, did so with decreasing prominence in the government of the country. As the monarchy became less of a political pinnacle, and ministerial government encroached on the governing functions of royalty, whilst a society outside the world of monarchy and aristocracy grew in public prominence, so the monarchy developed a new role as a social pinnacle, contributing more to public identity as it contributed less to the exercise of government. And whilst the domestic political role of monarchy continued to decline, its formal and rhetorical role at the head of an empire survived into the second half of the twentieth century. This transition was supported across the principal political parties, and accepted by left and right, so that in 1947 Stafford Cripps, chancellor of the exchequer in the first majority Labour government, was able vigorously to defend expenditure on the monarchy, albeit by suggesting that the 'pomp and ceremony' in Moscow was 'vastly greater' than in London.[11]

Britain has a complex history of monarchy (though not an instance, since history is not simply a series of expressions of universal essences) not only because its geographical extent has fluctuated, but because it gradually acquired, and then lost, an empire. The pageantry of empire, and particularly the pageantry of Indian empire, was distinct and spectacular. Between the two world wars Edwin Lutyens created splendid architectural images for the British Empire in India long after the imperial crown had ceased to exercise political rule. At the same time, a relationship between government and governed which for most people most of the time had been local and parochial was slowly shifting to engage a state which had been largely remote with a public social life which was becoming increasingly active and evident. As the governing role of the monarchy faded, its public presence grew.

The change had been neither simple nor steady, but the distances traversed both in the identity of the monarch and in the identities of the governed population, as they were cultivated, qualified, or changed in engagement with the monarchy, were substantial. The first audience for the monarch had been the monarch, and beyond that the court. The identity which was cultivated and expressed was one of lordship, and any challenge to the incumbent of the throne was an attempt to seize lordship. Richard III was ousted in 1485, like many of his predecessors, in a struggle for dominance and spoils. Religious leadership had engaged secular rule when its other involvement in the life of the population was limited. The irruption of religious dispute into government in the sixteenth century at a time when secular rule was itself being extended gave a dual dimension to the identities of monarchs. In the tumult of reformation and counter-reformation, monarchs identified themselves not solely in terms of royal splendour, but, as they had always done, in terms of religious faith. When the population was largely unmobilised, the cultivation and maintenance of religious orthodoxy had been the principal regular involvement of government with the lives of its subjects. The Reformation and Counter-Reformation conflicts within European Christianity merely intensified this involvement. A young Henry VIII, before he broke with the papacy, earned the title 'Defender of the Faith' from the pope in recognition of his tract against Luther. Religion still followed the monarch rather than vice versa, but though there was no novelty in religious dispute under Henry and his successors Edward VI, Mary, and Elizabeth, a conflict between the religious identity of the sovereign and that of subjects would frequently be resolved by imprisonment, death, or exile.

The civil wars of the seventeenth century revealed how far a clash of religious identities, and the other aspects of identity with which religion was interwoven, could threaten the loyalties of powerful subjects and the lordship of the sovereign. The dispute in England (and Scotland and Wales) in the seventeenth century over the monarch's religion was not simply a matter of what went on behind the windows into men's souls. It was in fact not about that at all, but about the structure of authority which corresponded to different conceptions of the church, and of authority and structures of government within both the church and society. Protestantism was not necessarily either tolerant or egalitarian, but Catholicism was – not necessarily in essence, but in that time and place – hierarchical, absolute, authoritarian, and paternalist. So while the royal presence of Henry VIII had been composed of kingship as a unique identity sustained by no characteristic other than royal grandeur and divine sanction, with purple and cloth of gold denied to all but the royal family and with a richness of dress which set him apart,[12] that of Charles II after the English Civil War and the execution of his father had a religious dimension which engaged, or attempted to engage, with the demanding religious aspirations of at least the mightier of his subjects. For Charles I to flirt with Rome was to flirt with absolutism. For James II to do so was to attempt an absolutist coup and risk rejection by powerful subjects. The restored monarchy after 1660 operated in a kingdom where the religious identities of subjects, or of powerful subjects, were a constraint on the public identity of the king. Charles II tempted Louis XIV with the possibility of his own conversion to Roman Catholicism and a return of Britain to the Roman church, but could do so only in secret, whilst the increasingly evident Catholicism of his brother, James, was an identity clash which threatened the regime in a way it would not have done for the Tudors. Charles found it expedient to instruct uncharacteristically fervent attendance at communion by whole swathes of his court and household in order to display the pious adherence of his regime to the Anglican church and the security of at least his powerful subjects from the threat of Rome.[13] The Glorious Revolution of 1688 was indeed a revolution if it marked the transition from *cuius regio, eius religio*, to *cuius religio, eius regio*.

Attempts by monarchy to, if not mirror the identities of its subjects, then at least to modify itself in such a way as to appear recognisable even if not familiar, could sometimes dismay as much as they reassured. George III's perambulations around Windsor in the undistinguished country dress of the upper classes or even the gentry was the subject of some ridicule. Nonetheless, a king who attempted to place himself if not on an even level with his subjects, then at least within reach of them, was very different from one who, like Charles II, touched thousands of suppliant sick in the healing ritual of the king's evil, an identity which, if it did not claim a divine dimension for monarchy, claimed powers beyond the capacity of ordinary humanity. By the reign of Charles's niece Anne, the numbers touched were only in the hundreds, and the practice was not continued by her successors. The fading of any magic or mystery other than social and political distinction in the monarch was a feature of the shifting of the monarchy's expressed identity from divine ruler to leader of the ruling class, and to the epitome of an 'Englishness' which was ostensibly classless but became increasingly class and culture specific in a society which was more and more diverse.

In this process monarchy was active in the invention of its own identity, and in cultivating its presence in this way it has been ingenious, imaginative, and ambitious. George III's perambulations as a rural gentleman may have jarred, but his granddaughter's appropriation and transformation of rebel attire was theatrically successful. The tartan, which in the eighteenth century had been associated with Jacobitism and the rebellion of Prince Charles Edward Stuart and was hence banned, became in the nineteenth century an expression of royal affinity with the monarchy's Scottish subjects. When in her northern kingdom, Queen Victoria chose architectural and human surroundings which were visibly and distinctively Scottish (figure 10). When Victoria and Albert visited their northern kingdom, they wore a courtly Scottish fancy dress with as much dedication as Marie Antoinette played the role of picturesque peasant around the Petit Trianon in the previous century.[14] The long reign of Victoria was a transitional monarchy, creating new forms of both public presence

10 Queen Victoria in Scotland

and privacy, a public presence which, after the death of Albert, was demanded from a monarch for whom privacy was a sought-for response to personal loss.

The accommodation of royal identity to a public, popular one could engage all aspects of royalty. Names not only described character, they could compose it, and the change of the royal family name from Saxe-Coburg Gotha to Windsor during the First World War illustrates how the monarchy had come to be defined by the nation, rather than vice versa. The monarchy drew its identity from the culture, language, and names of those whose state it symbolised, and so if its name associated it with a hostile nation, it was the name of the monarch, not the character of the nation, which had to adapt. A monarchy which attempted to amend the religion or dress of its subjects to its own tastes transmuted slowly towards public concessions to what was seen as the culture of its subjects.

The move from a ruling monarchy, whose rituals were principally for the governing elite, to a social and symbolic monarchy in an open and mobilised society was slow and fragmentary, but steadily proceeding through to the stage which Frank Prochaska has described as the 'welfare monarchy'[15]. Royal weddings, unlike coronations and royal funerals, continued throughout the nineteenth and into the twentieth century to be important contracts of state, but of a state which stood above and apart from the mass of the population, and what was necessary was that they be contracted with appropriate solemnity in the presence of representatives of social and political power and privilege. As David Cannadine puts it, 'great royal ceremonials were not so much shared, corporate events as remote, inaccessible group rites, performed for the benefit of the few rather than the edification of the many ... not so much a jamboree to delight the masses, but a group right in which the aristocracy, the church and the royal family corporately re-affirmed their solidarity (or animosity) behind closed doors.'[16] Not until the wedding of Prince Albert, later to be George VI, and Lady Elizabeth Bowes-Lyon in 1923, was a royal wedding staged as a theatrical event for public appreciation, and therefore held not in the secluded elegance of St James's Palace, but in Westminster Abbey. The groom's father, George V, though not a radical monarch, was aware of the claims that a democratising society might make on the family which provided its formal headship, and of the benefits for public satisfaction with the social and political order which might flow from the pomp and glamour of ecclesiastical and state theatre. Royal weddings thus followed the example of public spectacle already set by royal funerals. But it required the growth of swift and easy transport by rail, followed by the dramatic expansion of communication with radio and cinema, together with a steady shift of population from country to town, to make possible a degree of familiarity with the public face of monarchy which an earlier local and face-to-face society could not provide.[17]

The changes in the cultivation of monarchical identity both reflect and are part of changes in government and politics within the British Isles, and in the composition of the public identities of both subjects and political participants. Monarchy in a mobilised society is a different institution from monarchy in a merely ruled society, whilst developing aspects of democracy are accompanied and either sustained or obstructed by the changing identity of monarchy. The audience for the presentation of monarchical identity has changed from the small and elite occasions of the middle ages, through the grand and festive coronation of George III, to the popular festival of the coronation of Elizabeth II in 1953.[18] The funeral of Diana, Princess of Wales, would have been inconceivable even half a century earlier.

The transition since the Stuarts has been from the king's evil to the welfare monarchy. The relics of the former survive in the rituals of the latter, but nonetheless the essential move is from enchantment to secularism, and from divine right and grace to feudal or patriarchal care and philanthropy. The move from a reigning monarch to a caring monarch, from ruling splendour by right to a monarchy which donates time and resources and encourages others to do so, parallels the development of a representative rather than a hereditary power in government, despite the perseverance of a hereditary power in legislation.[19] Such a monarchy presents an unceremonial public face rather than an enchanted one. It is not only more on public display, but can perform that function more conveniently, less stiffly, and with less difference of identity between itself and its subjects. It is easier for a patron to visit a hospital in more or less ordinary clothes than for a divinely touched sovereign to do so. But the transition over the years has often been difficult, and the coils of protocol have tangled the path to a monarchical culture less alien to the culture of subjects and citizens. Bridging the divide between the life of royalty and the life of more ordinary subjects and citizens could frequently be a negotiation by means of minute and prosaic detail. One issue which the debate over the monarchy became contained within or diverted to, following the coronation of George VI in May 1937, was whether or not MPs could wear lounge suits to royal garden parties[20]. Tom Nairn has presented an account of the monarchy as exercising a residual and unobtrusive power, not to intervene in society or politics, but to sustain its hierarchies. In a mobilised society that power is exercised at every point of royal contact, just as much as it was when monarchs cured the king's evil, and so the importance of lounge suits lies in the fact that they can be thought to be important. In that case royal garden parties can be seen as a minor instrument of class dominance, a small burnisher of deference.

Insofar as the identity of monarchy contributes to the identities of its subjects, that contribution can range from a confirmation of distinction and privilege to a confirmation of loyal-subject status in a legitimised hierarchical society. The circle of people for whom the monarchy provides an element of their identity has extended as the governmental power of the monarchy has shrivelled. The extension of a citizen public has been met by a monarchy which, whilst it still performs to small and privileged audiences, increasingly does so in a private capacity, while its formal activities are on public display, and to a public which all may join and consider themselves a part of. The shift came late, and whilst it followed the slow increase of mobilisation into democracy, it lagged behind it. The presentation of young women to the sovereign as the starting gate of an upper-class 'season' had ended well before the close of the twentieth century. But at the start of the twenty-first century the British monarchy still practised male primogeniture.

The transition from dressing room and private life to stage can be a feature of any kind of regime, but its character is part of the regime's character, and so different regimes can be observed to have different relations between back and front of house, and different styles of identity in each place. Politicians in the United Kingdom, certainly since the advent of television, do literally step from the dressing room onto the stage, being made up before they perform in front of the cameras, and this can be true of any form of government and politics where television is used. But the freer or more democratic a society, the greater the openness of private lives – even the lives of rulers, presidents, and monarchs – to public scrutiny. A democratic politics, requiring a degree of representativeness in its rulers, and unfriendly towards too great a visible distance between the lives of monarchs and presidents and the lives of ordinary people, will pressure monarchy to close the gap both between its front of house and its back of house, and between both of these and the perceived identities of ordinary citizens. As the monarchy loses power, its members become, in that respect, more like other members of the population. But at the same time the symbolic role of their office continues, and so there is a potentially growing tension between their public and their private lives. The monarchs of Britain by the nineteenth century had a front of house and a back of house. Royal progresses, both within the country and around the world, are difficult for a monarchy which rules a centralised state, but are a feature of one which is on display. So what matters is not only how the monarchy displays itself, but to whom it displays itself. It may be the case that the Wizard of Oz scenario, prosaic behind the curtain and flamboyant in front of it, is more frequently found in purely formal roles than in effective ones, in monarchies where the monarch is merely a constitutional symbol than in monarchies where the monarch rules. In that case, one strand in the cultivation of the monarchy from Tudors to Windsors will be the move towards a responsibility to display in public which, because it is liturgical, places fewer constraints of coherence on private life.

The monarchy, like other institutions and other persons, has cultivated its identity under the two justifications of tradition and change, appealing to and often creating ancient precedents for current practice, while adapting existing forms of identity to perceived changes in the society within which it lives. Prince Charles crafted a subtle harmonisation of these two justifications when he made known his intention to be not 'Defender of the Faith' but 'Defender of Faith', adapting a 500-year-old title to a contemporary variety of religious practices and loyalties.[21] The royal family associated the monarchy with faiths beyond Anglicanism and Christianity in the celebrations of the Queen's golden jubilee, and its members, including the Queen, visited a wide range of faiths throughout the year.[22] The service commemorating the fiftieth anniversary of the coronation in Westminster Abbey in 2003 was attended by representatives of the Baha'i, Muslim, Zoroastrian, Hindu, Jewish, Jain, Sikh, and Buddhist faiths, in addition to those of the principal Christian denominations.[23] The royal identity was crafted both by association with a religious community wider than traditional Anglicanism, and by distinction within that community in fulfilling a special role of responsibility and guardianship.

The slow transition from a feudal and governing to a social and public monarchy has been the subject of much description and interpretation. The role of the monarchy in public life has been critically and closely examined, its contribution to national or public identity dissected, praised, and condemned. Nairn's account of monarchy sits alongside Bagehot in arguing that it maintains social order through rituals and rhetoric which, whilst they do not involve the exercise of power or privilege by the sovereign, mask and maintain the work of those who do in fact govern or enjoy social, political, or economic domination.[24] But there is perhaps another function of monarchy in sustaining a particular British identity. Monarchy can be regarded not as a model of decorum and taste, or an expression and justification of deference and hierarchy, but as a distinctive and eccentric feature of a nation which can thereby mark itself off from others who can, by contrast, be portrayed as lacking tradition or venerable features of public life. None of this means that those, like Nairn, who condemn the monarchy are mistaken in a way which would cancel their antipathy, but it does mean that the consequences which they oppose are not sufficiently described in the account which they give of them. If events such as the

1953 coronation can be seen, as Shils and Young have described them, as occasions when common values are 're-affirmed and fortified', it is not necessarily the case that those values are ones of deference or subordination.[25] Coronations have provided an occasion for street parties as well as collective watching of still far-from-universal television, a peaceable parallel to Hegel's going to war in associating people with something broader than their isolated identity, and owing at least as much to the radical and subversive traditions of carnival as to loyal address, and not at all necessarily subservient to class hierarchies. Both for conservative supporters and radical opponents of the government, politics, and privileges of Britain, the monarchy plays an important part, so that simply to describe that part is, without further aspirations or aversions, neither to approve nor condemn it. The crowds outside Westminster Abbey who applauded critical comments within the building at the funeral of Princess Diana were not evidently being cultivated in class subordination. When, in 2012, the year of the Queen's diamond jubilee, IPSOS/MORI asked people what aspects of the country's life made them most proud to be British, 28% named the monarchy, but 37% named the National Health Service.[26] It might be as accurate to see even that 28% as supporting a hereditary republic as much as inherited privilege.[27]

Officers of state

The changing of the balance of power and functions within government has been accompanied by a shift of public political attention from monarchs to prime ministers, while the interest in the public and private conduct of monarchs as social phenomena has grown. As power rumbled from monarch to ministers, so it moved too from the Lords to the Commons. Lord Salisbury, the last prime minister from the Upper House, left office in 1902. As political attention shifted increasingly to ministers, so their public identity developed, from councillors to statesmen, and from statesmen to public figures – politicians representative of an increasingly democratic society. But at the same time there was a countermovement of identity. The move towards equality was matched by a reaction in the contrary direction in order to distinguish leaders from led, and if leaders were more ordinary, they were ordinary in a way which still marked them off from those whom they represented and led, out of the ordinary in their distinguished representativeness.

During the nineteenth century, political leaders could be given an elevated status which at the same time strengthened the status or identity of the person who conferred it. Mugs and plates celebrating politicians such as Gladstone with images and exhortations were both saying that the user or owner supports or admires Gladstone, and that he or she is a person who is to be associated with Gladstone, a Gladstonian. The cultivation of identity was two-sided. But by the end of the twentieth century, such a form of identification was rare for domestic politicians, jarring as it did with a suspicion of deference and an equation of democratic politics with sceptical distance from political leaders. Such hero worship was limited to international politics and, ironically, to radicals who spoke the language of transformative equality. Che Guevara was a more familiar face on tee shirts and posters than was Margaret Thatcher.

Securing a convincing harmony between representativeness and distinctiveness was never easy, and a visible excess in either direction could lead to ridicule. Michael Foot, when leader of the Labour Party, was criticised for not dressing sufficiently formally at the Cenotaph on Remembrance Sunday, and Tony Blair was considered by his critics to be overdoing his play-acting vernacularism in claiming to be 'a pretty straight kind of guy',[28] whilst his lord chancellor Derry Irvin was ridiculed for the opposite, the alleged grandiose ambitions in his material surroundings and his choice of wallpaper.

But whatever the balance between ordinariness and extraordinariness, a public identity becomes a far greater dimension of a politician's life with the development of a public. One account of this describes a theatrical division between public life and private life, even if the latter is generally difficult and frequently impossible to veil entirely from an inquisitive media. Tony Blair, whose public image was that of 'a pretty straightforward guy', religious but not excessively so, an ordinary family man with ordinary family interests, took steps in 2007 to remove from the published diary of his former press aide Alastair Campbell passages which portrayed him as bad-tempered and foul-mouthed, and further fine-tuned his popular identity by avoiding wearing spectacles in public.[29] Harold Wilson's preferred nicotine was not from a pipe, but for public visibility a pipe was his preferred image;[30] the Conservative leader and prime minister David Cameron might cycle for public consumption, but could not conceal the fact that with friends and colleagues he preferred stirrups to pedals.[31] Even so, the distance between the two identities was in each case qualitatively different from the gulfs which made tales of princes disguised as paupers plausible. Each instance suggests a publicisation of the hitherto private aspects of political leaders, or rather of a public version of the private. This was a style possibly first employed by Attlee in the presentation of him as the man next door.

The entanglement of private and public, and the continual leakage of the one into the other, was neatly encapsulated in the function of Number 10 Downing Street, a house where the prime minister might not live, so that there is a house which is not a house where the prime minister acts out his public role (but not in public) and a flat in the house next door where he is the private person who happens to fill that role, though where he also conducts business relevant to that role. An awareness of the confusion, and a willingness to accept it, is breached only if the politicians themselves fail to perform as the duality of roles requires. The offence caused by Andrew Mitchell's alleged description of police officers as 'plebs' was not that he held himself, if he did, above ordinary voters, but that he was believed to have said that he did.

The 'private' lives of public figures are relevant in a democracy in a way they are not in autocracies, and 'private' actions and tastes are taken as an indicator of distance from or closeness to either the people, or the assumed character of the people. The more a population is mobilised, the greater the relevance of private lives to public office, since the greater and more widespread the desire that rulers and leaders be both typical of the population and distinguished within it.

The military

Before government does anything else, it wages war. It wages war even before it becomes a government, and does so both against other communities and against those over whom it seeks to govern. Subject populations are the first to understand this foundation of ruling, and soldiers have consequently been frequently and persistently regarded with a mixture of suspicions ranging from scepticism to hostility. One strand in popular sentiment has been a hostility to a standing army as an instrument of excessive state power, another a suspicion of soldiers, and particularly soldiers, as potential troublemakers when on leave and on the streets. This was the sentiment described by Kipling in his poem 'Tommy', with the sting in its tail against a public view which turns its sympathies and antipathies through 180 degrees when national security is felt to be militarily threatened.

> For it's Tommy this, an' Tommy that, an' 'Chuck him out, the brute!'
> But it's 'Saviour of 'is country' when the guns begin to shoot;[32]

The presentation and perception of the army, navy, and air force have been part of the presentation and perception of themselves by the various strands which make up the population. Kipling's polarity recurs again and again, and 'Saviour of 'is country' has many versions, from Kipling's, to Churchill's 'Never in the history of human conflict has so much been owed by so many to so few.' When the security and safety of the population are felt to be threatened then armed bodies with whom ordinary people can identify are looked on with solidarity. But whilst armed forces may in those circumstances be seen as a special part of the community of ordinary men and women, that perception, whilst strengthened by external threat, needs other sources as well. Before the mobilisation of the population, armed bands were no more likely to be welcome because they fought for the king than if they fought for one of the king's rivals, and could be seen as at best an incursion or a pest, at worst a menace to life and property. Identification between warriors and citizens can be strengthened by real or supposed enemies, but it requires some prior perception of common identity, some sense of common participation and membership of a governed community. Soldiers of the king may not necessarily be regarded as anything less alien than soldiers of invading warlords, and whilst the successor to the Royal Flying Corps in the twentieth century has a monarchical prefix, it was known only as the 'RAF', an acronym which relinquished any claims to aristocratic or monarchical legitimation.

If there is there a real move from soldiers of the king to soldiers of the country, it depended on a move in a democratic direction sufficient for not just generals and admirals, but ordinary soldiers and sailors, to be regarded as citizens, spouses, parents, or children in uniform. Once that happens, and the population as a whole is involved in and affected by a war, hostility can be replaced by a benign scepticism, and cartoonists such as Bruce Bairnsfather can mock the military life with the recommendation that 'If you knows of a better 'ole, go to it.'[33] When that happens, a heroic construction of fighting life can no longer enjoy a monopoly of public sentiment, but suspicion of members of the armed forces can transpose into sympathy and support.

The celebration and commemoration of the military parallels the history of deference in the rest of society. Up until the end of the eighteenth century, kings were commemorated in public display, and aristocrats in private memorials, but the celebration of military prowess stopped there. The Napoleonic Wars, despite the fact that they were fought under the banner of king and tradition against not only tyranny but also revolutionary equality, were marked by a slight move away from war being expressed as the king's alone. Admiral Lord Nelson was given a state funeral with rituals adapted from those used for royalty, and although in the celebration of heroism in the war against France no one below the rank of captain in the Royal Navy or major-general in the army was represented in funerary sculpture, though ordinary soldiers were displayed around their podiums in various poses of admiration, nonetheless the monopoly of single leadership had been eroded.[34] The first regimental memorials were placed in St Paul's after the Crimean War, and by the time of the Great War, the common soldier was precisely the person who was represented on war memorials, and the names of all those killed were listed, the only order in which they were ranked being alphabetical, the public successor to the former celebration of hierarchy in both life and death.[35]

The public identity of the armed forces of the crown increased both as the mobilisation of the population increased, and as the country was seen to be threatened by outside violence. But whilst mobilisation and democratisation eroded the remoteness of armed forces, they did not do so in any single or uniform way, and the nature of perceived threats and the extent and location of danger were a component of popular perceptions, responses, and degrees and character of identification with fighting men and women. During the Second World War, when the threat to life and security was felt by the whole population and all adults could be regarded as part of the conduct of the war, members of the armed forces were family members on special duties as much as they were members of a distinct and separate set of organisations. If on the other hand fighting was limited, involving the armed forces but not the population as a whole either as producers of war materials or as conscripts, then whilst popular support for the armed forces might be as strong, it was support for a distinct and separate element in the national community, rather than solidarity with men and women who were part of a single national mobilised war effort. In the case of the returning soldiers, sailors, and air-force personnel from the Falklands War, it was celebration of a popular assertion of identity against an attempted alien incursion; in the case of respect paid to the returning dead from Afghanistan, the popular response had the added element of sympathy for men and women who were being sent to a conflict for which popular support was rapidly being replaced by sceptical bewilderment and anger as to what British armed forces were still doing there and why their lives continued to be placed at risk. Armed forces can be seen as a constituent part of a nation and its identity when the bulk of the population are not involved in war or when the fighting is geographically remote, but only once the population has moved substantially in the direction of mobilisation or democratisation. Before that, 'the King's wars' are no more than a remote tale, like dragons and mermaids.

Toffs and the survival record of hierarchy

'Society' as an object of public interest, admiration, and gossip was replaced during the second half of the twentieth century by performers and entertainers and sportspeople, with the retention in the public eye of members of the royal family and growing attention, though not in the front rank, paid to politicians. This did not necessarily mean that society, with a lowercase 's', had levelled out or become more egalitarian, but it did mean that the character of the peaks had changed, as had their relation to ordinary people and distance from or closeness to them, and the possibility, or perceived possibility, of ordinary people scaling those peaks. It took a very elaborate set of expectations to see oneself as king or queen, but only energy and talent to aspire to the top ten or the premier football league. The public images with which ordinary people could identity and about which they could listen, watch, or read were simultaneously accessibly ordinary, and aspirationally different.

The markers of hierarchy and the character of hierarchy can change without a society becoming any more equal. Language, which used to distinguish sharply a socially and economically privileged minority, did so less and less after the first half of the twentieth century.[36] George Orwell had assured 'the sinking middle class', fearful of the proletariat below, that 'we have nothing to lose but our aitches'.[37] But very shortly afterwards the upper classes began acquiring their consonants. Whilst a single accent lost its privileged dominance and found itself mildly ridiculed instead, varieties of speech became components of a popular identity which, whilst it was not egalitarian, was not formally hierarchical either.

The common people: subjects and citizens

When Bede in the eighth century wrote his history of the church and people of England, the protagonists were kings, princes, and priests, and their actions, decisions, successes, and failures were presented as sufficient evidence of the history of all. The normal invisibility of the greater part of the population changed little over the following centuries. Popular irruptions into the world of secular and ecclesiastical lordship in the middle ages were just that, invasions from outside or below which might shake or damage the structures of political, social, and religious order, but were not part of them. By contrast, an account of a mobilised society, and even more an account of a democratising society, cannot pause at the borders of the elite, but must describe the culture which exists beyond those limits and which encroaches on those boundaries, and hence stretches and thins them and renders them more permeable. Each move in a democratic direction makes it more difficult to sustain accounts which either describe a uniformity of identity or, by not transgressing the boundaries of domination, give no account of the identity or identities of the mobilised. The greater the progress along the serpentine road through mobilisation to democratisation has been, the greater the potential variety of identities, and the greater their potential public salience. The social and political emergence of the mass of the population has been uneven, contested, and partial. The advance has taken many forms and has ascribed many titles to the participants: the people, the public, the working class, and, as the electorate has expanded, the voters and, more selectively, taxpayers. Each of these terms is more than simply a label, since it has contributed, by shaping perceptions, to shaping the things perceived, a broad-scale instance of dynamic nominalism.

A distinction of fundamental importance in this uneven process has been between mobilisation from above and mobilisation from below. On the one hand, governing and controlling elites have mobilised as human resources for economic or military ends those who previously were marginalised or anonymous. Such mobilisation has involved not only the enrolment of those who previously were excluded from or socially invisible in the exercise of political, economic, or social power, but, in the act of recruiting them, the creation of new or amended categories whereby the identity of the mobilised is itself amended, cultivated, or created. Mobilisation creates the raw materials for a public world. But whilst that public world is mobilised, it is not democratised, and the initiatives from above are to enrol rather than to enfranchise, to modify the identity of the population as a whole, but to do so in a way which maintains its subordinate position. On the other hand, demands from outside the governing elite, by no means all of them from the least privileged, have slowly and with mixed success increased the numbers of those who, by extending their identity into social visibility or social power, cultivate and become a public society.

Mobilisation from above

Elites in a society whose population is becoming mobilised begin to accommodate their identity to the growing presence of the wider population. But they do so both by increasingly including that population in the community by association with which they identify themselves, and at the same time by distinguishing themselves as exceptional instances of that community's character. Evolution of identities has accompanied evolution of the relations of leaders to subjects, and to subjects who were increasingly becoming citizens. The mobilisation of a population from above has been carried out to serve taxation, production, and war, and has involved both a greater public presence and identity for the mass of the population, and an extension of the institutions of government which regulate them. A major aspect of identity, religion, while it has always been a concern of government, has not been treated from above in a way which increased the public identity of the mass of the population, but rather in a manner which cultivated, with varying effectiveness, their docile compliance. Attempts to regulate, promote, or prohibit the various forms of religious observance, whilst they required government to engage with the mass of the population, did so in a way which maintained and strengthened the gap between rulers and ruled, and constrained rather than promoted a greater public identity and presence for the mass of the people. Taxation required people to pay, production required them to work, and war required them to arm and train, but religious compliance required no more than silent presence in churches. In the interests of taxation, production, and war, by contrast, government not only extended its regulation and organisation of the population but, by this action, shaped the social contours of its territory and cultivated and created collective identities.[38]

New or enhanced public identities had many aspects, but one of the most immediately apparent features of greater social visibility is the actual visibility of dress. The mobilisation of the population, or sections of it, created or enhanced public roles which acquired a distinctive dress that indicated the public function as distinct from the social status of the person filling it. But the boundary between clothing as indicating public function and clothing as indicating social superiority has frequently been permeable and imprecise. Ecclesiastical, judicial, and military dress have long, though not unbroken, histories of distinctiveness, but ones which moved from individual distinction to collective identity as government expanded and the population was increasingly mobilised lacked such a clear resource of traditional costumery. Medieval warriors distinguished themselves with heraldry, but they also disguised themselves, if kings, with duplication, an early response to the lethal or potentially lethal consequence of the extremes of identity distinction. Heraldry says who you are, uniform, like livery, says whom you serve. There have been times when senior clergy dressed not distinctively as clergy, but distinctively as rich and powerful members of a superior layer of the population. Uniforms are a feature of societies where identity is validated by association with a group, person, or institution. As long as a society is uniform and hierarchical, with a recognisable elite, livery serves to cultivate the identity of those outside the elite who serve its members and draw a part of their identity from that service. The role of uniform is different from that of livery in that only subordinates wear livery, whilst leaders can and do wear uniform, even though they do so in a way which indicates their elevated status as distinguished individuals within the broader association. Whole sections of society move into uniform as a public space becomes created and occupied by the adult populace. The mobilisation of a population from above moves from an elite which has put its servants and supporters in livery, to a state which puts its population in uniform. Livery is part of subordination to an employer, uniform of both subordination to a state or eminence in the exercise of the state's power. There is a wide range of public functions for which a mobilised or mobilising society may provide uniforms, but the two functions which involve the greatest numbers and in the most visible way, are the police and armed forces.

The slow shift from an agricultural to an urban and industrial population was associated with a new salience of the identity of this population, not only or principally because of the different ways of living and working which this involved, but because new ways of living required definition, organisation, and identification in a way which existing ones did not. As a categorised resource in the social planning and management of industrial reformers – Owen, Salt, Lever, and Cadbury – 'the people' or 'the working classes' were given a new prominence in towns and suburbs built to model and cultivate a social order. This was not a neat or uniform movement and has had uneven and fragmentary progress. The incorporation of 'the people' into military consciousness became a part of government with the introduction of conscription in the First Word War from 1916, and the celebration after it of all adult combatants as equal in the anonymity of the unknown warrior. Incorporation into 'Britishness' develops with passports in something approaching their contemporary form from 1855 and in a more standard produced form with the British Nationality and Status of Aliens Act in 1914, before further mobilisation into citizenship.

The shift of power away from the monarchy enhanced the public status of those, however limited as a proportion of the adult population, whose electoral mandate supplied the members for one of the two chambers of parliament. The move to add an active and public dimension to the status of 'subject' drew a society in its wake, and is accompanied by a growing public identity of people outside the circles of the political and governing elite.

Whilst changes in public identity and the emergence of a slowly expanded and diversified public have had a multiplicity of causes, government has been active in the process. In late twentieth-century Britain, the ascendancy of market and economic liberal ideology was accompanied by a further twist in identity cultivation from above, with the renaming of a clutch of previously distinct roles as 'customers', a title eclipsing the specific and distinguishing descriptions: clients, patients, audiences, passengers. The linguistic strategy of narrowing the scope of politics and widening the scope of commerce as far as it was possible to do retained only two designations beyond the embrace of cash transaction: voters, and worshippers.

One aspect of the cultivation of an identity of customers rather than citizens meant that identity by association and by distinction redefined the associated population in such a way as to marginalise substantial layers of it, heightening the distance in identity between those people and the distinguished minority. If the customer is always right, the customer is also always to blame since all outcomes are the result of free consumer choice, and inequality is simply the result of lack of aspiration or lack of determination. Whole sections of the population could be stigmatised as chavs, an identity which Owen Jones has presented as serving to justify inequality.[39] But it functions also to maintain the identity of the more privileged as rooted in their association with the population as a whole, while at the same time sustaining their distinction and difference from that population by marginalising a section of it.

Mobilisation from below: economic discontents in the public arena

The slow, irregular, and obstacle-strewn progress from a mobilised population towards a democratic one was constituted by the emergence first of subjects, then of civil society, then of citizens. Whilst a formal political identity has grown for wider and wider sections of the population, a converse desire to control and limit the vigour or potential vigour of citizen politics – cultivating a quiet, orderly, and uncomplaining citizen identity rather than an active, unpredictable, and assertive one – has been a persistent feature of government and politics. It is feature of citizen identity which, conversely, has been continually challenged, and principally from below. At the same time as the political identity, through citizenship, was slowly extended, so too the economic identities of the population, which if they had impinged on government had done so in an invasive manner with riot, sabotage, or disorder, became a part of the political public world, and the concerns of ordinary workers became a part of their enhanced public identity.

By the eighteenth century, a new or greater public identity for sections of the adult population had been achieved sporadically and outside the established rubric, by demonstration as in support of Wilkes, or riot as in support of Lord George Gordon. But in the nineteenth century there were also movements of a more sustained nature, on the one hand advocating political reform and campaigning for the Charter, on the other demanding improved conditions and wages for employees, not only – as with Luddism and protests by workers in such domestically based forms of production as weaving – in defence of old systems, but increasingly by those employed in the new expanding factory-based forms of production. Whereas the first was a contribution to the cultivation of a purely political and constitutional element in developing public identities, the second was an extension of the identity of sections of the population from an economic world which still remained private, into a public dimension of economic claims and economic grievances.

The movement towards democracy has never been completed. A democratic constitution requires a democratic society to give it substance, and the degree to which this has been achieved has been uneven if democratic politics are to extend beyond freedom at election times. A population with a limited franchise had few peaceful entries into politics beyond demonstrating, lobbying, and heckling. The carnivalesque possibilities of the last of these at election hustings where candidates were nominated, and at the election meetings where politicians met not only the electorate but those who were excluded from the electorate, were frequently vigorously exploited not only before but after the extension of the franchise towards formal democracy. As late as 1959, Robin Day, standing in Hereford, had his platform taken over and his microphone broken by not always sober citizens.[40]

Carnival is never something leaders welcome unless they have already tamed and organised it. When it is unpredictable, uncontrolled, or spontaneous, even in well-established democratic polities, professional politicians resent and resist such democratic inroads from the population outside. In London in the twenty-first century, Brian Haw, a single protestor camped on the grass outside the Houses of Parliament, caused unusual annoyance to professional politicians, and provoked laborious attempts to remove him wholly out of proportion to any actual political impediments his posters and placards caused.[41] The prodigious legal and political energies directed against Haw were a striking illustration of the thinness of political skins. A similar sensitivity was revealed at the 2005 Labour Party Conference when a cry of 'Rubbish!' from Walter Wolfgang, an elderly party member, during a speech on Iraq by Foreign Secretary Jack Straw resulted in a rush of security guards and the forcible expulsion of the dissident pensioner from the hall.[42] Lack of predictability or uniformity is a component (which is much stronger than an indicator) of democracy and civil society. It is both the necessary vital energy of democracy, and a phenomenon which can flourish only in a democratic state.

The slow loosening, though not disappearance, of the divisions between the terrace levels of a relatively homogeneous social hierarchy has been associated not with growing uniformity of identity, but with greater diversity. The horizontal divisions of an earlier mobilised population have been complemented by vertical ones. The identities of class have been joined by, amongst others, more substantial and numerous identities of religion. At the same time there has been a decline of a popular or working-class political identity – no more banners or brass bands; the miners' dispute of 1984–85 was the last grand occasion for this instance of political celebration and collective ritual proclamation. But the assertion of citizen identity from below, in however fragmented ways, has persisted as both an active contribution to and an active component of the identity of a democratic demos.

Mobilisation from below: clothing

The mobilisation of the population from above was conducted in part by putting people into uniform. The mobilisation, and democratisation, of the population from below was similarly conducted in part by the cultivation of styles of clothing and of uniforms which challenged explicitly or implicitly the monopolies of the state and the hierarchies of fashion. This was done in two ways: by adopting the modes of dominant groups and hence transgressing social borders and challenging the monopolies of stylistic identity, and by ignoring dominant conventions and dressing in ways thought, at least from above, as improper, slovenly, or stylistically subversive. In the case of the first challenge, a common complaint about the clothing of the lower strata of society had frequently been that they sought to dress like their 'betters', often with cast-offs or cheap imitations. This was a matter of alarm for the more privileged at a time when clothing could be an immediate sign of social status and a swift way of distinguishing between acceptable or admissible, and unacceptable or inadmissible persons. But whilst innovation or disruption might come from below, elites were able to develop their own refined versions of the vernacular, dealing with the challenge by assimilating it and raising it to a level of expense or sophistication where exclusivity was re-established. In the course of the eighteenth century there was an apparent shift from the lower orders seeking to dress like the upper, to elite fashion following and glamorising the popular in a mode at least as widespread as, and perhaps more so than, Marie Antoinette and her entourage dressing as peasants in the Petite Trianon.[43] Similarly, in the twentieth century the paper clips as earrings of punk were assimilated by the gilded, plated, and bejewelled versions of the prosaic interloper.

Dressing in defiance or simple disregard of convention could, if nothing else, cause great disturbance with little effort. Political and constitutional democracy had still advanced to include only a minority of the adult population by the beginning of the twentieth century. Social democracy was similarly restrained. Class remained a physical and sartorial dimension of visible public life, and whilst by the 1920s the boundaries were being breached, those who breached them risked being seen, at least by those into whose territory they climbed, either as 'impostors' or as hooligans. *The Times* reported with outrage that the participants in the Kinder Scout mass trespass of 1932 were a 'mob of young men and women – hatless, raucous, yellow jerseyed, slung with concertinas'.[44]

But in a class society which recognises but does not admire horizontal divisions, there can be a radical politics which makes a point of dressing in 'King's couture', if that is the equivalent of the King's English. In the

1930s there were radicals who took care to avoid the kind of appearance which had so shocked *The Times* on the occasion of the Kinder Scout trespass. The Communist Party allegedly instructed its sometimes bohemian members to adopt 'smart' dress, so as not to give the impression of being outside the social pale.

Gillray's cartoon of George III traumatising an agricultural worker by dressing across social borders illustrates the sartorial cultures of the eighteenth century existing within horizontal divisions of class. Those of the late twentieth and twenty-first centuries do not have such clear distinctions. The change was slow but substantial. Writing in the middle of the twentieth century, Richard Hoggart was able to observe that:

> Cheap mass-produced clothing has reduced the immediately recognizable differences between classes, but not as greatly as many think. A Saturday-night crowd leaving the cinema in the city centre may look superficially one. A closer glance from an expert of either sex, from a middle-class woman or man particularly conscious of clothes, will usually be sufficient even nowadays for them to 'place' most people around them.[45]

Anthony Crosland, at the same time, was able to argue that:

> different social classes can be instantly distinguished by their dress (especially men's clothes; though only a very insensitive person can share the now popular view that one cannot tell a woman's background by her clothes), eating (and even drinking) habits, taste in furniture, type of house, style of entertainment, sporting tastes, and leisure activities generally.[46]

But by the 1960s class no longer existed as an immediately visible physical and sartorial dimension, although there was a range of subcultures. Teddy boys had already presented an image which seemed to have little to do with class, either as a snub to convention or a flamboyance of expenditure. Duffle coats, initially associated with naval heroism, illustrated the flexibility of the meanings attached to dress, as they were adopted as the costume of frequently politically demonstrating radicalism. As the twentieth century progressed into its second half, Britain increasingly moved from a society stratified by dress, demeanour, and physique to a variegated bazaar. Extravagance in dress or appearance continued, indeed flourished, but was no longer the expression of class or caste, but only of either eccentricity or flamboyant wealth.

The state of clothes by the end of the twentieth century

The assertion of public identities from below, or from outside the circle of elites, has regularly caused concern and sometimes attempts at regulation from above. The more mobilised a society, and the greater the potential variety of associations and of possible conflict between them, the greater the likelihood of attempts to regulate, restrain, or prohibit livery. The livery of servants to the wealthy, the aristocratic, or the powerful does not threaten social peace or social cohesion. The livery of mass political organisations may, in contrast, challenge existing hierarchies or the peaceful coexistences of public life. The 1936 Public Order Act asserted and enforced the state's monopoly of uniforms, save when they could not be conceived as challenging political or public uniforms – the Salvation Army, Girl Guides, Boy Scouts.

There is the possibility of a less obvious but more substantial dilution of government initiative and control through the fading or erosion of distinctions as a result of the proliferation of uniforms – armed forces, post office, police, fire brigade, prison service, transport staff, traffic wardens, community support officers, or private security staff – in a way which partly dissolves the boundaries between the crown and society, so that a uniformed person may be a constable, but is nonetheless recognisably also an ordinary citizen and householder, and may be a private security guard either under contract to the crown or displaying the authority of his or her uniform for a profit-seeking commercial organisation. The more people are mobilised, the greater the possible blurring and fading of the differences between livery, uniform, and fashion. But the resulting distribution of clothing between livery, uniform, and fashion is both flexible and malleable. In a state where the dominant, or aspiring, ideology places a high value on markets and profit-seeking, the authority of dress may be extended well beyond the frontiers of public service and public office. A regime which replaces a variety of functions – passenger, audience, client, patient – with the single title of 'customer' has also been marked by a privatisation of uniform, whilst livery has become a mark of corporate rather than of domestic employment. At the same time, the service role of the liveried servant in domestic employment has been transferred to service roles in the market and in the collective provision of service roles. Road sweepers, coffee-shop assistants, and postal-delivery workers will wear company livery; their managers will not. Rather than assert its monopoly of uniform, government has cultivated a gradual progression from the uniform of public service to the uniform of private employment, diluting thereby the unique authority of public service, but potentially enhancing that of profit-seeking. This is a shift of emphasis, not a unique or novel innovation. Those employees of railway companies who dealt directly with the public wore company uniform in the nineteenth century. But with a shift of public functions to profit-seeking organisations, exercisers of coercive functions which had formerly been the monopoly of government were marked by uniforms which on the one hand laid claim to governing authority or public service but on the other marked a loyalty not to the state but to commercial organisation: prison officers, security guards, postal-delivery workers.

As clothing became less and less effective as a way of proclaiming privilege, extravagance by the end of the twentieth century was increasingly expressed in jewellery and cars, rather than in clothes. When affordable clothing was not available, the mere fact of having anything more than the functional minimum of 'ordinary' dress, with the possibility of Sunday best for special occasions, could proclaim wealth. Once mass-produced clothing makes the constituency of purchasers the larger part of the population, so that 'Sunday best' is universalised and diversified, distinction becomes a choice of style which indicates, not wealth, but dissent, or religious affiliation, or social group. Abstemiousness in clothing had always performed this function, and the sombreness of Puritanism was continued into the eighteenth century with Quaker and Methodist admonishments for the faithful to dress simply. But now not only simplicity but extravagance was widely available. In all these changes in clothing, the broader identity paradox flourishes. On the one hand it is a search for individual distinctiveness, on the other a cultivation of identity by means of association, the brand or label being more important than the quality or character of the product. The visible identity of dress proclaims both identity as part of a wider constituency and identity as unlike anyone else.

Walk

Lear's fool's advice never to walk if you could ride was aimed at social and political success and survival, not at weight reduction or health. The development of the railways and later of the public tram and omnibus created a society in which riding rather than walking was not something necessarily and obviously enjoyed only by a few, or by small numbers, of the privileged in an expensive carriage, but was, as the title omnibus indicated, a possibility if not for all then for large sections of the population. The device of retaining hierarchy within mass transport by the division into first, second, and third class did so within a system which nonetheless ended the privilege of the minority to be the only ones who habitually did not, or need not, walk. Nor is social distinction ever simply a matter of wealth or expenditure. In the early years of the twenty-first century, cycling flourished not as a cheap alternative for those who could not afford a car, but as a lifestyle choice. At the same time, privilege and the advantages purchased by greater wealth were in some areas concealed rather than flaunted. Whilst railways and airlines retained the complimentary title of 'first class' to reassure the fortunate of their good fortune, second-class and lower designations and facilities were veiled in titles such as 'standard' and 'tourist', ensuring that whilst the privileged were assured of their distinction, the less privileged were not stigmatised, since, whatever their lesser wealth, they were still necessary as customers. The use of titles in this way to assure the larger proportion of travellers that they were not discriminated against was an illustration at one and the same time of the techniques available for the maintenance of privilege, and of the need to avoid alienating the majority.

Talk

What was expressed in clothing and transport was expressed equally clearly in speech. Like visible appearance, audible evidence contributes to public identity, and so gives an impression of permanence, whilst being as fluid as fashion, and of as little significance in itself until combined with all the other aspects of identity. Playwrights have always been aware of this fluid power of speech, and have been adept at employing it in portraying the complexities of character and identity. Edgar in Shakespeare's *King Lear* is able to move swiftly between one identity and another simply by a change of accent. At the start of the twentieth century, in Shaw's *Pygmalion* an East-End flower seller could, by no more than a change of accent, pass as an aristocrat. *Pygmalion* is a satire on both the importance and the superficiality and conditionality of speech. The transformation of Eliza Doolittle into an aristocrat was accomplished without altering one jot of the substance of what she said. The role of speech as a badge of social position continued long after Shaw's mockery of it, and at the mid point of the twentieth century Anthony Crosland could remark on 'the most supremely unmistakable of all symbols of social standing – differences of accent and vocabulary. In no other country is it possible in the same way to assess a person's class standing the moment he opens his mouth.'[47] Crosland goes beyond Shaw, in suggesting that whilst what is said may not change with class, not just the accent but the words used may. He was writing at the same time that Nancy Mitford, with tongue in cheek, was describing the differences between elite and popular words which she termed U and non U, and of the significance of saying napkin rather than serviette. But by then language had none the less moved a long way beyond the King's English of Shaw's 1912, and from his manipulative linguist Professor Higgins who, in the musical *My Fair Lady* derived from *Pygmalion*, and at the same time as Crosland and Mitford, demands in exasperation 'Why can't the English learn how to speak?' But the English – and the Scots, the Welsh, and the Irish – had always known how to speak. What had already changed by the time of Crosland, Mitford, and Lerner and

Loewe was that they had increasingly gained confidence in the manner in which they did so, as part of their public identity. This development marked the end of the King's English in the Queen's Britain, and the emergence of a multilingual and multiaccented populace. Localised language became a component of social decentralisation and the departure of any single national linguistic hierarchy. The growth of pride in diversity accompanied the public presence of a substantial range of accents in the British Isles. Nor is any one accent found, and only found, with other aspects of identity. People of different religions and ethnicities may speak with similar accents, and inhabitants of the same city with different voices. The proliferation of publicly established accents provides, in shifting combinations with other aspects of identity, a population which is far more diverse than the term 'multicultural' can encompass.

'Posh' remains as a national rather than a local style, and you cannot tell where a posh person comes from by his or her voice. Ross McKibbin has argued that a distinct upper-class manner of talking began to be eroded and dissolved after the First World War, being replaced under influence from the upper middle class by phonetic pronunciation which no longer ignored consonants or telescoped words.[48] But whilst the tones of hierarchy might mutate, and even fashionably imitate or parody tones from other social regions, just as with Marie Antoinette in the pastures of the Petit Trianon an aristo dressing as a shepherd was still very obviously not a horny- handed daughter of toil, so a politician or a banker adopting an accent from the outer fringes of London still could not pass as a man or woman of the people.

Language as exclusion was not a preserve of those at the top of the scale of class, status, or advantage, and could be used with equal force and effectiveness by those challenging the social order from below or from the margins. Members of the Young Communists League in the 1930s reported how they sang songs on trains in German and Russian, not knowing what the words meant, but that it was 'real sectarianism' because the other passengers couldn't understand it either, whilst assuming that the young revolutionaries could.[49] Distinction could work against existing hierarchies as well as in support of them.

Eating British, eating English, but also eating Scottish, eating Welsh, and eating Irish

Food is not only one of the principal components of identity, but an apt metaphor for its complex, contingent, and cultivated character. Cuisine is always a combination, mixture, and juxtaposition of ingredients, methods of preparation, ways of presenting, and modes of consuming. It cannot be reduced to some single principle or essence, and in this respect is like the identity of a whole society – the sum, consequence, and interaction of its parts. Like other dimensions of identity, food serves both to distinguish one population from another, and to distinguish groups and individuals within a population from each other. Food both unites and divides.

For an emerging professional and commercial middle class resentful of the restraints and inequalities it felt in a society which still retained heavy layers of aristocratic privilege, feasting provided far more than just sustenance. By the end of the eighteenth century, a 'traditional' celebration of Christmas by the middling classes who both honoured traditions and did their duty of hospitality towards the poor was being contrasted with the effete, dissolute, or negligent treatment of the festival by an aristocracy which failed in its obligations to charity and the less fortunate and to the honouring of a tradition of which its critics claimed, and ate to prove the case, to be the true maintainers and cultivators.[50] So long before Dingley Dell or Scrooge, Christmas was being celebrated, and charity and entertainment dispensed, as an active contrast with the dissolute and failed life of the upper classes. Celebrating Christmas both within the family as convivial fellowship and outside the household as charitable social responsibility cultivated identity both by contrast with the irresponsible and less traditional privileged, and by the exercise of a culture of one's own which asserted distinctiveness and claimed the legitimacy of tradition. Food took its place in the assertion of public identity and the waging of class competition.

The ways in which people eat have changed and developed, and are the culinary dimensions of a population for whom the term 'multiculturalism' is inadequate or simply misleading. Multiculturalism suggests a range of autonomous and comprehensive cultures whose members will share common characteristics in all aspects of their identity. The condition of the people of the British Isles is far more complex, varied, and flexible than this and offers far more opportunities for the creative and innovative cultivation of identity.

Eating, like other dimensions of identity, cultivates both association and distinction through a range of practices which are, or are presented as being, foreign, traditional, rational, or esoteric. As with identity cultivation by other means, identification through food both associates with a broad category of others, and refines that same category to distinguish individuals within it. I eat, therefore I am. The upper classes, and those who cultivated a distinction from the mass, ate in French, or at least did so in restaurants and on formal public or corporate occasions. In the popular public sphere, away from the culture of the elite, foreign food, let alone foreign names, was disdained, and insofar as it was considered to display precise and excessive concern with the preparation and consumption of food, was contrasted with the plain fare and no-nonsense cuisine of the British Isles. Even the term for elite cuisine was foreign – *haute cuisine* not high cuisine. But a softening and diversification of social ranks in the second half of the twentieth century involved a change in the use of foods whose origin, or alleged origin, was in other parts of the world. The end of empire and the withdrawal of the British state to the British Isles was followed by the arrival of cuisines from around the world, and not only from places whose maps had previously been coloured red. Menus in French continued to signify a claim to distinctive refinement, but the arrival of Chinese, Indian, Italian, and Asian restaurants and takeaways was part of a growth of popular eating which eroded and transcended the former class distinction between eating in English and eating in French. Curry had had a place on some dining tables much earlier, but as an exotic sauce added to conventional dishes, initially in the homes of those who had brought the novelty back from India. Empire in the eighteenth and nineteenth centuries had surprisingly little impact on this pattern. Curry may have represented the culinary lessons of India, but those lessons, or an appropriately processed version of them, did not become a significant part of eating in the British Isles until the end of empire was followed by the arrival of the children of former imperial subjects. Actual foreign menus, or versions of them accommodated to current popular tastes in Britain, were brought directly by those from whose cultures the cuisine derived. The new arrivals in British high streets sold both at their own tables and for takeaway, joining the prepared-food market at its most popular level, and sharing company with fish and chips. Foreign eating, which had previously marked off those at the top of the social and income scale, like clothes, no longer served to distinguish, or easily distinguish, privilege.

The popularity of Indian, Chinese, and Italian restaurants from the 1950s was paralleled, or at least accompanied, by a heightened interest in indigenous British cuisine, and the works of Theodora Fitzgibbon or Gary Rhodes were a small antiphonal response to the arrival of foreign tastes. The assertion of culinary identity responds to innovation, difference, and the challenge of the unfamiliar or the foreign. The English did not discover that they had a cuisine until the arrival of Chinese and Indian restaurants and French cookery books. And, paradoxically, the search for roots and tradition in the tables of the nineteenth century or the kitchens of the eighteenth or seventeenth, whilst recovering earlier ways of eating, recovered also the fact that menus are the result of choice, change, invention, and innovation. The Christmas turkey was an import from the United States, the Burns Night haggis a nineteenth-century invention rapidly exported south across the border.

For this reason the presence of ways of eating which have been imported does not signify that there is no indigenous cuisine. The cuisine is the whole complex, and is necessarily and always made up of distinct elements, many of which, taken by themselves, will be recent and foreign, or will appear to be so. Distinction depends on and is nurtured by contrast. It would not make sense to go to a café for a full English breakfast before the arrival of croissants. It is not chips, but chips with everything, that distinguishes a particular identity for both the observer and the consumer, and the celebration of the chip shop had to wait until rival food outlets were on the street. The history of chips illustrates the flexibility of meaning. Chips with everything could be regarded with horror from above as a sign of the cultural poverty of the masses. Fish and chips by the seaside could, at another time, be the elites' application of the games of Mary Antoinette, or the cultural patriots' celebration of the uniqueness of British popular cuisine.

Eating and drinking, both what is consumed and where it is consumed, have carried both assurance and stigma. A combination of consumption in public and consumption by people whose identity jars with dominant modes provides occasion for elite dismay and disapproval. Coffee houses in the eighteenth century provided forums for radical and oppositional politics, and coffee bars in the second half of the twentieth century attracted distrust as havens of loud music, unorthodox clothes and hair, and unpredictable juvenile exuberance. They were each seen, both by those who frequented them and by those who abhorred them, as part of a culture at one remove from the normal, for the frequenters one remove up or out, for the abhorrers one remove beyond. The coffee house, the pub, the fish-and-chip shop, all stand halfway between the privacy of the household and the publicness of the street. The human traffic of this public eating and drinking ebbs and flows, and by the start of the twenty-first century had spread to even more public and visible forms as urban midday meals were sold at a busy turmoil of temporary street stalls. Eating in the street, which had long been considered amongst the socially aspiring as the mark of the uncouth, became the lunchtime sophistication of busy workers of all kinds. Cuisine, like all the other components of identity, carried no inherent significance, but was flexible to the point of reversal in the associations and distinctions it announced.

Public and private spaces

An Englishman's home may be his castle, and an Englishwoman's commune hers, but public identity, whilst nurtured in the household, is cultivated and created in the spaces between households, the public spaces which architecture defines and which practice and custom can reinterpret. Public space, and the architecture which shapes and occupies it, is more permanent than clothing, or diet, or language, and rather more difficult to alter or remove. But its meaning is not solid and fixed in the way that its structure is, and even its most blatant or vociferous symbols and statuary can fade from the notice of later generations, or be seen by them in new and surprising ways.

The use of space is both an assertion of a right derived from identity, and the cultivation or announcement of identity. People who have access to a restricted space say both that their identity entitles them to the privilege, and that they are to be identified as people who occupy such a privileged space. Occupying the space is both an entitlement of privilege and a component of it, a claim to a privilege and a public display of a privileged identity. The use of space in a hierarchical or an unmobilised society is critically different from its use in mobilised or democratising ones. In an unmobilised society there is no public space. Space is the monopoly of the dominating elite, and the mass of the population has access to it only by permission, and in a subordinate role.

The absence of public space is not the same as the absence of any form of collective space. In an unmobilised society, or more precisely a population in which there is no society in the sense of a comprehensive collective identity, there will be social territories, patches of collective, private, space. These are spaces where private activities are carried out – streets, markets, bridges. But unless use is necessary to a particular purpose such as market-stall trading, an elite will claim privileged use whether by the actual exclusion of the majority of the population, or by the assertion of various forms of preference in use and access. Where members of the population at large do exercise rights of access and use, they will be most likely to do so as sharers in an association with local common rights.

Public space is more than space outside the privacy of a household or workplace, and the term 'public' indicates more than that the ground is simply in potential sight of other people; it indicates a dimension which is common to a whole population, or to a sufficiently large part of it to deserve being treated as comprehensive. In that sense, a social space outside households and workplaces which excludes children might still be considered public; one which excluded on the basis of gender, ethnicity, language, or religion not at all, or in only a limited and compromised way. The adjective 'public' indicates universality, the whole population, and not only universality, but equality.

Even where public spaces exist, there is continual negotiation and contest to define who are the public, and who are to be considered marginal or alien – who may properly be in public spaces, and who should be regarded as interlopers. There is a constant search for distinction, one aspect of which is the narrative of aliens – the excluded, the threatening, the rabble – contrasted with ordinary decent folk. The language of social hierarchy is never very far from the language of social demonology. Accounts in the early twenty-first century of chavs, whose dress and demeanour made them seem, to some, unwelcome and inappropriate in public places, were an instance of a recurring theme, and the alarms and disapprovals recorded by Owen Jones echoed the report by Mass Observation of the celebrations in Glasgow of George VI's coronation in 1937. There was a delicate hint of distant disapproval in the description of crowds:

> running about with no aim or purpose. There are a great many drunks. Women in shawls and girls are rubbing their faces with 'make-up' that is used for branding cattle in the market. Streaked with blue or red they look like Maoris, or painted savages in a war-dance. They seem capable of anything.
>
> Small gangs in side streets are lighting fires that may become definitely dangerous in congested areas like these. The atmosphere is electric. The people seem to feel that to-night the police are powerless. They can do what they like.[51]

A society in which all may in principle use public spaces will be, unless it is characterised by an unusual degree of cultural uniformity, one in which the consequent varieties of human public identity will forever provoke complaints, dismay, and attempts at regulation and exclusion. But such a society will be one in which identity, which might be regulated or constrained from above, will at the same time be asserted and cultivated from below.

Space is defined by the ways in which people use it, and by who uses or may use it, and who does not or may not. At the same time, people are defined by their use of space, and rights over space are a dimension of who people are. Whilst public space appears within a mobilised society, and expands in a democratic one, the boundaries between public and private are fluid and shifting. The enclosure of common land in Britain over several hundred years from the sixteenth century redefined both those who profited from enclosure and those who were excluded by it. To enjoy rights over land, to be a landowner, is to cultivate an identity which is marked in part by the contrast with those who enjoy no such rights. In the cities which grew with rational town planning and orderly squares from the eighteenth century, the status of householder and property owner was enhanced by exclusive access to the parks within the squares, land publicly visible but not publicly accessible. The key square followed into the new spaces of enlightenment cities the monopoly and exclusions of space which parks, grouse moors, and enclosed commons constituted in the country.

In the use of space to cultivate identity, other dimensions contribute. Whilst access to space is itself a dimension of identity, it can be further regulated by stipulated forms of dress, so that one dimension of identity sustains another. Kensington Gardens in the eighteenth century, whilst open to 'gentry', were barred to those who were 'meanly dressed'.[52] Glyndebourne requires evening, and the private spaces at Ascot morning, dress. Space is occupied not only by those who are distinguished by their right to occupy it, but by the attire which both permits their occupation and enhances its distinction.

Common land, whilst never the property of those who enjoyed its use, was a resource used and a space acted in by particular agricultural communities. The enclosure of common land and its creation as private space illustrates how the creation of public spaces was not a homogeneous or unqualified linear progress. Whilst some forms of public space were emerging in the seventeenth and eighteenth centuries, others were being destroyed by enclosure. A public space precedes or accompanies or contributes to the creation of a public, so that phrases such as 'members of the public' or 'the public' have meaning only as a social category emerges of people who – whilst not part of a ruling elite – are, aspect by aspect and in a growth which is neither simple, nor irreversible, nor necessarily coherent, more than mere subjects. The emergence of the public, of civil society, of 'the people' is the result in part of the broadening downwards of the politically visible and active, and in part of demands upwards from the aspirant but excluded. This was not only a demand to join a world from which they had been barred, but also for the creation of a world in which they played an active, visible, and prominent part. The mass trespass on Kinder Scout in 1937 was an attempt, eventually successful, to shift boundaries and to make public what had previously been private, or what was seen as having been improperly appropriated as private. A claim for a new world could readily be married with an appeal to ancient rights of the people.[53] The boundary between public and private remains mobile; the number of key squares has steadily fallen as they have become public parks, but gated estates have slowly appeared in British cities, as one form of privacy is succeeded by another.

The boundaries between private and public are equally mobile between government and people. By the close of the twentieth century, Buckingham Palace could be visited, as could, though only after decommissioning, the royal yacht *Britannia*. Members of the public were no longer classified as 'strangers' when visiting the House of Commons, and the new premises of the Greater London Authority had glass-walled passages which enabled the people to look down on their representatives. On the other hand,

Downing Street, where the official residence of the prime minister is one of a short terrace of houses, was closed to the people, and in the early years of the twenty-first century the Blair government moved to limit public use of public spaces, in terms of both access and what might be done, in an extended area around the Houses of Parliament. Whatever the reasons for these measures, their effect was to visibly accentuate the distance between elected rulers and the populace.

Riot is the most evident incursion into public spaces of either new participants or participants behaving in new and disruptive ways. Disorder and destruction, frequently a mixture of spontaneous and organised actions, have occurred in towns and cities at all times, from before the Gordon Riots of 1780 to the poll-tax riots of the twentieth, and the riots throughout English cities in 2011 in the early years of the twenty-first century. The streets are the resort of those who do not or cannot exercise power or cultivate identity in legislatures, government offices, courts, or the media, and riot the actions of those who, by the very act or rioting, are excluded or outlawed. Riot is a raid on public space, not an occupation or extension of it, and is an incursion from outside the boundaries of the civil and political order. Riot differs, therefore, from another form of law-breaking in public and private spaces – civil disobedience. Theatrical law-breaking, with an intention and assumption that the law will be enforced and penalties imposed, identifies those who carry it out as placing themselves clearly within the existing political and legal order, whilst presenting their dissent from some of the policies pursued there, and at the same time challenging the existing conventions of both public and private space. When women demonstrating against the situating of American cruise missiles at Greenham Common entered the base and picnicked on the missile silos, they were both redefining governed space as citizens' space, and using active satire to ridicule and call into question the identity and policy of those who deployed nuclear weapons.

Where civil disobedience employs the law against itself, other uses of public places to question policy and extend the public identity of the protestors remain within the law. The use by radicals and trade unionists of processions, banners, assemblies, demonstrations, brass bands, and the street theatre which these provided was not only a claim to inhabit an existing social space, but the creation of a new space. It was the assertion and cultivation of a public identity by those who took part, a vigorous demonstration of a claim not only to occupy an existing space, but to do so in a way which showed new identities of the population and new dimensions of the public space which it now used. The public space thus created or claimed was part of an authoritative, secure, and permanent change, in contrast with the temporary gesture of misrule in rioting. As

Mansfield puts it, at a time 'when radicals and others outside the formal political nation had limited access to the public sphere where permanent monuments were erected, banners provided an important means, not only of ideological declamation, but also of commemoration and memorial.'[54]

The protocols of public spaces are in this way a measure of the protocols of society. Who is seen in public spaces; what distinctions of class, age, and gender are visible; and how, if at all, these distinctions change are a part of who has a public identity, or claims one, or is denied one. The hostile responses of male politicians and journalists to early twentieth-century demonstrations by female suffrage campaigners was not only a disagreement with their policies or demands, but an attempt to deny their claim, expressed in the act of demonstrating, to be public persons and citizens on at least the same terms as men. Later in the same century, feminist campaigns to 'reclaim the streets' were similarly propaganda by the deed; the act of walking at night and in collective confidence in public places was an expression of a right claimed and exercised, and an expression more visible and forceful than the wording of a pamphlet or a placard. The dress which is thought appropriate or inappropriate in public spaces, the persons who wear it, and the identity which they thereby express, are important components of the identities by which society is constituted.

The various uses of the street are mixed and muddled, and real events do not fit exclusively into one category to the exclusion of all others. The unruliness of the coronation crowds in 1937 was a middle point between the misrule of riot and the authoritative assertion of marches, banners, placards, and demonstration. But whatever the character of the actions and behaviour in streets and places public or private, they will both declare and cultivate the identities of those involved, both in their own eyes and in the eyes of those who, with reactions ranging from enthusiasm to outrage, will observe, hear, and report on them. If homes are people's castles, streets are their terraces and pleasure grounds.

Religion, churches and faiths; the return of God, and of religious controversy

In 1750 Charles Edward Stuart travelled incognito to London and received Holy Communion in the church of St Mary le Strand.[55] Five years earlier, his Jacobite army had been massively defeated at Culloden Moor, after he had failed to raise any significant or effective support for his claim to the throne once he had crossed the border into England. The political opposition to a Roman Catholic on the throne had been given legislative expression in the 1701 Act of Settlement, and the monarch was required to be in communion with the Church of England. So Bonnie Prince Charlie was maintaining an option, however precarious, on the crown which his grandfather James II had relinquished or been expelled from. The sacrament of Holy Communion was an instrument of dynastic ambition alongside the secular weapon of highland armies. The course of most forms of identity in Britain has, whilst never approaching uniformity, moved away from rigid and ostentatious distinctions of rank, class, or wealth. Religious identity has moved in different directions, and whilst there was never uniformity, equality in variety was only approached in the twentieth century. It might be responded that religious identity is something occasional, active at the passage rites of birth, marriage, and death, but dormant for much of the rest of life or the rest of the week. Yet a decline in regular attendance at Sunday worship in Christian churches has not been paralleled by a decline in the salience of religious identity in public life.

The Vicar of Bray is a much more important figure than suggested in the satirical song which records a succession of opportunistic changes of theological and liturgical loyalties. Changes in the character and prevalence of religious observance which had, for much of the twentieth century, been dismissed as of little public importance, had returned by its end to be treated as an essential strand in the social weave. And approaching religion from the human rather than the divine side, it is the cultivated identities which are most salient. But the other significant fact about the Vicar of Bray is that he is untypical in the severance of religious actions from other aspects of his identity. For much of the period being reviewed, the intractability rather than the fluidity or mere convenience of religious faith and religious identity is what is striking. But whilst religious observance is a component of identity, its relation with other aspects of identity is flexible and unpredictable; in worship and religious practice and ritual, people may parallel, challenge, reject, or transcend other aspects of who they are.

Religion is the ultimate identity by association with another or others, since it is identity with the ultimate other, an identity which has the potential to deny all self-interest. It therefore has a continuing power in relation to other aspects of identity, and the twentieth century, insofar as it can be described as a secular century, was untypical, and the revival of religion, or of awareness of religion, by the century's end is a return to a more usual human practice.

The severity of puritan dress was an expression of a larger identity, but its casting off, and the reaction against it, after 1660 was not simply and solely a symptom of something else. It was itself part of, a dimension of, a cause and a reflection of, a fuller, more many-textured set of actions. People rejected drab because it was Puritan, but they at the same time rejected Puritan because it was drab. Severity of dress was not a reflection of an inner Puritanism, but a part of what it was to be Puritan. It is for this reason that 'external' actions and expressions are as much constituents of identity as are 'internal' values, thoughts, aversions, or aspirations. What is significant is not simply how people construct their public, social, political selves, but what differences, if any, there are between the constructions in one circumstance and another. There is a further dimension to Puritanism: it followed from the priesthood of all believers, in that any one of the faithful could, and should, express his or her faith through appearance.

The eighteenth century, whilst frequently seen as a time of fading religious enthusiasm whose character was simply emphasised by the contrary zeal of Methodism, began with legislative assertion of religious identity at the pinnacle of public life. No one could ascend to or occupy the throne who was a Roman Catholic, and the monarch must be in communion with the Church of England. To be English was to be Anglican, and below the monarchy communion with the established church was a condition of admittance to the universities or the professions. This legally maintained uniformity of national identity became more difficult to sustain the greater the number of the country's inhabitants who were included as part of its public life. Within an elite, uniformity is more readily achieved than with larger numbers of the population, where the two most accessible alternatives are either toleration and diversity, or coercive orthodoxy. The more a population is mobilised, the greater the potential diversity of religious identity. At the same time, greater mobilisation increases the likelihood of mobilisation within any particular faith. The authority of priesthood is not undermined of necessity in a mobilised society, and can survive and flourish there. But the possibilities of its being qualified by greater lay participation are increased, as are the diversity of forms it may take. In the eighteenth century, as Methodism set out to increase the numbers of those incorporated in the life of the church, it began to assign to the newly mobilised a role which had previously been reserved for the priesthood. Local preachers were laymen and laywomen, who extended their public identity from their existing familial and occupational roles to include that of the preacher and leader of a congregation in worship.

But whilst religious belief and practice may be intense at the start of the twenty-first century, it is both fragmented and a series of minority identities, rather than a comprehensive national identity. The disputes which took place in the sixteenth century over religious identity took place in a society where religious practice, in its smallest particulars, defined a whole people and where government sought, and needed for its own security, orthodoxy of religious practice enforced by law. *Cuius regio, eius religio* was not only a description of general European practice in the sixteenth and seventeenth centuries, but a recognition of the dependence of government on agreement between the religious loyalties of princes and those of their subjects. Hence not only physical behaviour, but the meaning to be attached to that behaviour was a matter of deep concern and controversy. The so-called 'Black Rubric' of the 1552 and 1662 Books of Common Prayer described what people were doing, and what they were not doing, when they knelt to receive Holy Communion. The controversy surrounding the comings and goings of this descriptive paragraph was part of a society whose identity was cultivated by religious actions and religious beliefs in the smallest particular.[56]

The diversity of Britain was presented as regional rather than as class or cultural in the official handbook to the Festival of Britain in 1951, which nonetheless told its readers, 'Britain is a Christian Community. The Christian Faith is inseparably a part of our history. It has strengthened all those endeavours which this Festival has been built to display.'[57] But the identity of the population was neither homogeneous nor unchanging. On the one hand distinctive tastes in working-class life may have been slowly eroded by the greater availability of films and lending libraries, but at the same time cultural and regional diversity became more pronounced.[58] Heresy makes sense only in a uniform population, and the charge of blasphemy is a feature of a homogeneous society, or of an attempt to create one. Although the last blasphemy trial in the United Kingdom was as recent as 1992, and blasphemy was not removed from the criminal law until 2008, religion in a democratising state no longer created homogeneity. On the one hand was a growth of indifference, on another a move within patriarchal Christianity towards greater lay participation, with lay participation in the Roman Catholic Mass. The tension between patriarchal churches and a society which was edging towards gender equality further broadened the range of beliefs and practices within the population, and the diversity of religious, and non-religious, identities. Within other faiths, particularly Islam, there was both a reassertion of patriarchy and a questioning of male privilege and of the orthodox relations between the sexes.

By the twentieth century, clothing had long ceased to be significant for religious identity in the Christian churches. Different conceptions of church and faith were still cultivated in part by differences in dress, which not only distinguished between genders, but assigned different roles, responsibilities, and duties to them. A priest in clothes indistinguishable from those worn by ordinary members of the public creates an identity distinct from that of a colleague wearing a cassock, whilst a biretta contributes to yet another identity. But by the end of the century the importance of clothing within elements of Islam had become publicly apparent and a matter not just of personal identity but of collective doctrine and controversy. Where in the vestments controversy of the sixteenth century it was the clothing of priests that was the issue, in the twentieth century controversy within and beyond Islam, the clothing of laywomen was the issue, both for Muslim women wishing to wear distinctive clothing and for Christian women wishing to wear distinctive ornaments. The identity of the ordinary faithful in a mobilised and democratising society had achieved an importance which in less mobilised times was most heavily evidenced in concern over the identity of the religious elite – priests, ministers, and pastors.

Conclusion

Appearance may not be the most important aspect of identity at times of revolution, uncertainty, and transition, but its importance is most frequently discussed at such moments. The French Revolution throughout its course was the occasion for intense discussion of everything from hats to sashes, from playing cards to crockery. The course of events in the British Isles has been less churned about by revolution, but the role of appearance in constituting that change has been no less important, if not always so evident. At times of transition and uncertainty, the concern for presentation and display can be intense, demanding, and uncompromising; in settled periods it is likely to be assured, confident, and resistant to change. By the final quarter of the twentieth century in the British Isles, uncertainty had intensified both the assertion of varied identities and the demand for at least recognition, and at most auxiliary status, in others. At the point furthest away from governing elites, this took the form of the demand for 'respect' in teenage gangs. A mark of the uncertainty with which identity is cultivated can be the ferocity with which demands are made on others to acknowledge it. And while debates over the place of religion in public life and over the identities which doctrine and tradition required or made possible were not violent, they were conducted with intense and divisive passion.

One contribution to the passions which were aroused in the politics of identity was the fact that familiar comprehensive packages, while they had never been as universal or as neat as some hoped, no longer provided easy keys to identity. Whilst the smallest aspects of identity may be taken as indicative of an entire personality, there was increasingly no simple, rigid, or universal correspondence between one aspect and another. It is a measure of the fragmentation of identity by the end of the twentieth century that these apparently predictable correspondences were dissolving, and that following the hounds said nothing about views on nationalisation or nuclear deterrents, or tweed suits about knowledge or ignorance of contemporary pop.

What the experience of the British Isles illustrates is that the ways in which identity is cultivated shift and mutate, and that a dimension of identity which is important at one time can be marginal at another. Clothing can be more important than language, language than clothing. But the shifting and turbulent course of public identities also undermines any account of social character which argues or assumes that change is linear, simple, irreversible, predictable, or along a single track from which no deviation occurs. Even the attempts to reverse changes or impose allegedly traditional uniformities bear witness to the certainty of continual flux.

The British Isles contain a vertically diverse as well as a horizontally stratified population. There is ironic truth in Margaret Thatcher's remark about the abstractness of the idea of 'a society', for a single homogeneous culture, 'society', was exactly what she valued, but not only had this never existed, but 'society' at the time of her remark was moving towards growing cultural and individual variety and unpredictability. Voices protesting against multiculturalism, whether in Olympic ceremonies or varieties of faith, as alien to British tradition illustrate, by their own particular narratives, the prevalence of that very cultural diversity which they denounce, and the role of constantly asserted and innovated identities in its creation and cultivation. The identity of the people of the British Isles has always been shifting and vigorously varied; by the start of the twentieth century it was flourishing, a full orchestra of identities producing both polyphony and cacophony.

Notes

1 Becky E. Conekin, *The Autobiography of a Nation: The 1951 Festival of Britain* (Manchester: Manchester University Press, 2003), pp. 96, 97.
2 Shaw, *Pygmalion*, p. v.
3 Hoock, 'Nelson Entombed', p. 134.
4 Eric Hobsbawm, 'Introduction: Inventing Traditions', in Eric Hobsbawm and Terence Ranger (eds), *The Invention of Tradition* (Cambridge: Cambridge University Press, 1983).
5 Randall Hansen, *Citizenship and Immigration in Post-War Britain* (Oxford: Oxford University Press, 2000), p. 212.
6 Paul Rich, 'Patriotism and the Idea of Citizenship', in Ursula Vogel and Michael Moran (eds), *The Frontiers of Citizenship* (London: Macmillan, 1990), p. 101.
7 Anthony Howard, '"WE ARE THE MASTERS NOW": The General Election of July 5th 1945', in Michael Sissons and Philip French (eds), *Age of Austerity* (London: Hodder and Stoughton, 1963), p. 15.

8 Calder Walton, *Empire of Secrets: British Intelligence, the Cold War and the Twilight of Empire* (London: Harper, 2013), p. 26.
9 Krishan Kumar, *The Making of English National Identity* (Cambridge: Cambridge University Press, 2003).
10 David Cannadine, 'Last Night Fever', *London Review of Books*, 29:17, (2007), 21–4.
11 Prochaska, *Republic of Britain*, p. 198.
12 Maria Hayward, *Dress at the Court of King Henry VIII* (Leeds, UK: Maney, 2007), pp. 9–10.
13 Anna Keay, *The Magnificent Monarch: Charles II and the Ceremonies of Power* (London: Continuum Books, 2008), pp. 160–5.
14 Hugh Trevor-Roper, 'The Invention of Tradition: The Highland Tradition of Scotland', in Hobsbawm and Ranger, *The Invention of Tradition*.
15 Frank Prochaska, *Royal Bounty: The Making of a Welfare Monarchy* (New Haven, CT: Yale University Press, 1995).
16 David Cannadine, 'The Context, Performance and Meaning of Ritual: The British Monarchy and the "Invention of Tradition", c. 1820–1977', in Hobsbawm and Ranger, *The Invention of Tradition*, pp. 101, 116.
17 Cannadine, 'The Context, Performance and Meaning', p. 110.
18 Holger Hoock, *Empires of the Imagination: Politics, War and the Arts in the British World, 1750–1850* (London: Profile, 2010), pp. 21–36.
19 Prochaska, *Royal Bounty*.
20 Prochaska, *Royal Bounty*, p. 192.
21 Andrew Pierce, 'Prince Charles to be known as Defender of Faith', *Daily Telegraph*, 13 November 2008, www.telegraph.co.uk/news/uknews/theroyalfamily/3454271/Prince-Charles-to-be-known-as-Defender-of-Faith.html (accessed 2 April 2013).
22 Jonathan Petre, 'Queen to visit British mosque for first time', *Daily Telegraph*, 21 April 2002, www.telegraph.co.uk/news/uknews/4181908/Queen-to-visit-British-mosque-for-first-time.html (accessed 13 May 2016).
23 Rodney Barker, 'The Pluralism of British Pluralism', *Journal of Political Ideologies*, 14:1 (2009), 36.
24 Nairn, *The Enchanted Glass*; Walter Bagehot, *The English Constitution* (London: Chapman and Hall, 1867).
25 Edward Shils and Michael Young, 'The Sociological Meaning of the Coronation', *Sociological Review*, New Series, 1 (1953), 63–81.
26 IPSOS/MORI, 'Britons are more proud of their history, NHS and army than the Royal Family', *IPSOS/MORI*, 21 March 2012, www.ipsos-mori.com/researchpublications/researcharchive/2939/Britons-are-more-proud-of-their-history-NHS-and-army-than-the-Royal-Family.aspx.
27 Prochaska, *Royal Bounty*, pp. xvi, 161.
28 Fran Abrams, 'Blair: "I think I'm a pretty straight sort of guy"', *Independent*, 17 November 1997, www.independent.co.uk/news/blair-i-think-im-a-pretty-straight-sort-of-guy-1294593.html (accessed 2 April 2013).
29 Andrew Rawnsley, 'Why Alastair Campbell has deleted Blair's expletives: The former spinmeister's diaries have been heavily censored but they still threaten

to damage the departing Prime Minister', *Observer*, 27 May 2007, http://observer.guardian.co.uk/comment/story/0,2089087,00.html#article_continue (accessed 7 June 2007).

30 Ben Pimlott, *Harold Wilson* (London: Harper Collins, 1992), p. 266.

31 BBC News, 'Tony Blair focuses on his new look', *BBC News*, 23 December 1999, http://news.bbc.co.uk/1/hi/uk/576445.stm (accessed 20 May 2013).

32 Rudyard Kipling, 'Tommy', in *A Choice of Kipling's Verse made by T. S. Eliot* (London: Faber and Faber, 1941), pp. 172–4.

33 Holt and Holt, *In Search of a Better 'Ole.*

34 Hoock, 'Nelson Entombed', pp. 123–4.

35 Hoock, 'Nelson Entombed', p. 134; Alex King, *Memorials of the Great War in Britain: The Symbolism and Politics of Remembrance* (Oxford and New York: Berg, 1998).

36 McKibbin, *Classes and Cultures*, p. 36.

37 Orwell, *The Road to Wigan Pier*, p. 203.

38 Raeff, 'The Well-Ordered Police State and the Development of Modernity'; Raeff, *The Well-Ordered Police State.*

39 Owen Jones, *Chavs: The Demonization of the Working Class* (London: Verso, 2011), p. 10.

40 Jon Lawrence, 'The Culture of Elections in Modern Britain', *History*, 96:324 (2011), 466.

41 David McKittrick, 'Brian Haw: veteran peace campaigner who occupied Parliament Square for a decade in protest at war', *Independent*, 20 June 2011, www.independent.co.uk/news/obituaries/brian-haw-veteran-peace-campaigner-who-occupied-parliament-square-for-a-decade-in-protest-at-war-2299874.html (accessed 16 March 2012).

42 Marcel Berlins, 'When a slogan equals terrorism', *Guardian*, 3 October 2005, www.guardian.co.uk/politics/2005/oct/03/terrorism.immigrationpolicy (accessed 16 March 2012).

43 Styles, *The Dress of the People.*

44 *The Times*, 7 March 1939, quoted in Harker, '"The Manchester Rambler"', p. 223.

45 Richard Hoggart, *The Uses of Literacy* (Harmondsworth, UK: Pelican, 1959), p. 10.

46 C. A. R. Crosland, *The Future of Socialism* (London: Jonathan Cape, 1956), p. 177.

47 Crosland, *The Future of Socialism*, p. 178.

48 McKibbin, *Classes and Cultures*, p. 36.

49 Harker, '"The Manchester Rambler"', p. 225.

50 Neil Armstrong, *Christmas in Nineteenth-Century England* (Manchester: Manchester University Press, 2010), pp. 5–6.

51 McKibbin, *Classes and Cultures*, pp. 10–11.

52 G. D. H. Cole and Raymond Postgate, *The Common People 1746–1946* (London: Methuen, 1961), p. 59.

53 Squires, 'The Mass Trespass', 1–3; Harker, '"The Manchester Rambler"', p. 225.

54 Nicholas Mansfield, 'Radical Banners as Sites of Memory: The National Banner Survey', in Pickering and Tyrell, *Contested Sites*, p. 81.
55 Paul Kléber Monod, *Jacobitism and the English People, 1688–1788* (Cambridge: Cambridge University Press, 1989), p. 154.
56 Diarmaid MacCulloch, *Thomas Cranmer: A Life* (New Haven, CT: Yale University Press, 1996), pp. 525–30.
57 Conekin, *The Autobiography of a Nation*, p. 118.
58 Robert James, *Popular Culture and Working-Class Taste in Britain, 1930–1939: A Round of Cheap Diversions?* (Manchester: Manchester University Press, 2010).

Conclusion

Masks and faces: what you see is what you get

Shakespeare's King Lear appears to complain that the artefacts with which people clothe, house, and surround themselves conceal their true nature: 'robes and furred gowns hide all'.[1] But the public performance is at least as real as any private one. It is conducted in relation to other people, and is the one which affects them and with which they have to deal. It is not secret selves, but active, overt, social selves that constitute the human environment. When Lear tore off his clothes he was not revealing a true nature which lay beneath the robes and furred gowns, but cultivating or dramatically bringing to birth a different, additional, or differently stressed nature. His denunciation of authority can be read as an analysis of authority, not as a revelation of a reality beneath the surface:

> Thou hast seen
> a farmer's dog bark at a beggar?
> …
> And the creature run from the cur? There thou
> Mightst behold the great image of authority: a
> dog's obeyed in office[2]

The robes and furred gowns which constitute the human dogs against whom Lear roars are part of, not props to, the social identity of rulers and command givers. A dog in office is still, amongst other things, a dog, but not merely a dog.

To observe that human identity is cultivated in this way is the very opposite of saying that it is a mere mask. A mask can be put on and put off at will, whereas human identity is the face, the reality which is seen and heard, and the more it is cultivated, the more it is composed of many elements, each one of which constrains at the same time as it identifies. In that sense, 'cultivation' is a more illuminating word to use in relation to social identity than 'construction' or even 'creation', since what is cultivated begins with but is not constrained or determined by already-existing components; it grows and becomes entrenched, and develops as the context and condition of its own existence and future growth. The complexity and potential dynamism of human nature are such that art – whether as fiction, poetry, painting, sculpture, music, or film – can often express or indicate what bare theory can only point at from a great distance. Cultivation provides, too, an alternative description to an account of people as trapped in a choice between intentionality, where everything that is done is part of a plan, and spontaneity, where actions burst suddenly from nowhere.

The irresolvable paradoxes of cultivated identity and the possibilities of autonomy, action, and choice

Feathers are part of the bird. But the bird's plumage will change only with the shifts of evolution. People choose their own plumage, but they choose it in circumstances not of their own making; human feathers are chosen, or chosen within limits. That is one of the enduring tensions of identity. We may cultivate our own identities, but they are at the same time cultivated for us.

There is another paradox to add to the conflict between human agency and the unavoidable role of circumstance and social situation: we make identities by association with collectivities, whilst at the same time seeking to distinguish ourselves from others – the two dimensions of what Veblen called invidious comparisons.[3] Veblen does not develop this tension, but it is a part of a dynamism which means that identity is never fixed, but is always shifting and adjusting. Identification is cultivated by association with a real or imagined group, whilst at the same time negative contrasts are devised which distinguish one group from another. The impetus for distinctiveness does not stop at the boundaries between groups, but operates within the group as well, so that whilst in relation to other groups an individual cultivates an identity as a group member – a Christian, a Muslim, a German, an Italian – within the group the cultivation of individual identity distinguishes one Christian from other Christians, one Italian from other Italians. Identity is pulled in two directions, towards association and towards distinction. Identity is subject to continual adjustment, both to its own internal contradictions since no identity is ever wholly coherent or internally consistent, but is composed of competing and potentially conflicting elements, and to the inherent contrasts and comparisons with others and the tension between association and singularity. And while the individual is not sovereign nor autonomous in this continuous flux, he or she nonetheless has possibilities of action and choice, however those may be shaped and constrained by circumstance. Such action is composed of both emulation and distinction, following examples, and distinguishing oneself from them. Association with others cultivates equality; individual distinction cultivates inequality. Both for individuals and for groups and associations of individuals, equality and inequality are forever exercising their contrary gravitational pulls.

One feature in particular of identity and its cultivation enhances the potential for significant human action. The more a person cultivates and enhances his or her identity by collective identification, the greater the complexity and plenitude of that identity. And therefore the greater its individuality, since the more aspects there are to an identity, the more unique it becomes. This means that it makes good sense to talk of human action and human will. Whatever the constraints, what humans are is what they do, and every action therefore confirms, develops, departs from, or transcends their identity as it was up until that point. This claim allows for human agency including, crucially, the agency of the self, of an individual who is, in however restricted a way, making decisions and pursuing choices. Identity is constructed out of many circumstances and many actions and events, and whilst that means there is no single lever which can steer everything, any single change will alter the character of the whole, not necessarily radically, but in reality nonetheless, and such change is always a possibility for human innovation, invention, reform, and even transformation. How identity is at any current moment does not determine everything that follows. However small the openings for identity-shaping action, they are always there. Consequently all the things that people do can be of significance, and giving an account of them is far more than simply stating that that is how things are, since the qualification must always be an acknowledgment of the ways in which things can be otherwise through the continual response to tensions and contradictions. Such an account, far from being merely descriptive, is an identification of the flux and flexibility of human identity, and of the perpetual possibilities of change, both benign and corrupting.

Such changes in identity can be slow and imperceptible, or sudden and dramatic. Michael Rosen has discussed the latter in examining the circumstances in which significant numbers of people may reject the orthodoxies within which convention, convenience, or coercion have constrained them. Such can be the force of convention, or of a rational calculation about the likely success and possible penalties of individual as opposed to collective dissent, that it may require what can appear as irrational or even deranged dissent by a minority before a larger number will together act in a way which they would previously have been deterred from but can now pursue because circumstances have been altered by eccentric or irrational individuals. Eccentric irrational individual heterodoxy may be the necessary detonator for collective change with which an individual may then associate, shifting identity from passive or powerless subject to active citizen or insurgent.[4] But such instances not only require a revision of conceptions of rationalism to accommodate the rationalism of eccentricity, they also require a broadening of the perceptions of identity and interest which are the starting point for any rational action, whether conscious and reflective, or instinctive.

The description and prediction of human nature and the limitations of universal theory

Whatever metaphor is used, whether of fauna or flora, all appearances and all aspects of appearance are relevant in an account of identity. By their fruits ye shall know them, but by their fur and feathers as well. And one element in cultivating identity, which the biological metaphor points up, is the environment within which an identity is cultivated. But the function of conditions beyond an individual in cultivating identity does not mean that there is an absence of choice. All factors are dependent upon each other, but they are not determined. Choices can be made, but their outcomes cannot be predicted. They are still worth making. This creates difficulties in the way of a science of human action, or even of human behaviour. The fullest account will always be a particular one, having more of the character of history or a novel than of a scientific treatise. That does not mean that general analyses have no purpose. Their contribution is to refine the language which is then applied to specific phenomena. Nor does it mean that, in any particular circumstances, predictions cannot be made about what might happen next. But they will be predictions in terms of the particular and unique situation about which they are made, and will always be tentative since any one general consequential relationship is likely to be qualified by others, so that its contribution will be just that, a contribution, not a determinant.

This makes a universal science of human conduct unlikely or unreliable, and predictions dangerous. It is better to expect unexpected and creative identities. This limits the usefulness of both Marxism and utilitarian rational-choice accounts. The jibe has been made that social history was no more than the history of the crinoline. But that underrates, entirely misses, the character of identity both individual and social or political. People will die for an article of clothing, a word, or a culinary detail. This is not to dismiss materialist or rationalist accounts of history, past, present, or future, but to insist that humans are more than physical survivalists, that the purposes which are a dimension of their identities, without being arbitrary or transient, are varied and not readily predictable, and that generalisations can never go beyond setting out the range of expectations, and limitations on expectations, which can be brought to the understanding of actual instances, actions, and situations.

The role of elites in the cultivation of identity

Identity is cultivated rather than created insofar as creation suggests making something from nothing, and unless actions or initiatives are taken spontaneously by large numbers, they will be taken in the first instance by small numbers or by individuals. In that sense, action is always the action of elites if the term 'elites' is used to indicate minorities. But the law of small numbers is also a claim which is justified only if the effects of individual or small-group actions are evident in the eventual actions of large numbers. While it can be claimed that identity is cultivated, and is most actively cultivated by elites of one kind or another, the reverse statement may be more accurate: those who devote most energy to the cultivation of identity constitute an elite. It is the initiative in cultivating identity which makes the label 'elite' appropriate. Nonetheless, a dominant or powerful role in the cultivation of identity is one of the characteristics of groups who are in this and other ways marked off from the majority and enjoy a privileged position in relation to that majority. Once again the image of a mask is misleading, however contrived actions, constructions, and ritual and rhetoric are. Asking whether the cultivation of identities by an elite is a deliberate manipulation of identity to serve other ends is to fragment human action unrealistically. The celebration of military heroes in the statuary of St Paul's Cathedral was part of the cultivation of a narrative of national virtue and glory.[5] One of the many accounts given by those whose efforts placed the memorial statuary was that national character, national achievement, and national aspiration were thereby expressed and recorded. But whilst this contributed to a public imagination of empire, it is inadequately understood if it seen as only and entirely a conscious and manipulative strategy to promote that imagination. The conscious strategy may be there, but it is part of a wider action, and an action which both cultivates and constitutes the identity of the actor. The imagination was already there in the character of the memorialists. There may have been an expectation that the celebratory statues would promote national pride and deference to heroic leaders, but the pride and the deference were also there in the act of artistic creation and the concepts which drove artistic intentions.

If, as Herbert Morrison remarked, socialism is simply what Labour governments do, so is human nature what humans do.[6] That is not an observation which goes very far, since it is qualified both by the limitations of contingent context and by the possibilities of human action, but it can exclude the need to spend time on biological or social determinism, or on the concept of untrammelled agency. It identifies both constraints – humans cannot fly unaided or spend long periods underwater without artificial breathing apparatus – and opportunities – human nature is not confined to what can so far be observed. The observation is morally neutral in that it has both liberating and corrupting implications: nothing that humans do and no aspect of human identity can be dismissed as unnatural. Nor are any aspects of human identity excluded from critical appraisal. Democratic empiricism does not preclude ethical judgment, it rather requires it.

Talking the world into existence

Because human identity is cultivated, the cultivators are both the possessors of the identity and those amongst whom they live. There is not therefore a single identity for any person, since the identity as perceived by one will be different from that perceived by another. And since all we can ever know are accounts of identity, it is misleading to seek a true or real identity beyond the accounts given of it by people – the statements, actions, sights, sounds, and artefacts which are experienced and reported.

None of this means that human identity can be constructed or altered at will. But it does mean that there is no single character that can usefully be described as an essential human identity. Nor can an account of human identity be anything more than an account of what, up to now, can be said about accounts of identity in all times and in all places. Identity is in part the sum of what a person does. But what a person does is in part what a person is seen to do. There is thus a further dimension to identity, which is pointed out in the perception of things that Ian Hacking has described as 'dynamic nominalism'.[7] The lenses and filters of social perception cultivate and create identity; they are part of the circumstances in which identity is nurtured and pollarded. This power of naming is dramatically, indeed melodramatically, portrayed in Ray Bradbury's short story '*Referent*', where the infinite potential relationships and patterns of sensed phenomena are shaped and constricted by the perceptions of observers. A traveller through space is trapped in an alien (human) culture by the perceptions of the small child whom he meets, and by whom he is identified, and hence shaped and trapped, as a small child.[8] A referent is similarly imagined by Jorge Luis Borges in his short story '*Tlön, Uqbar, Orbis Tertius*', in which a parallel world of phenomena both natural and social is brought into existence by being described and recorded in an encyclopaedia.[9] It is precisely for this reason that Anthony Appiah has raised queries and objections in the debate over 'recognition', arguing that he does not wish to be 'recognised' by others as an instance of social categories, since this constrains and distorts, and even more radically shapes and forms, a public identity which is not of his choosing.[10] A distinction in practice between affirmative recognition and constraining or oppressive presentation or description can be as finely balanced as, within theory, are the linguistic distinctions between recognition and reification, and expression and distinction. Yet the clarification of language is necessary if at the level of practice the cultivation of identity is to be carried out by individual persons, rather than imposed on them. Theologians have always been aware of this dimension: 'In the beginning was the word',[11] and the very title of their discipline, theology, the word of God, gives the divine word creative primacy.

Humans are builders and makers, but so are beavers. But there is an added and transforming dimension: humans reflect on and describe what they have made, and in so doing describe and make themselves, and others.[12] It is in the addition of 'and others' that the further dimension, and possible tension, arises. There may or may not be a tension, but there will necessarily be a conversation or some degree of dialogue, between who I am to myself and who you construct me as. Human nature is in part what humans describe themselves as being, or as not being, and that is not only the construction of the costumes and the set that cultivate human identity, but the comments of the audience and the critics. The story told instantly becomes part of what it purports only to describe. This both extends the complex contingency of identity and extends into language the opportunity for continual cultivation of identity by individuals and groups, not only by the linguistic dimension of identity, but by the ability of that dimension to shape other aspects of the social world. Everything that is done, and every description in whatever form, has consequences for the 'moving target' of identity. There is no certainty in those consequences, but there is a certainty that there will be consequences, and that stasis is impossible. So human responsibility remains, and inaction is only a particular species of action. There is no such thing as 'a mere observer' and the highest and shiniest of ivory towers is as much a part of the human market place as the loudest huckster's stall.

The dimensions of identity and the character of change

To argue that the accounts we give instantly both affect the objects and persons to which they refer, and themselves become a part of that which is described, the reference becoming a referent, is already to have provided answers, or partial answers, to some of the questions which immediately leap out from the account of cultivated identity. The most obvious questions will be two. First, what is the function of the costumes and scenery and ways of acting which constitute social identity in human life, and if they are not epiphenomenal, how do they change? Second, is there an escape from saying that everything is affected by everything else, and that there is no single independent variable or cause, that all we can ever say is that at one moment and place these are the identities which can be observed, and at another, others?

One response, or one starting point, is to say that the costumes and scenery are not an indication of, or cause of, or sustainers of something else, they are something in themselves, the major dimension of reality. That means that identity cannot be divided into accidents and essences. One qualification to this might be that there may indeed be a distinction between 'pretended' identity and 'real' identity, an instance of incoherence which is not only accepted, but consciously cultivated. People may deliberately present one identity to one audience, and another to another. But the theatre of deceit can be more transparent than its protagonists realise. Those who strut on the political stage saying they are the people's friend can be judged by all their strutting as well as by all their words. It is necessary to ask about other components of their identity: how and where they move in relation to their subjects, whether on foot or in convoys of large black limousines; what kinds of spaces they inhabit, and who else has access to those spaces and on what terms. Sometimes the rupture between one identity and another may be deliberately concealed. There are those who seem consciously and for effect to construct a public personality which is different from their 'private' or 'normal' self: Blair's public good temper, Wilson's pipe. But it would be a mistake to conclude that one identity is real, the other false. Both are real, but are severed from each other by the different functions which they serve.

But whilst costumes and scenery, walking and talking, constitute identity, no particular evident component has a universal significance. What appear as similar feathers can relate to other, very different, aspects of behaviour. As Darwin realised when studying the Galapagos finches, context is crucial. And whilst the feathers are important, they do not constitute the entire identity of the bird. There may be a difference in ideology between Leninist/Stalinist architectural monuments and Nazi ones, whilst the systems and relations of power which they compose are closely similar. And in considering the similarities and differences between identities, any answer depends on the criteria used for the taxonomy. If the whole constructed identity is built into the taxonomy or the comparison, then there are real differences as well as real similarities. And if no identity can be reducible, or adequately understood, by giving an account of one only of its dimensions or features, if attempts at parsimony of any kind are like playing a piece of music written for choir and orchestra on a single penny whistle, then identity is never a matter of some dissected-out feature or features, but only of the whole.

Insisting on the complexity and contingent location of identity, on identity as composed of many aspects in relation with each other, might appear to make change difficult or impossible. The opposite can be the case. An entire identity, because of its complex variety, will be characterised by tensions, contradictions, and discord. It will be constantly subject to a gravitational pull towards coherence, though a pull which is never resolved, which is forever shifting the objects on which it operates, and the intensity with which it exerts its demands. A wolf in sheep's clothing is as rare as a sheep in wolf's clothing. In most cases what you see is what you get, provided you know what to look for. This constant impetus towards coherence, in circumstances where complete coherence can never be achieved and where, therefore, the impetus will never entirely expire, provides the dynamism for identity to change.

If the relation between identification and meaning and justification – feathers and nests and foraging – and other dimensions of social action is symbiotic rather than causal, how is change explained? The answer is that the relation between the various dimensions of action is never entirely coherent, and that the search for coherence will involve adaptation of one dimension or another, so that the symbiosis is dynamic, and its tensions and incoherencies never fully resolved. All variables are both dependent and independent in this sense, and whilst a political intervention to change one dimension of identity may well lead to other changes, it will not have the status of an irreversible and iron causal injection, since it will itself be subject to continuing adjustment to other dimensions of the situation. The history of interventions, whether medical or social, political or economic, illustrates not only that the expected effects of x on y can frequently not accurately be predicted, but that x may have effects on other aspects which had not been imagined.[13] Even worse, the character of x will be a feature of its relationship with other factors, and in influencing those other factors and hence its own environment, x, too, will change. An explanation, therefore, unless it is of a severely limited event and chronology, will always be an interpretation, narrative, or description. To fully describe a change is not to explain why something happened, but to give the fullest account of what did in fact happen. This is all that is possible, though it is no small thing, and all accounts which claim to be explanations are more accurately seen as fuller accounts or descriptions. So, for instance, an account of the changed character of the Japanese polity and of the place of the imperial family in it is not explained by talking either about the different presentations of the family, or about the check to Japanese power, or about the post-war US occupation, or about the growth of democratic sentiment, since all these are elements or dimensions of the whole complex and dynamic history, elements in the complex weave, not causes of something other than themselves. They are fuller answers to the question 'What is meant or indicated by the phrase "changes in Japan"?'

The conclusion of such a narrative is not a cheerful, or lugubrious, '*que sera, sera*'. Some regularities, or at least recurrences and familiarities and ubiquities, can be observed, though the most powerful prediction that can be made is that there are no grounds to expect that a single-factor account of identity will apply universally, or even in any particular instance. Such assumptions about what can be said cannot avoid being informed by value judgments or by preferences which are the starting point of speculation, not its conclusion. So I will state a preference for freedom, variety, tolerance, and innovation. All of those involve both planning and a refusal to plan. Innovation cannot be planned for since, as Humphrey Lyttelton allegedly once replied to a query as to what the future of Jazz would be, 'If I knew that, I'd be there.' But the circumstances which make innovation, variety, and useful choices more likely require equality of possibility with the avoidance of any orthodoxy as to outcome. The starting point, though not the conclusion, of an understanding is that nothing is peripheral, and everything that people do should be considered.

The importance of context

Rituals and actions possess different meanings as parts of identity in different circumstances. The parading of the liberty cap, which at the beginning of the nineteenth century was treated by government as subversive and challenging, would, a hundred years later, be either incomprehensible or quaint. A similar flexibility is enjoyed by carnival, which can function in the way that Simmel envisaged conflict functioning, or can be, as in the late sixteenth century in south-eastern France, a vehicle for rebellion.[14] It can, also, be neither of these things, but a means of pursuing grievances in unconventional ways which, while challenging custom and hierarchy, do not confront or threaten established government or social order.[15]

Because artefacts and feathers, stage props and scenery, are made or chosen, none of them have any inherent meaning. A swastika which symbolises well-being in its Sanskrit and Hindu form, symbolises something entirely different in its Nazi employment. Dark glasses can express laid-back casualness, or authoritarian reserve. Murals of the mythical hero Cúchulainn depict him in one part of Northern Ireland as the defender of Ulster and an ancestor of loyalists and unionists, in another part of the country as the symbol of nationalism.[16] Analyses remain in an abstract realm until they are applied. Once they are applied, the resulting account is distinct in two ways: first, it is specific and contingent, in that the total mix of aspects or dimensions identified by analytical categories makes each interpretation unique. Second, as with 'A sharp', which is and is not the same as 'B flat', the presence of other dimensions and the relation between the dimensions forms the character not only of the whole but of the dimensions. Mark Anthony's description of Caesar's assassins as 'all honourable men'[17] takes its meaning from all the other things which he said, and the occasion on which he said them, and the audience to which they were addressed.

Identity and autonomy: auxiliaries and the ethics

Humans are social beings, and identity is cultivated not only in isolation but also in relation to others. There is a constant and continuing tension between the cultivation of an individual identity and the attempt to both sustain and distinguish that identity by shaping the identities of other people, on the one hand seeking to shape them to the individual's view of the world and of his or her own character, on the other seeking to cultivate an inferior though not hostile identity in others as an expression of the individual's superiority. Identity by association always limits difference by cultivating others within the association, however inferior they are presented as being, as friends and allies. Other associations, by contrast, can be presented as antagonists or enemies whose negative qualities throw into relief the virtues of one's own community.

There is an inherent conflict in the manipulation of the identity of others as a means of cultivating one's own, though one which rarely reaches the point where the entire enterprise collapses. The greater the claim, the greater the effort invested in cultivating the identity. When the claim is to political or collective identity, the effort can be immense. And, paradoxically, the cultivation of the identity of others may then be pursued by excluding them and marking them off from the identity of leaders, rulers, or elites, as readily as enlisting them as auxiliaries to the identity at the top of the political hierarchy. This exclusion, in its most extreme form, can lead to a cultivation of identity which is solipsistic and narcissistic. However, at this point the two dimensions of identification conflict, since some common identity is a feature of society and polity; the distinction of an elite or a leader has become isolation. If everyone speaks a different language there is no society.

There is no resolution of the conflict between the desire to enrol or subordinate others in the cultivation of a person's identity and the presumption that the individual is sovereign over himself or herself, apart from severe liberal restraint in the face of a constant temptation. Far from precluding such restraint, a recognition of the nature of human identity cultivation provides the foundation for it. If there is no human essence, whatever exists or has existed is human, and the condemnation of unnaturalness fails. It would seem at first as if this commits one to accepting any and all forms of life and conduct, however abhorrent. But this is not so. If there is no universal humanity, there is no justification for determining the life of anyone but oneself. Tyranny over oneself is a personal choice; tyranny over anyone else lacks any justification. Individuals may define and cultivate their own identities, but only insofar as that does not require the subordination of others to their self-identification. This is not because of an inalienable right to determine one's own identity and therefore not to have it determined by anyone else, but because, since the only human reality is the actions of individuals, there is no principle which privileges any one individual to subordinate others' identification to his or her own, or treat them as auxiliaries to his or her identity. In that sense, the only person who can impugn or challenge individual honour or esteem, is the individual himself or herself. The actions of others are irrelevant to it. This individualism conflicts with the ways in which identity is cultivated. But an understanding of human identity cultivation which precludes any conception of essential human nature also precludes any justification of impinging on the autonomy of others, or subordinating their identity to one's own. The absence of empirical universals does not block the making of ethical judgments – it makes them possible.

Interests and identity

It may be that the politics of the twenty-first century will increasingly become a series of contests, often bitter and violent, over natural resources: water, oil, minerals, and land capable of producing food. In a world approaching or entering a time of limited resources and continued population growth, the contests for food, water, and fuel could become a dominant element in human action. In that case it might appear that a politics of identity will be replaced by a politics of interest or of biologically grounded needs and responses. That would be to misrepresent the relation between interest and identity, and between ubiquitous needs and their particular expression and pursuit. The preceding discussion has presented human life as being about meaning, justification, identity, and esteem. The acquisition and use of material goods has been presented as carried out as part of this activity, not as a separate or prior or fundamental activity. It might seem a cruel luxury of the richer parts of the world to treat identity as important when for large portions of humanity, life is a continual and stressful effort to secure enough food, water, shelter, warmth, health care, or education for minimal survival. But the accounts given of the varied classes and categories of humanity, and of the distribution of rights amongst them, would be matters of identity cultivation, creation, and description. Narratives of identity would provide the language for the distribution, and the restriction of the distribution, of resources between the various classes, groups, and categories into which competing claimants divide the human population. Identity would be a means of restricting access to resources which are insufficient to provide subsistence for everyone. Identification will not cease to be a human concern or a human activity, but its function and its relation to other dimensions of life will alter. Humans wish to survive, and to survive and flourish physically, materially. But the way in which they wish to survive and flourish can be as important to them as the mere fact of survival and flourishing. This is the point of Hegel's master-and-slave parable, in which the slave initially submits and the master does not, because for the master flourishing, and flourishing through a constructed and articulated identity, transcends mere physical existence.[18] Material survival is never simply material survival with no further human dimension, it is always the survival of real people, whose life is cultivated in their identities amongst the deprived no less than amongst those more fortunate sections of the world's population. Human political activity will never be a simple reflection of objective and universally recognised and accepted economic interests. The parties to any contest will be shaped by shared identities, and the resources for understanding the world and for justifying aspirations, aversions, and actions within it will be used and developed in the cultivation of identity. Human identity, as an infinitely variable and changing presence, will shape and constitute human action as it has always done.

In times of hardship, explanations for distress are sought in the supposed actions of those whose identity differs from that of the distressed: foreigners, or subordinate or marginal categories of people. The narratives may differ, from witches in the seventeenth century to immigrants in the twenty-first, but the demonisation reflex of seeing alien identities is the same. Identity cultivation as a dividing up of humanity is the language of conflict over material resources. This takes the form of both invoking alien identities as threatening, and of subordinating and exploiting those whose identity is contrasted with that of the more fortunate. The continual recruitment of others in the cultivation and use of identity, either as auxiliaries or as contrasting subordinates or aliens, suggests that the competition for scarce resources will be conducted with the armoury of ideology and all the passion of identity, raising conflicts over material well-being or survival to the level of cultural survival. The sanctity of identity provides justification for expropriation and exploitation. Battles over water, or food, or energy will be ruthless even if they are only market commercialism carried to extremes, but they will be shaped, justified, and enhanced by conflicts between identities which will raise them to even more intense levels.

The destructive power of identity

A recognition of the apparently irrational, eccentric, or deranged element in identity cultivation can make sense of all the 'hopeless' insurrections, resistances, and protests from the Pilgrimage of Grace to the 1989 revolts in Eastern Europe, which Michael Rosen presents as the 'irrational' catalysts of transformation, or at least of disruption.[19] Such eccentricities are irrational only within the limits of a narrow conception of interest and a narrow conception of identity. But they can also point towards an understanding of movements such as radical Islamism, which appears to place no value on any beliefs, practices, or persons other than its own, and to pursue a policy of the physical destruction of those alien beliefs, practices, and persons. Patriots do not wave flags because they are patriots; they are patriots because, among other things, they wave flags. 'Patriot' is a shorthand way of describing all the things they do. This is to say more than that a person is what they do. They are also what they make, cultivate, and preserve. It is because what people do constitutes who they are, and is not reducible to some deeper or more 'objective' or material reality, that religion is again and again so prevalent. Associating who one is with a human society gives solidity and dimension, but associating who one is with a superhuman or metaphysical dimension gives something else again. Genuflexion is grasping the hand of infinity. But it is always human beings who do the grasping, and whether one sees religion as a human creation, or sees knowledge of the divine as necessarily expressed through and by finite human capacity, all that can be known is human action. The question of both the cultivation and maintenance, and the destruction, replacement, and change of human identity is thus answerable only in terms of that identity itself, making understanding and interpretation possible, if difficult, but explanation and prediction a rainbow's end. The resurgence of militant, coercive, and intolerant religious movements in the twenty-first century demonstrates in murderous and destructive form the overwhelming power of the search for and the cultivation of identity, and of the unavoidable dependence of even the most apparently anti-materialist persons and movements on evident action and tangible resources.

Beyond face to face

The resurgence of religion is not the only set of events which has made identity both fluid and unpredictable. Visible identity has grown and become both more accessible and more frequent. Portraiture enabled a few people to see a fabricated image of an aristocrat, a monarch, a cleric, crafted, if the sitter was powerful or fortunate enough, to show piety, heroism, beauty, or wisdom. Photography placed sometimes less manicured images before a wider public; cinema and then television gave the images life, and made even more, potentially, fragile the image which the object of the vision sought for. But that slow erosion of control by the subject over the image was reversed with the rapid expansion, from the end of the twentieth century, of the Internet. Social media enabled all with access to a computer, a phone, or a tablet to present whatever images they wished of themselves, to the point where the gap between what could be seen in face-to-face contact and what was presented in an electronic world of virtual reality was so deep and broad that any evident connection between one side and the other disappeared. The conclusion of this chasm between the face-to-face person and the electronically presented person was the avatar in a virtual world of computer gaming.

But a potential universal power of not simply identity cultivation but of identity creation was challenged, as it developed and spread, by increasingly well-funded and extensive operations, principally though not exclusively by the rulers of states, to control, limit, or suppress a form of creation, cultivation, and publishing abroad over which, unlike all other forms of identity cultivation, they had no immediate control. The challenge which a freely accessible World Wide Web made to autocracy was not only the free dissemination of information and ideas, but the free proclamation of identities.

Paradoxes of identity

The man who, when delayed at the theatre box office, demanded 'Don't you know who I am?' was illustrating one of the many paradoxes of identity. On the one hand he was claiming the superiority of his identity, on the other revealing that it depended on recognition from those whom he considered below him. Human identity is full of tensions and contradictions. People cultivate identity both by associating themselves with others and by distinguishing themselves from them. Underlying competition for material resources is the paradox of public identity: individuals not only identify themselves in the sight of others, those others are frequently a part of the scenery which they construct or cultivate for the performance of their drama of identity. But in so doing, they subvert the equal dramatisation of those others. Mutual recognition is difficult when it involves recognising and acknowledging that others have identities which do not confirm your own preferences and values, and when, therefore, confident identity is reliant principally on a drama without a stage or a supporting cast.

So the cultivation of political identity, of persons, nations, and rulers, is an instance of a wider human activity, whereby identity is cultivated across the whole plane of individual and social life. And just as in political life, others are constantly being recruited, coerced, or attacked as part of the supporting cast of the drama, so in all the other dimensions of human life, authority can mean not only the autonomy and sufficiency of an author, but the extension of power over others. The cultivation of identity is not innocent. It gives meaning and justification, but frequently does so by privileging some cultivated group at the expense of some other cultivated group. The positive features of such identities are sustained by contrast with their negative reversals in the cultivated identities of dominated, managed, or controlled groups. These positive and negative identifications most familiarly are shaped as class, race, ethnicity, gender, religion, or nationality. The practices by which others are treated as auxiliaries to identity can vary from shaping the identity of those who can be controlled or managed, to telling stories about those who are beyond the narrator's control or influence. In the first case, members of the dominant person's group, community, or nation are subordinated to his or her identity. In the second case, narratives are cultivated about those who may live in other communities or countries, or who may not exist at all. The two practices can overlap or merge when people within a state are placed in geographical or social ghettos both to subordinate them and to cultivate an identity both alien and stigmatised. This subordination and exclusion can then be further intensified by a narrative which links people to real or imaginary external or supernatural enemies.

To observe the negative function of identity is not to condone it or be unable to affect it

What has been said and argued in the preceding chapters is not a claim about causes but about character. The various dimensions of human action which have been described are presented as constituting social character, not causing it. In that sense, an explanation is presented not in terms of causality but in terms of the various components of identity which, while they may sustain each other, do not have temporal precedence over each other. The more the particular character of an identity is described, the more elements are identified any one of which, by its absence, would have meant that the identity was different, and so whether seen as cause or constituent of the identity, each part or aspect is essential to the character of the whole.

People cultivate identity both by associating themselves with others and by distinguishing themselves from others. This creates a perpetual tension. The more precisely, despite these difficulties, an identity is established, the greater the contrast with surrounding identities. In these circumstances, distinguishing involves both describing and heightening a difference from others, yet the greater the difference, the more others can be seen, paradoxically, not as by their difference sustaining one's identity, but as threatening it by the very authority which their own identity enjoys. At the same time, their alleged difference is supportive of the identity with which they are contrasted by the very illumination, through contrast, of the identity from which they differ.

Recognition of the function of identity cultivation does not preclude either recognition of the harm it causes, or the making of ethical judgments about its operation and consequences. It both perceives the nature of the difficulty and provides incentives and justification for confronting it. The insistence on the possibility and reasonableness of equal respect for all identities qualifies the demand for recognition by excluding some of its forms. If others may not be subordinated as auxiliaries to identity or treated unequally because of differences of identity, recognition is available only from an equal, and the difference between the recogniser and the recognised strengthens the identity of each by combining the authority of an independent and different identity with the illuminating contrast which that difference entails. This provides for the possibility of applying ethical judgment, though not of empirical solutions, to the likely negative or harmful functions of identification in the twenty-first century. To record these processes and tensions is not to condone them, and an appreciation of their character makes possible an ethical assessment. This will not solve let alone remove the problems, but it provides a reason and a justification for confronting them. But in order to confront them effectively, it is necessary to recognise the role of identity cultivation, assertion, and preservation in providing the language and the perceptions within which competition for resources is carried on, which are the elements that enable it to be carried on. Confronting these tensions is thus an intensified instance of the universal and ubiquitous need to confront the paradoxes of identity, whose cultivation is the generator both of human progress and of human conflict.

Notes

1 Shakespeare, *King Lear*, Act IV, Scene 6.
2 Shakespeare, *King Lear*, Act IV, Scene 6.
3 Veblen, *The Theory of the Leisure Class*, p. 40.

4 Rosen, *On Voluntary Servitude*, pp. 261–2.
5 Hoock, *Empires of the Imagination*.
6 I am indebted to George Jones for this information. The remark is reported to have been made by Morrison at a seminar at the London School of Economics in the late 1950s in response to a question from Ralph Miliband.
7 Ian Hacking, *Historical Ontology* (Cambridge, MA: Harvard University Press, 2002); Hacking, 'Making up People'.
8 Ray Bradbury, 'Referent', in *The Day it Rained Forever* (London: Rupert Hart-Davies, 1959).
9 Jorge Luis Borges, 'Tlön, Uqbar, Orbis Tertius', in *Labyrinths: Selected Stories and Other Writings* (Harmondsworth, UK: Penguin, 1970).
10 K. Anthony Appiah, 'Identity, Authenticity, Survival: Multicultural Societies and Social Reproduction', in Charles Taylor and Amy Gutmann (eds), *Multiculturalism: Examining the Politics of Recognition* (Princeton, NJ: Princeton University Press, 1994), pp. 149–63; Appiah, *Ethics*, pp. 105–10.
11 *The Bible, Authorized King James Version* (Oxford: Oxford University Press, 2008), John 1:1.
12 It may not be possible to assert with unqualified confidence that no animals do so. But it is possible to assert that humans do.
13 Helen Roberts, *What Works in Reducing Inequalities in Child Health?* (Bristol, UK: Policy, 2012), pp. 40–1.
14 Humphrey, *The Politics of Carnival*.
15 Humphrey, *The Politics of Carnival*.
16 Bill Rolston, *Drawing Support 2: Murals of War and Peace* (Belfast: Beyond the Pale, 1995).
17 William Shakespeare, 'Julius Caesar', in *The Complete Works*, edited by Stanley Wells and Gary Taylor (Oxford: Oxford University Press, 1986), Act III, Scene 2.
18 Taylor, *Hegel*, pp. 153–7.
19 Rosen, *On Voluntary Servitude*, pp. 261–2.

Bibliography

Abel, Chris, *Architecture and Identity: Responses to Cultural and Technological Change*, 2nd ed. (Routledge: London, 2000).

Abrams, Fran, 'I think I'm a pretty straight sort of guy', interview with Tony Blair, *Independent*, 17 November 1997, www.independent.co.uk/news/blair-i-think-im-a-pretty-straight-sort-of-guy-1294593.html (accessed 2 April 2013).

Agence France-Presse, 'Obama forced to apologise to Karzai for Koran burnings in Afghanistan', *The Australian*, 24 February 2012, www.theaustralian.com.au/news/world/obama-forced-to-apologise-to-karzai-for-koran-burnings-in-afghanistan/story-e6frg6so-1226280166800, (accessed 25 January 2015).

Agulhon, Maurice, 'Politics, Images, and Symbols in Post-Revolutionary France', in Sean Wilentz (ed.), *Rites of Power: Symbolism, Ritual and Politics since the Middle Ages* (University of Pennsylvania Press: Philadelphia, PA, 1985).

Akerlof, George A., and Kranton, Rachel E., *Identity Economics: How Our Identities Shape Our Work, Wages, and Well-Being* (Princeton University Press: Princeton, NJ, 2010).

Alexander, Jeffrey C., and Lara, Maria Pia, 'Honneth's New Critical Theory of Recognition', *New Left Review*, 220 (November/December 1996).

Alofsin, Anthony, *When Buildings Speak: Architecture as Language in the Habsburg Empire and its Aftermath, 1867–1933* (University of Chicago Press: Chicago, 2006).

Altman, Robert, *Gosford Park* [film] (Sheperton Studios: Sheperton, UK, 2001).

Anderson, Benedict, *Imagined Communities: Reflections on the Origin and Spread of Nationalism* (Verso: London, 2006).

Appiah, K. Anthony, 'Identity, Authenticity, Survival: Multicultural Societies and Social Reproduction', in Charles Taylor and Amy Gutmann (eds), *Multiculturalism: Examining the Politics of Recognition* (Princeton University Press: Princeton, NJ, 1994).

Appiah, Kwame Anthony, *The Ethics of Identity* (Princeton University Press: Princeton, NJ, 2005).

Armstrong, Alexander, and Miller, Ben, *RAF fighter pilots sketch*, www.armstrongandmiller.co.uk/video_raf_pilots.html (accessed 22 June 2011) [now available at www.youtube.com/watch?v=r_b1Y-Rl_Uo].

Armstrong, Neil, *Christmas in Nineteenth-Century England* (Manchester University Press: Manchester, 2010).

Aubrac, Lucie, *Outwitting the Gestapo*, translated by Konrad Bieber and Betsy Wing (University of Nebraska Press: Lincoln, NE, and London, 1993).

Austen, Jane, *Emma*, (J. M. Dent: London, 1922).

Avineri, Shlomo, *Hegel's Theory of the Modern State* (Cambridge University Press: Cambridge, 1972).

Axel, Gabriel, *Babette's Feast* [film] (Nordisk Film: Copenhagen, 1987).

Ayres, Alyssa, *Speaking Like a State: Language and Nationalism in Pakistan* (Cambridge University Press: Cambridge, 2009).

Babington, Charles, 'Senate rejects flag desecration amendment', *Washington Post*, 28 June 2006, www.washingtonpost.com/wp-dyn/content/article/2006/06/27/AR2006062701056.html (accessed 21 February 2017).

Bagehot, Walter, *The English Constitution* (Chapman and Hall: London, 1867).

Barker, Rodney, 'Hooks and Hands, Interests and Enemies: Political Thinking as Political Action', *Political Studies*, 48:2 (2000).

Barker, Rodney, *Legitimating Identities: The Self-Presentations of Rulers and Subjects* (Cambridge University Press: Cambridge, 2001).

Barker, Rodney, *Making Enemies* (Palgrave Macmillan: Basingstoke, UK, 2007).

Barker, Rodney, 'The Pluralism of British Pluralism', *Journal of Political Ideologies*, 14:1 (2009).

Barmé, Geremie, *The Forbidden City* (Profile Books: London, 2008).

Barrie, J. M., *Peter Pan* (Oxford University Press: Oxford, 2006).

BBC News, 'Tony Blair focuses on his new look', *BBC News*, 23 December 1999, http://news.bbc.co.uk/1/hi/uk/576445.stm (accessed 20 May 2013).

BBC News, 'Global net censorship "growing"', *BBC News*, 18 May 2007, http://news.bbc.co.uk/1/hi/technology/6665945.stm (accessed 19 May 2007).

BBC News, 'North Korea threatens war on US over Kim Jong-un movie', *BBC News*, 26 June 2014, www.bbc.co.uk/news/world-asia-28014069 (accessed 8 November 2016).

BBC News, 'Sony hack: North Korea threatens US as row deepens', *BBC News*, 22 December 2014, www.bbc.co.uk/news/world-asia-30573040 (accessed 8 November 2016).

Beacham, Richard C., *Power into Pageantry: Spectacle Entertainments of Early Imperial Rome* (Yale University Press: New Haven, CT, 1999).

Beard, Mary, 'Highway Codes: What Romans Thought Walking Was For, and What They Might Have Talked About as They Walked', *The Times Literary Supplement*, 5693 (11 May 2012).

Bede, *A History of the English Church and People*, translated by Leo Sherley-Price (Penguin: Harmondsworth, UK, 1955).

Belchem, John, '"An Accent Exceedingly Rare": Scouse and the Inflexion of Class', in John Belchem and Neville Kirk (eds), *Languages of Labour* (Ashgate: Aldershot, UK, 1997).

Belchem, John, and Kirk, Neville, *Languages of Labour* (Ashgate: Aldershot, UK, 1997).

Bell, Quentin, *On Human Finery* (Hogarth Press: London, 1976).

Berlins, Marcel, 'When a slogan equals terrorism', *Guardian*, 3 October 2005, www.theguardian.com/politics/2005/oct/03/terrorism.immigrationpolicy (accessed 16 March 2012).

Bettenson, Henry, *Documents of the Christian Church* (Oxford University Press: London, 1959).

Bevan, Robert, *The Destruction of Memory: Architecture at War* (Reaktion: London, 2006).

The Bible, Authorized King James Version (Oxford University Press: Oxford, 2008).

Bisson, Thomas N., *The Crisis of the Twelfth Century: Power, Lordship, and the Origins of European Government* (Princeton University Press: Princeton, NJ, 2009).

Borges, Jorge Luis, 'Tlön, Uqbar, Orbis Tertius', in *Labyrinths: Selected Stories and Other Writings* (Penguin: Harmondsworth, UK, 1970).

Borowczyk, Walerian, *Blanche* [film] (Abel & Charlton, Télépresse Films, 1971).

Bosanquet, Bernard, *The Philosophical Theory of the State* (Macmillan: London, 1965).

Boulting, John, and Boulting, Roy, *The Guinea Pig* [film] (Pilgrim Pictures: London, 1948).

Bourdieu, Pierre, *La Distinction: Critique Sociale du Jugement* (Editions de Minuit: Paris, 1979).

Bourdieu, Pierre, *Distinction: A Social Critique of the Judgment of Taste*, translated by Richard Nice (Routledge: London, 1984).

Bourdieu, Pierre, *Language and Symbolic Power*, edited by John B. Thompson, translated by Gino Raymond and Matthew Adamson (Polity: Cambridge, 1991).

Bowan, Kate, and Pickering, Paul A., '"Songs for the Millions": Chartist Music and Popular Aural Tradition', *Labour History Review*, 74:1 (2009).

Bowlby, Chris, 'Ambassador, you are really spoiling us', *BBC News*, 10 October 2006, http://news.bbc.co.uk/1/hi/magazine/6034687.stm (accessed 8 November 2016).

Bradbury, Ray, 'Referent', in *The Day it Rained Forever* (Rupert Hart-Davies: London, 1959).

Brauman, Leigh, 'Border Country', *Cambridge Alumni Magazine*, 62 (Lent, 2011).

Brooks, Mel, *The Producers* [film] (MGM: Beverly Hills, 1968).

Browning, Robert, 'The Lost Leader', in Tom Paulin (ed.), *The Faber Book of Political Verse* (Faber and Faber: London, 1986).

Burke, Jason, 'Saudi women get behind wheel in protest against driving ban', *Guardian*, 18 June 2011.

Burns, Robert, *The Poetical Works of Robert Burns*, edited by J. Logie Robertson (Oxford University Press: Oxford, 1921).

Burnside, John, Crawford, Robert, and Jamie, Kathleen, *Penguin Modern Poets 9* (Penguin: London, 1996).

Buruma, Ian, 'The Indiscreet Charm of Tyranny', *New York Review of Books*, 52:8 (2005).

Cañeque, Alejandro, *The King's Living Image: The Culture and Politics of Viceregal Power in Colonial Mexico* (Routledge: London, 2004).

Cannadine, David, 'The Context, Performance and Meaning of Ritual: The British Monarchy and the "Invention of Tradition", c. 1820–1977', in Eric Hobsbawm and Terence Ranger (eds), *The Invention of Tradition* (Cambridge University Press: Cambridge, 1983).

Cannadine, David, 'Last Night Fever', *London Review of Books*, 29:17 (2007).

Cavallaro, Dani, and Warwick, Alexandra, *Fashioning the Frame: Boundaries, Dress and the Body* (Berg: Oxford and New York, 1998).

Cawsey, Suzanne F., *Kingship and Propaganda: Royal Eloquence and the Crown of Aragon, c.1200–1450* (Oxford University Press: Oxford, 2002).

Chaucer, Geoffrey, *The Works of Geoffrey Chaucer*, edited by Alfred W. Pollard, H. Frank Heath, Mark H. Liddell, and W. S. McCormick (Macmillan: London, 1925).

Cienski, Jan, 'Cross proves catalyst for Polish church crisis', *Financial Times*, 14 September 2010, www.ft.com/cms/s/0/8cfd1fec-c004–11df-9628–00144feab49a.html (accessed 29 September 2010).

Clark, Ian, *Legitimacy in International Society* (Oxford University Press: Oxford, 2005).

Clark, Jonathan, *A World By Itself: A History of the British Isles* (Heinemann: London, 2010).

Clunas, Craig, 'At the Royal Academy', *London Review of Books*, 27:23 (2005).

Cohen, Deborah, *Household Gods: The British and Their Possessions* (Yale University Press: New Haven, CT, 2006).

Cole, G. D. H., and Postgate, Raymond, *The Common People 1746–1946* (Methuen: London, 1961).

Colley, Linda, *Britons: Forging the Nation 1707–1837* (Yale University Press: New Haven, CT, 1992).

Conekin, Becky E., *The Autobiography of a Nation: The 1951 Festival of Britain* (Manchester University Press: Manchester, 2003).

Coole, Diana, 'Experiencing Discourse: Corporeal Communications and the Embodiment of Power', *British Journal of Politics and International Relations*, 9:3 (2007).

Cosgrove, Denis, *Social Formation and Symbolic Landscape* (University of Wisconsin Press: Madison, WI, and London, 1998).

Crawford, Margaret, *Building the Workingman's Paradise: The Design of American Company Towns* (Verso: London, 1993).

Crawford, Robert, 'Us', in John Burnside, Robert Crawford, and Kathleen Jamie, *Penguin Modern Poets 9* (Penguin: London, 1996).

Crisp, Quentin, in performance at the Duke of York's Theatre, London, *An Evening With Quentin Crisp*, 1978.

Crosland, C. A. R., *The Future of Socialism* (Jonathan Cape: London, 1956).

Davis, David, 'Designing Out Crime', *BBC One, Politics Show*, 3 December 2006, http://news.bbc.co.uk/1/hi/programmes/politics_show/6193304.stm (accessed 1 February 2012).

De Botton, Alain, *The Architecture of Happiness* (Pantheon: London, 2007).

De Charny, Geoffroi, *A Knight's Own Book of Chivalry* (Pennsylvania University Press: Philadelphia, PA, 2005).

Delphy, Christine, interview with Andrea Catherwood, *BBC 4 Woman's Hour*, 19 February 2016, www.bbc.co.uk/programmes/b070hscm (accessed 18 May 2016).

Diski, Jenny, *A View from the Bed and Other Observations* (Virago: London, 2003).

Disraeli, Benjamin, *Sybil, Or The Two Nations* (Oxford Paperbacks: Oxford, 2008).

Douglas, Mary, 'Deciphering a Meal', *Daedalus*, 101:1 (1972).

Douglas, Mary, *Purity and Danger* (Russell Sage Foundation: New York, 1984).

Douglas, Mary, 'Standard Social Uses of Food: Introduction', in Mary Douglas (ed.), *Food in the Social Order: Studies of Food and Festivities in Three American Communities* (Russell Sage Foundation: New York, 1984).

Drabble, Margaret (ed.), *The Oxford Companion to English Literature* (Oxford University Press: Oxford, 1985).

Dryzek, John S., *Deliberative Democracy and Beyond: Liberals, Critics, Contestations* (Oxford University Press: Oxford, 2000).

Dunleavy, Patrick, 'Party Competition: The Preference-Shaping Model', in *Democracy, Bureaucracy and Public Choice: Economic Explanations in Political Science* (Harvester Wheatsheaf: Hemel Hempstead, UK, 1991).

Eco, Umberto, *The Name of the Rose* (Harcourt: London, 1983).

Edelman, Murray, *The Symbolic Uses of Politics* (University of Illinois Press: London, 1964).

Edelman, Murray, 'Space and the Social Order', *Journal of Architectural Education*, 32:3 (1978).

Eggen, Dan, and White, Josh, 'Inmates alleged Koran abuse', *Washington Post*, 26 May 2005, www.washingtonpost.com/wp-dyn/content/article/2005/05/25/AR2005052501395.html (accessed 9 August 2010).

Eisenstein, Sergei, *Ivan the Terrible, Part 2* [film] (Mosfilm: Moscow, 1958).

Elias, Norbert, *The Court Society*, translated by Edmund Jephcott (Blackwell: Oxford, 1983).

Ellenberger, Nancy, *Balfour's World: Aristocracy and Political Culture at the Fin de Siècle* (Boydell: London, 2015).

Epstein, James, *Radical Expression, Political Language, Ritual, and Symbol in England 1790–1850* (Oxford University Press: Oxford, 1994).

Fenske, Gail, *The Skyscraper and the City: The Woolworth Building and the Making of Modern New York* (University of Chicago Press: Chicago, 2008).

Finnane, Antonia, *Changing Clothes in China* (Hurst & Co: London, 2008).

Franck, Thomas M., *The Power of Legitimacy Among Nations* (Oxford University Press: New York, 1990).

Frick, Carole Collier, *Dressing Renaissance Florence: Families, Fortunes, and Fine Clothing* (Johns Hopkins University Press: Baltimore, MD, 2002).

Gardiner, Patrick, *The Nature of Historical Explanation* (Oxford University Press: Oxford, 1968).

Geertz, Clifford, *Negara: The Theatre State in Nineteenth Century Bali* (Princeton University Press: Princeton, NJ, 1980).

Gerth, H. C., and Mills, C. W., *From Max Weber: Essays in Sociology* (Routledge & Kegan Paul: London, 1948).
Goffman, Erving, *The Presentation of Self in Everyday Life* (Penguin: London, 1971).
Goldstein, Judith, and Keohane, Robert O. (eds), *Ideas and Foreign Policy: Beliefs, Institutions, and Political Change* (Cornell University Press: Ithaca, NY, and London, 1993).
Goodsell, Charles, *The Social Meaning of Civic Space: Studying Political Authority through Architecture* (University Press of Kansas: Lawrence, KS, 1988).
Goody, Jack, *Cooking, Cuisine and Class: A Study in Comparative Sociology* (Cambridge University Press: Cambridge, 1982).
Goody, Jack, 'Bitter Icons', *New Left Review*, Second Series, 7 (January/February 2001).
Gormley, Charles, *Heavenly Pursuits* [film] (Channel Four Films: London, 1985).
Greenfeld, Liah, *Nationalism: Five Roads to Modernity* (Harvard University Press: Cambridge, MA, and London, 1992).
Hacking, Ian, *Historical Ontology* (Harvard University Press: Cambridge, MA, 2002).
Hacking, Ian, 'Making Up People', *London Review of Books*, 28 (2006), www.lrb.co.uk/v28/n16/hack01_.html (accessed 5 May 2007).
Hansen, Randall, *Citizenship and Immigration in Post-War Britain* (Oxford University Press: Oxford, 2000).
Harding, Luke, 'The joke's on Saddam', *Guardian, G2*, 14 March 2003.
Harker, Ben, '"The Manchester Rambler": Ewan MacColl and the 1932 Mass Trespass', *History Workshop Journal*, 59:1 (2005).
Hawthorn, Geoffrey, *Plausible Worlds* (Cambridge University Press: Cambridge, 1991).
Hawthorn, Geoffrey, *Thucydides on Politics: Back to the Present* (Cambridge University Press: Cambridge, 2014).
Hayward, Maria, *Dress at the Court of King Henry VIII* (Maney: Leeds, UK, 2007).
Herrin, Judith, *Women in Purple: Rulers of Medieval Byzantium* (Princeton University Press: Princeton, NJ, 2004).
Hobsbawm, Eric, 'Introduction: Inventing Traditions', in Eric Hobsbawm and Terence Ranger (eds), *The Invention of Tradition* (Cambridge University Press: Cambridge, 1983).
Hobsbawm, Eric, *Age of Extremes: The Short Twentieth Century 1914–1991* (Michael Joseph: London, 1994).
Hobsbawm, Eric, and Ranger, Terence, *The Invention of Tradition* (Cambridge University Press: Cambridge, 1983).
Hocart, Arthur Maurice, *Kings and Counsellors: An Essay in the Comparative Anatomy of Human Society*, edited by Rodney Needham (University of Chicago Press: Chicago, London, 1970).
Hogg, Quintin, *The Case for Conservatism* (Penguin: West Drayton, UK, 1947).
Hoggart, Richard, *The Uses of Literacy* (Pelican: Harmondsworth, UK, 1959).
Hollis, Edward, 'Reality Checkpoint', *Cambridge Alumni Magazine*, 57 (Easter Term 2009).

Holloway, Hilton, 'Volvo plays party politics', *Autocar*, 10 June 2011, www.autocar.co.uk/blogs/autocarconfidential/archive/2011/06/10/volvo-plays-party-politics.aspx (accessed 18 June 2011).

Holt, Tonie, and Holt, Valmai, *In Search of a Better 'Ole: The Life, the Works and the Collectables of Bruce Bairnsfather* (Pen & Sword Books/Leo Cooper: Barnsley, UK, 2001).

Honey, John, *Does Accent Matter? The Pygmalion Factor* (Faber: London, 1989).

Hoock, Holger, 'Nelson Entombed: The Military and Naval Pantheon in St Paul's Cathedral', in David Cannadine (ed.), *Admiral Lord Nelson: Context and Legacy* (Palgrave Macmillan: Basingstoke, UK, 2005).

Hoock, Holger, *Empires of the Imagination: Politics, War and the Arts in the British World, 1750–1850* (Profile: London, 2010).

Howard, Anthony, '"WE ARE THE MASTERS NOW": The General Election of July 5th 1945', in Michael Sissons and Philip French (eds), *Age of Austerity* (Hodder and Stoughton: London, 1963).

Humphrey, Chris, *The Politics of Carnival: Festive Misrule in Medieval England* (Manchester University Press: Manchester, 2001).

Hunt, Lynn, *Politics, Culture and Class in the French Revolution* (University of California Press: Berkeley, CA, 1984).

Hunt, Lynn, 'Freedom of Dress in Revolutionary France', in Sara E. Melzer and Kathryn Norberg (eds), *From the Royal to the Republican Body: Incorporating the Political in Seventeenth- and Eighteenth-Century France* (University of California Press: Berkeley, CA, 1998).

Hunt, Lynn, 'A Touchy Lot', *London Review of Books*, 32:5 (2010).

Hunt, Tristram, *Building Jerusalem: The Rise and Fall of the Victorian City* (Weidenfeld and Nicolson: London, 2004).

Huntington, Samuel P., 'The United States', in Michel Crozier, Samuel P. Huntington, and Joji Watanuki, *The Crisis of Democracy: Report on the Governability of Democracies to the Trilateral Commission* (New York: New York University Press, 1975).

Hyde, Jenni, 'Culture Shock: The Arrival of the Conquistadores in Aztec Mexico', *The Historian*, 104 (winter 2009).

IPSOS/MORI, 'Britons Are More Proud of Their History, NHS and Army than the Royal Family', *IPSOS/MORI*, 21 March 2012, www.ipsos-mori.com/research-publications/researcharchive/2939/Britons-are-more-proud-of-their-history-NHS-and-army-than-the-Royal-Family.aspx.

James, Robert, *Popular Culture and Working-Class Taste in Britain, 1930–1939: A Round of Cheap Diversions?* (Manchester University Press: Manchester, 2010).

Jamie, Kathleen, 'The Queen of Sheba', in *Mr and Mrs Scotland Are Dead: Poems 1980–1994* (Bloodaxe Books: Tarset, UK, 2004).

Joerges, Bernward, 'Do Politics Have Artefacts?', *Social Studies of Science*, 29:3 (1999).

Jones, Ann Rosalind, and Stallybrass, Peter, *Renaissance Clothing and the Materials of Memory* (Cambridge University Press: Cambridge, 2000).

Jones, Martin, *Feast: Why Humans Share Food* (Oxford University Press: Oxford, 2007).

Jones, Owen, *Chavs: The Demonization of the Working Class* (Verso: London, 2011).

Joyce, James, *Ulysses* (Bodley Head: London, 1962).

Kadman, Noga, *Erased from Space and Consciousness: Israel and the Depopulated Palestinian Villages of 1948* (Indiana University Press: Bloomington, IN, 2015).

Kantorowicz, Ernst H., *The King's Two Bodies* (Princeton University Press: Princeton, NJ, 1957).

Keay, Anna, *The Magnificent Monarch: Charles II and the Ceremonies of Power* (Continuum Books: London, 2008).

Keller, Marcello Sorce, 'Why Is Music So Ideological, and Why Do Totalitarian States Take It So Seriously? A Personal View from History and the Social Sciences', *Journal of Musicological Research*, 26:2 (2007).

Kildea, Gary, and Leach, Jerry, *Trobriand Cricket: An Ingenious Response to Colonialism* (Royal Anthropological Institute: London, 1974).

King, Alex, *Memorials of the Great War in Britain: The Symbolism and Politics of Remembrance* (Berg: Oxford and New York, 1998).

Kipling, Rudyard, 'Tommy', in *A Choice of Kipling's Verse made by T. S. Eliot* (Faber and Faber: London, 1941).

Krahl, Regina, 'The Yongzheng Emperor: Art Collector and Patron', in Evelyn S. Rawski and Jessica Rawson (eds), *China: The Three Emperors 1662–1795* (Royal Academy of Arts: London, 2006).

Kumar, Krishan, *The Making of English National Identity* (Cambridge University Press: Cambridge, 2003).

Ladurie, Emmanuel Le Roy, *Carnival: A People's Uprising at Romans 1579–1580*, translated by Mary Feeney (Scolar: London, 1979).

Lampedusa, Giuseppe Tomasi Di, *The Leopard* (Vintage: London, 2007).

Land, Isaac, 'What Are We at War About?', *London Review of Books*, 27:23 (2005).

Lasswell, Harold D., and Fox, Merritt B., *The Signature of Power: Buildings, Communication, and Policy* (Transaction Books: New Brunswick, NJ, 1979).

Lawrence, Jon, 'The Culture of Elections in Modern Britain', *History*, 96:324 (2011).

Lepore, Jill, *The Name of War: King Philip's War and the Origins of American Identity* (Random House: New York, 1999).

Lester, Richard, *Help!* [film] (United Artists: Los Angeles,1965).

Linehan, Thomas, *Communism in Britain, 1920–39: From the Cradle to the Grave* (Manchester University Press: Manchester, 2007).

Linehan, Thomas, 'Communist Activism in Interwar Britain: Motivation, Belonging and Political Religion', *Socialist History*, 32 (2008).

Linehan, Thomas, 'Space Matters: Spatialising British Fascism', *Socialist History*, 41 (2012).

Loncraine, Richard, *Richard III* [film] (United Artists: Beverly Hills, 1995).

MacCulloch, Diarmaid, *Thomas Cranmer: A Life* (Yale University Press: New Haven, CT, 1996).

MacCulloch, Diarmaid, *Christianity: The First Three Thousand Years* (Allen Lane: London, 2009).

Mace, Rodney, *Trafalgar Square, Emblem of Empire* (Lawrence & Wishart: London, 1976).

Macintyre, Ben, *Agent Zigzag* (Bloomsbury: London, 2007).
Mackenzie, W. J. M., *Political Identity* (Penguin: Harmondsworth, UK, 1978).
Mann, Michael, *The Dark Side of Democracy: Explaining Ethnic Cleansing* (Cambridge University Press: Cambridge, 2005).
Mansel, Philip, *Dressed to Rule: Royal and Court Costumes from Louis XIV to Elizabeth II* (Yale University Press: New Haven, CT, 2005).
Mansfield, Nicholas, 'Radical Banners as Sites of Memory: The National Banner Survey', in Paul A. Pickering and Alex Tyrell (eds), *Contested Sites: Commemoration, Memorial and Popular Politics in Nineteenth-Century Britain* (Ashgate: Aldershot, UK, 2004).
Mantel, Hilary, *The Assassination of Margaret Thatcher: Stories* (Henry Holt & Company: London, 2014).
Markus, Thomas A., 'Introduction', in Thomas A. Markus (ed.), *Order in Space and Society: Architectural Form and Its Context in the Scottish Enlightenment* (Mainstream: Edinburgh, 1982).
Markus, Thomas A., 'The School as Machine: Working Class Scottish Education and the Glasgow Normal Seminary', in Thomas A. Markus (ed.), *Order in Space and Society: Architectural Form and its Context in the Scottish Enlightenment* (Mainstream: Edinburgh, 1982).
Markus, Thomas A., *Visions of Perfection: Architecture and Utopian Thought* (Third Eye Centre: Glasgow, 1985).
Markus, Thomas A., *Buildings and Power: Freedom and Control in the Origin of Modern Building Types.* (Routledge: London, 1993).
Markus, Thomas A. (ed.), *Order in Space and Society: Architectural Form and Its Context in the Scottish Enlightenment* (Mainstream: Edinburgh, 1982).
Marx, Karl, 'The Eighteenth Brumaire of Louis Bonaparte', in Karl Marx and Frederick Engels, *Selected Works in Two Volumes,* Volume 1 (Foreign Languages: Moscow, 1962).
Masur, Louis, *The Soiling of Old Glory: The Story of a Photograph that Shocked America* (Bloomsbury: London, 2008).
McCormick, Ted, *William Petty and the Ambitions of Political Arithmetic* (Oxford University Press: Oxford, 2009).
McCurry, Justin, 'Japan upholds rule that married couples must have same surname', *Guardian,* 16 December 2015, www.theguardian.com/world/2015/dec/16/japanese-court-rules-married-women-cannot-keep-their-surnames (accessed 14 January 2016).
McDonald, Maryon, *'We Are Not French': Language, Culture and Identity in Brittany* (Routledge: London, 1989).
McKibbin, Ross, *Classes and Cultures: England 1918–1951* (Oxford University Press: Oxford, 1998).
McKittrick, David, 'Brian Haw: Veteran peace campaigner who occupied Parliament Square for a decade in protest at war', *Independent,* 20 June 2011, www.independent.co.uk/news/obituaries/brian-haw-veteran-peace-campaigner-who-occupied-parliament-square-for-a-decade-in-protest-at-war-2299874.html (accessed 16 March 2012).

Melzer, Sara E., and Norberg, Kathryn, 'Introduction', in Sara E. Melzer and Kathryn Norberg (eds), *From the Royal to the Republican Body: Incorporating the Political in Seventeenth- and Eighteenth-Century France* (University of California Press: Berkeley, CA, 1998).

Mill, John Stuart, 'On Liberty', in *Three Essays* (Oxford University Press: Oxford, 1975).

Miller, David, 'Reflections on British National Identity', *New Community,* 21:2 (1995).

Milmo, Cahal, 'Why the FO had to buy a double bed for Kennedy', *Independent,* 27 February 2002.

Mintz, Sidney W., *Tasting Food, Tasting Freedom: Excursions into Eating, Culture, and the Past* (Beacon: Boston, MA, 1996).

Mitchell, W. J. T., *Landscape and Power,* 2nd ed. (University of Chicago Press: Chicago, 2002).

Mitford, Nancy, *Noblesse Oblige: An Enquiry into the Identifiable Characteristics of the English Aristocracy* (Hamish Hamilton: London, 1956).

Monkonnen, Eric H., *America Becomes Urban: The Development of U.S. Cities and Towns, 1780–1980* (University of California Press: Berkeley, CA; Los Angeles; and London, 1988).

Monod, Paul Kléber, *Jacobitism and the English People, 1688–1788* (Cambridge University Press: Cambridge, 1989).

Monroe, Kristen Renwick, *The Heart of Altruism: Perceptions of a Common Humanity* (Princeton University Press: Princeton, NJ, 1996).

Monroe, Kristen Renwick, 'Identity and Choice', in Kenneth R. Hoover (ed.), *The Future of Identity: Centennial Reflections on the Legacy of Erik Erikson* (Lexington Books: Lanham, MD, 2004).

Monroe, Kristen Renwick, *The Hand of Compassion: Portraits of Moral Choice during the Holocaust* (Princeton University Press: Princeton, NJ, 2004).

Montefiore, Simon Sebag, *Stalin: The Court of the Red Tsar* (Weidenfeld & Nicolson: London, 2003).

Moore, Rowan, 'The Space Station of the Steppes', *Observer, New Review,* 8 August 2010, www.theguardian.com/world/2010/aug/08/astana-kazakhstan-space-station-steppes (accessed 21 February 2017).

Moore, Rowan, 'We think we shape the homes we live in, but how much do they shape us?', *Observer, New Review,* 12 August 2012.

Morahan, Christopher, *Clockwise* [film], screenplay by Michael Frayn (Studio Canal: London, 1986).

Morgan, Craig, 'Crisis, Patriotism and the Growth of Fascism: the British Union of Fascists in the Midlands, 1932–34', *Socialist History,* 41 (2012).

Morone, James, 'The Triumph of Plunder', *London Review of Books,* 26:18 (2004).

Morris, Desmond, *The Naked Ape* (Jonathan Cape: London, 1967).

Morris, William, 'Useful Work versus Useless Toil', in A. L. Morton (ed.), *The Political Writings of William Morris* (Lawrence and Wishart: London, 1973).

Morrison, Herbert, *Herbert Morrison: An Autobiography* (Odhams: London, 1960).

Mount, Ferdinand, *The Theatre of Politics* (Weidenfeld & Nicolson: London, 1972).

Nairn, Tom, *The Enchanted Glass: Britain and its Monarchy* (Radius: London, 1988).

Narayan, R. K., *My Dateless Diary: An American Journey* (Penguin Books India: New Delhi, 1988).

Nettl, J. P., 'The German Social Democratic Party 1890–1914 as a Political Model', *Past and Present*, 30 (1965).

Nicolson, Harold, *Diaries and Letters 1930–39*, edited by Nigel Nicolson (William Collins: London, 1966).

O'Connell, Sean, *The Car and British Society: Class, Gender and Motoring 1896–1939* (Manchester University Press: Manchester, 1998).

Orwell, George, *Homage to Catalonia* (Penguin: London, 1962).

Orwell, George, *The Road to Wigan Pier* (Gollancz: London, 1937; Penguin ed. Penguin: London, 1962).

Orwell, George, 'In Defence of English Cooking', *The Collected Essays, Journalism and Letters of George Orwell*, Volume II: *My Country Right or Left, 1940–1943*, edited by Sonia Orwell and Ian Angus (Penguin: Harmondsworth, UK, 1970 [1968]).

Orwell, George, 'The Lion and the Unicorn', *The Collected Essays, Journalism and Letters of George Orwell*, Volume II: *My Country Right or Left, 1940–1943*, edited by Sonia Orwell and Ian Angus (Penguin: Harmondsworth, UK, 1970 [1968]).

Owen, David, 'Self-Government and "Democracy as Reflexive Co-operation": Reflections on Honneth's Social and Political Ideal', in Bert van den Brink and David Owen (eds), *Recognition and Power: Axel Honneth and the Tradition of Critical Social Theory* (Cambridge University Press: Cambridge, 2007).

Owen, David, 'Reification, Ideology and Power: Expression and Agency in Honneth's Theory of Recognition', *Journal of Power*, 3:1 (2010).

Paine, Thomas, *Rights of Man: Being an Answer to Mr. Burke's Attack on the French Revolution* (Watts: London, 1937).

Parks, Tim, 'A Most Delicate Invention', *London Review of Books*, 33:18 (2011).

Paulin, Tom, *The Faber Book of Political Verse* (Faber and Faber: London, 1986).

Peake, Mervyn, *Gormenghast* (Eyre and Spotiswood: London, 1950).

Petre, Jonathan, 'Queen to visit British mosque for first time', *Daily Telegraph*, 21 April 2002, www.telegraph.co.uk/news/uknews/4181908/Queen-to-visit-British-mosque-for-first-time.html (accessed 13 May 2016).

Philo, C., 'Edinburgh, Enlightenment and the Geographies of Unreason', in D. N. Livingstone and C. W. J. Withers (eds), *Geography and Enlightenment* (University of Chicago Press: Chicago, 1999).

Pickering, Paul A., 'The Chartist Rites of Passage: Commemorating Feargus O'Connor', in Paul A. Pickering and Alex Tyrell (eds), *Contested Sites: Commemoration, Memorial and Popular Politics in Nineteenth-Century Britain* (Ashgate: Aldershot, UK, 2004).

Pickering, Paul A., and Tyrell, Alex, 'The Public Memorial of Reform', in Paul A. Pickering and Alex Tyrell (eds), *Contested Sites: Commemoration, Memorial and Popular Politics in Nineteenth-Century Britain* (Ashgate: Aldershot, UK, 2004).

Pickering, Paul A., and Tyrell, Alex (eds), *Contested Sites: Commemoration, Memorial and Popular Politics in Nineteenth-Century Britain* (Ashgate: Aldershot, UK, 2004).

Pierce, Andrew, 'Prince Charles to be known as Defender of Faith', *Daily Telegraph*, 13 November 2008, www.telegraph.co.uk/news/uknews/theroyalfamily/3454271/Prince-Charles-to-be-known-as-Defender-of-Faith.html (accessed 2 April 2013).

Pilapil, Renante D., 'From Psychologism to Personhood: Honneth, Recognition, and the Making of Persons', *Res Publica*, 18:1 (2012).

Pimlott, Ben, *Harold Wilson* (Harper Collins: London, 1992).

Podoksik, Efraim, 'Overcoming the Conservative Disposition: Oakeshott vs. Tönnies', *Political Studies*, 56:4 (2008).

Pope, Alexander, *The Rape of the Lock* (Oxford University Press: Oxford, 2007).

Powers, William K., and Powers, Marla M. N., 'Metaphysical Aspects of an Oglala Food System', in Mary Douglas (ed.), *Food in the Social Order: Studies of Food and Festivities in Three American Communities* (Russell Sage Foundation: New York, 1984).

Prochaska, Frank, *Royal Bounty: The Making of a Welfare Monarchy* (Yale University Press: New Haven, CT, 1995).

Prochaska, Frank, *The Republic of Britain 1760–2000* (Allen Lane: London, 2000).

Puwar, N., *Space Invaders* (Berg: London, 2004).

Raeff, Marc, 'The Well-Ordered Police State and the Development of Modernity in Seventeenth- and Eighteenth-Century Europe: An Attempt at a Comparative Approach', *American Historical Review*, 80:5 (1975).

Raeff, Marc, *The Well-Ordered Police State: Social and Institutional Change through Law in the Germanies and Russia, 1600–1800* (Yale University Press: New Haven, CT, 1983).

Rawnsley, Andrew, 'Why Alastair Campbell has deleted Blair's expletives: the former spinmeister's diaries have been heavily censored but they still threaten to damage the departing Prime Minister', *Observer*, 27 May 2007, http://observer.guardian.co.uk/comment/story/0,2089087,00.html#article_continue (accessed 7 June 2007).

Rawski, Evelyn S., and Rawson, Jessica, *China: The Three Emperors 1662–1795* (Royal Academy of Arts: London, 2006).

Reuters in Tokyo, 'Japanese women in court fight to keep their surnames after marriage', *Guardian*, 11 December 2015, www.theguardian.com/world/2015/dec/11/japan-supreme-court-rule-one-surname-law-married-couples (accessed 14 January 2016).

Rich, Paul, 'Patriotism and the Idea of Citizenship', in Ursula Vogel and Michael Moran (eds), *The Frontiers of Citizenship* (Macmillan: London, 1990).

Ringmar, Erik, *Identity, Interest and Action: A Cultural Explanation of Sweden's Intervention in the Thirty Years War* (Cambridge University Press: Cambridge, 1996).

Roberts, Helen, *What Works in Reducing Inequalities in Child Health?* (Policy: Bristol, 2012).

Rock, Paul, and Cohen, Stanley, 'The Teddy Boy', in Vernon Bogdanor and Robert Skidelsky (eds), *The Age of Affluence 1951–64* (Macmillan: London, 1970).

Rolston, Bill, *Drawing Support 2: Murals of War and Peace* (Beyond the Pale: Belfast, 1995).

Rolston, Bill, *Drawing Support: Murals in the North of Ireland*, 2nd edition (Beyond the Pale: Belfast, 2010).

Rosen, Michael, *On Voluntary Servitude: False Consciousness and the Theory of Ideology* (Polity: Cambridge, UK, 1996).

Roth, Philip, *Portnoy's Complaint* (Vintage: London, 2005).

Rublack, Ulinka, *Dressing Up: Cultural Identity in Renaissance Europe* (Oxford University Press: Oxford, 2010).

Runciman, David, *Pluralism and the Personality of the State* (Cambridge University Press: Cambridge, 1997).

Runciman, David, *Political Hypocrisy: The Mask of Power, from Hobbes to Orwell and Beyond* (Princeton University Press: Princeton, NJ, 2008).

Ruoff, Kenneth J., *The People's Emperor: Democracy and the Japanese Monarchy, 1945–1995* (Harvard University Press: Cambridge, MA, 2001).

Rushdie, Salman, *Shame* (Picador: London, 1984).

Rushdie, Salman, *The Satanic Verses* (Allen Lane: London, 1988).

Sacks, Jonathan, *The Home We Build Together: Recreating Society* (Continuum: London, 2007).

Sandler, Lucy Freeman, 'The Wilton Diptych and Images of Devotion in Illuminated Manuscripts', in Gillian Gordon, Lisa Monnas, and Caroline Elam (eds), *The Regal Image of Richard II and the Wilton Diptych* (Harvey Miller: London, 1998).

Savage, Michael, '"Living goddess" has deity stripped after US trip', *Independent*, 4 July 2007.

Scales, Len, 'Bread, Cheese and Genocide: Imagining the Destruction of Peoples in Medieval Western Europe', *History*, 92:307 (2007).

Schorske, Carl E., *Thinking with History: Explorations in the Passage to Modernism* (Princeton University Press: Princeton, NJ, 1998).

Schumpeter, Joseph A., *Capitalism, Socialism, and Democracy*, 5th ed. (George Allen and Unwin: London, 1976).

Searle, John, *The Construction of Social Reality* (Allen Lane: London, 1995).

Searle, John, *Making the Social World: The Structure of Human Civilization* (Oxford University Press: Oxford, 2010).

Seaton, Jean, *Carnage and the Media: The Making and Breaking of News about Violence* (Allen Lane: London, 2005).

Shakespeare, William, 'Julius Caesar', in *The Complete Works*, edited by Stanley Wells and Gary Taylor (Oxford: Oxford University Press, 1986).

Shakespeare, William, *King Lear* (London: Methuen, 1957).

Shaw, George Bernard, *Ruskin's Politics* (Ruskin Centenary Council: London, 1921).

Shaw, George Bernard, 'First Aid to Critics', in *Major Barbara* (Constable: London, 1926).

Shaw, George Bernard, *Pygmalion* (Penguin: London, 1946).

Shils, Edward, and Young, Michael, 'The Sociological Meaning of the Coronation', *Sociological Review*, New Series, 1 (1953).

Simmel, Georg, *Conflict* and *The Web of Group-Affiliations*, translated by Kurt H. Wolff and Reinhard Bendix (Free Press: New York, 1964).

Smith, Hannah, *Georgian Monarchy: Politics and Culture, 1714–1760* (Cambridge University Press: Cambridge, 2006).

Squires, Mike, 'The Mass Trespass of Kinder Scout: How Breaking the Law Achieved Change', *Socialist History Society Newsletter*, New Series, 1:1 (2012).

Stevens, Wallace, 'Theory', in Wallace Stevens, *Harmonium* (Faber: London, 2001).

Stone, Jon, 'Tory grandees angry as BBC chooses Hilary Mantel's "The Assassination of Margaret Thatcher" for Book at Bedtime', *Independent*, 14 December 2014, www.independent.co.uk/news/uk/politics/tory-grandees-angry-at-bbc-for-serialising-thatcher-assassination-book-9923514.html (accessed 21 February 2017).

Styles, John, *The Dress of the People: Everyday Fashion in Eighteenth-Century England* (Yale University Press: New Haven, CT, 2007).

Sudjic, Deyan, *The Edifice Complex: How the Rich and Powerful Shape the World* (Penguin: New York, 2005).

Sumner, B. H., *Survey of Russian History* (Methuen: London, 1961).

Tait, Robert, 'Iranian police give barbers the chop to enforce Islamic dress code', *Guardian*, 25 August 2007.

Tawney, R. H., 'The Choice before the Labour Party', in *The Attack and Other Papers* (George Allen & Unwin: London, 1953).

Taylor, Andrew, *A Plum in Your Mouth* (Harper Collins: London, 2006).

Taylor, Charles, *Hegel* (Cambridge University Press: Cambridge, 1975).

Terrill, Ross, *R. H. Tawney and His Times: Socialism as Fellowship* (Harvard University Press: Cambridge, MA, 1973).

Thompson, E. P., *Whigs and Hunters* (Allen Lane: London, 1975).

Thompson, Ian, *The Sun King's Garden: Louis XIV, André Le Nôtre and the Creation of the Gardens of Versailles* (Bloomsbury: London, 2007).

Thorne, Will, *My Life's Battles* (George Newnes: London, 1925).

Toensing, Gale Courey, 'First destroy the archives', *Counter Punch*, 31 July 2006, www.counterpunch.org/toensing07272006.html (accessed 5 June 2011).

Trevor-Roper, Hugh, 'The Invention of Tradition: The Highland Tradition of Scotland', in Eric Hobsbawm and Terence Ranger (eds), *The Invention of Tradition* (Cambridge University Press: Cambridge, 1983).

Turits, Richard Lee, 'A World Destroyed, A Nation Imposed: The 1937 Haitian Massacre in the Dominican Republic', *Hispanic American Historical Review*, 82:3 (2002).

Tyrell, Alex, 'Preserving the Glory for Preston: The Campo Santo of the Preston Teetotalers', in Paul A. Pickering and Alex Tyrell (eds), *Contested Sites: Commemoration, Memorial and Popular Politics in Nineteenth-Century Britain* (Ashgate: Aldershot, UK, 2004).

Tyrrell, Alex, and David, Michael T., 'Bearding the Tories: The Commemoration of the Scottish Political Martyrs of 1793–94', in Paul A. Pickering and Alex

Tyrell (eds), *Contested Sites: Commemoration, Memorial and Popular Politics in Nineteenth-Century Britain* (Ashgate: Aldershot, UK, 2004).

Uglow, Jenny, *A Little History of British Gardening* (Random House: London, 2005).

Upton, Dell, *Another City: Urban Life and Urban Spaces in the New American Republic* (Yale University Press: New Haven, CT, 2008).

Vale, Lawrence J., *Architecture, Power and National Identity* (Yale University Press: New Haven, CT, 1992).

Van den Brink, Bert, and Owen, David, *Recognition and Power: Axel Honneth and the Tradition of Critical Social Theory* (Cambridge University Press: Cambridge, 2007).

Veblen, Thorstein, *The Theory of the Leisure Class: An Economic Study of Institutions* (Allen & Unwin: London, 1924).

Vickery, Amanda, *Behind Closed Doors: At Home in Georgian England* (Yale University Press: London, 2009).

Walker, Harriet, 'If the cap fits, wear it. But not if your name is William Hague', *Independent*, 24 August 2010, http://www.independent.co.uk/news/people/news/if-the-cap-fits-wear-it-but-not-if-your-name-is-william-hague-2061171.html (accessed 18 March 2016).

Walsham, Alexandra, *The Reformation of the Landscape: Religion, Identity and Memory in Early Modern Britain and Ireland* (Oxford University Press: Oxford, 2011).

Walton, Calder, *Empire of Secrets: British Intelligence, the Cold War and the Twilight of Empire* (Harper: London, 2013).

Walton, Charles, *Policing Public Opinion in the French Revolution: The Culture of Calumny and the Problem of Free Speech* (Oxford University Press: Oxford, 2009).

Waquet, Françoise, *Latin, or the Empire of a Sign*, translated by John Howe (Verso: London, 2001).

Watt, Gary, *Dress, Law and Naked Truth: A Cultural Study of Fashion and Form*, Kindle ed. (Bloomsbury: London).

Waugh, Auberon, *Will This Do?* (Carroll and Graf: London, 2003).

Webb, Sidney, and Webb, Beatrice, *Soviet Communism: A New Civilisation?* (The authors: Liphook, UK, 1935).

Weber, Max, 'The Social Psychology of the World Religions', in H. C. Gerth and C. W. Mills, *From Max Weber: Essays in Sociology* (Routledge & Kegan Paul: London, 1948).

Weber, Max, *Economy and Society*, edited by Guenther Roth and Claus Wittich, two vols (University of California Press: London, 1978).

Webster, Philip, '"Blair Force One" is on order, but it's for the Queen and Brown', *The Times*, 23 May 2007, www.timesonline.co.uk/tol/news/politics/article1826731.ece (accessed 30 November 2010).

Weil, Patrick, *How to be French: Nationality in the Making Since 1789*, translated by Catherine Porter (Duke University Press: Durham, NC, 2009).

Wesker, Arnold, *Roots* (Penguin: Harmondsworth, UK, 1959).

Weston, R. P., and Lee, Bert, 'Brahn Boots', *All Poetry*, https://allpoetry.com/Brahn-Boots [originally published 1940] (accessed 21 February 2017).

Wilder, Thornton, *Our Town and Other Plays* (Penguin: London, 2000).

Willes, Margaret, *The Gardens of the British Working Class* (Yale University Press: New Haven, CT, 2014).

Williams, Rowan, 'The Formation of Christendom', *New Left Review*, 170 (July–August 1988).

Willis, Jonathan, '"By These Means the Sacred Discourses Sink More Deeply into the Minds of Men": Music and Education in Elizabethan England', *History*, 94:315 (2009).

Willis, Jonathan, *Church Music and Protestantism in Post-Reformation England: Discourses, Sites and Identities* (Ashgate: Aldershot, UK, 2010).

Winner, Langdon, 'Do Artifacts Have Politics?', *Daedalus*, 109:1 (1980).

Wise, Robert, *Two for the Seesaw* [film] (United Artists: Beverley Hills, 1962).

Woolf, Virginia, *Orlando* (Penguin: London, 1974).

Woolf, Virginia, *Three Guineas* (Penguin: London, 1993).

Wrangham, Richard, *Catching Fire: How Cooking Made Us Human* (Profile: London, 2009).

Wright, Jeffrey, 'Capitalism and Working-Class Acquiescence', *Socialist History*, 36 (2010).

Wrigley, Richard, *The Politics of Appearance: The Symbolism of Dress in Revolutionary France* (Berg: Oxford, 2002).

Yeats, W. B., 'Coole and Ballylee 1931', in *The Collected Works of W.B. Yeats, Volume I: The Poems*, revised 2nd ed. (Simon & Schuster: New York, 2010).

Yeo, Eileen Janes, 'Gender and Class: Women's Languages of Power', *Labour History Review*, 60:3 (1995).

Young, Wayland, *The Profumo Affair: Aspects of Conservatism* (Penguin Books: Harmondsworth, UK, 1963).

Younge, Gary, and Henley, Jon, 'Wimps, weasels and monkeys: the US media view of "perfidious France"', *Guardian*, 11 February 2003, www.theguardian.com/world/2003/feb/11/pressandpublishing.usa (accessed 7 February 2017).

Yovel, Yirmiyahu, *The Other Within. The Marranos: Split Identity and Emerging Modernity* (Princeton University Press: Princeton, NJ, 2009).

Zakim, Michael, *Ready-Made Democracy: A History of Men's Dress in the American Republic, 1760–1860* (University of Chicago Press: Chicago and London, 2003).

Zitser, Ernest A., *The Transfigured Kingdom: Sacred Parody and Charismatic Authority at the Court of Peter the Great* (Cornell University Press: Ithaca, NY, and London, 2004).

Permissions

All chapters in this book were first published in CPPIWPM, by Manchester University Press by Rodney Barker; hereby published with permission under the Creative Commons Attribution License or equivalent. Every chapter published in this book has been scrutinized by our experts. Their significance has been extensively debated. The topics covered herein carry significant information for a comprehensive understanding. They may even be implemented as practical applications or may be referred to as a beginning point for further studies.

We would like to thank the editorial team for lending their expertise to make the book truly unique. They have played a crucial role in the development of this book. Without their invaluable contributions this book wouldn't have been possible. They have made vital efforts to compile up to date information on the varied aspects of this subject to make this book a valuable addition to the collection of many professionals and students.

This book was conceptualized with the vision of imparting up-to-date and integrated information in this field. To ensure the same, a matchless editorial board was set up. Every individual on the board went through rigorous rounds of assessment to prove their worth. After which they invested a large part of their time researching and compiling the most relevant data for our readers.

The editorial board has been involved in producing this book since its inception. They have spent rigorous hours researching and exploring the diverse topics which have resulted in the successful publishing of this book. They have passed on their knowledge of decades through this book. To expedite this challenging task, the publisher supported the team at every step. A small team of assistant editors was also appointed to further simplify the editing procedure and attain best results for the readers.

Apart from the editorial board, the designing team has also invested a significant amount of their time in understanding the subject and creating the most relevant covers. They scrutinized every image to scout for the most suitable representation of the subject and create an appropriate cover for the book.

The publishing team has been an ardent support to the editorial, designing and production team. Their endless efforts to recruit the best for this project, has resulted in the accomplishment of this book. They are a veteran in the field of academics and their pool of knowledge is as vast as their experience in printing. Their expertise and guidance has proved useful at every step. Their uncompromising quality standards have made this book an exceptional effort. Their encouragement from time to time has been an inspiration for everyone.

The publisher and the editorial board hope that this book will prove to be a valuable piece of knowledge for students, practitioners and scholars across the globe.

Index

CPSIA information can be obtained
at www.ICGtesting.com
Printed in the USA
LVHW082311100122
708212LV00001B/26

9 781639 895427